MANY VOICES

MANY VOICES

Bilingualism, Culture and Education

Jane Miller

Routledge & Kegan Paul

London, Boston, Melbourne and Henley

First published in 1983
by Routledge & Kegan Paul plc
39 Store Street, London WC1E 7DD,
9 Park Street, Boston, Mass. 02108, USA,
296 Beaconsfield Parade, Middle Park,
Melbourne, 3206, Australia, and
Broadway House, Newtown Road,
Henley-on-Thames, Oxon RG9 1EN
Set in 10/12pt Times
Printed in Great Britain by
Billing & Sons Ltd
Worcester

Library of Congress Cataloging in Publication Data

Miller, Jane, 1932–
Many voices.
Bibliography: p.
Includes index.
1. Education, Bilingual.   2. Bilingualism.
I. Title.
LC3719.M54 1983   371.97   82–20433

ISBN 0–7100–9331–4
ISBN 0–7100–9341–1 (pbk.)

For Karl, Daniel, Sam and Georgia

Contents

Acknowledgments   viii
Introduction   ix
1 The dimensions of bilingualism in London schools   1
2 'So I think I'll stay halfway'   15
3 'Urdu has very deep manners'   46
4 'It's a positioning of the self within the language'   77
5 The social perspectives of bilingualism   110
6 Learning first and second languages   127
7 Do bilinguals think better?   143
8 The educational implications of bilingualism   153
9 Writing in a second language   173
Notes   194
Bibliography   199
Index   211

Acknowledgments

I have many people to thank. Christopher Ricks first suggested I write about bilingualism, and John Hardcastle and Heather Sutton were the first to show me how language diversity might be used in the classroom. Mike Raleigh and Terry Furlong have been collaborators on many undertakings. I want to thank them generally as well as for the particular help they gave me with arrangements to talk to their bilingual pupils. Then there are the bilingual speakers themselves, who gave me so much time and help. Both my family and my colleagues in the English Department at the Institute of Education deserve my gratitude for their support and forbearance. It has been invaluable having, in Shyama Iyer, a bilingual speaker who has been involved in the work from the beginning. I also want to thank Mary Taubman for her constant friendship and interest. Finally, I want to thank Tony Burgess, for his encouragement, time and advice. My interest in the subject grew out of the work I did with him and with Harold Rosen and many other teachers and students who have worked on the *Language and the Inner City* project.

Earlier versions of Chapter 1 have appeared in *The State of the Language*, edited by Leonard Michaels and Christopher Ricks, and in *Trends in Education*, spring issue 1980. An earlier version of the last chapter appeared in *Raritan*, vol. 2, no. 1, summer 1982. There are also parts of Chapter 8 which I originally wrote for *Languages and Dialects of London Schoolchildren* by Harold Rosen and Tony Burgess. I would like to thank all those concerned for allowing me to use that material for this book.

Introduction

There is already a vast literature on bilingualism. It may be necessary, therefore, to start by establishing why I should have the temerity to add to it, especially as I do so neither as a linguist nor as a specialist teacher of English as a second language, nor, indeed, as a bilingual. As a student I learned French, German and Russian, so that for a time I read a good deal more in those languages than in English. I remember returning with relief to literature written in English, as if I had come home after an immersion in other languages, aspects of which would always elude me. Until the mid 1970s I taught English in a London school with an exceptionally high proportion of bilingual pupils. I had daily contact there with young people who appeared to be as at home in two or more languages as I was only in my mother tongue. I was intrigued even then by their possession of second and third languages, while I, who had studied other languages seriously and for a long time, had never known that kind of ownership. I do not want to suggest that in those days I, or many other teachers in London schools, went beyond a general admiration for the speed and ease with which these young people learned English. I rarely, if ever, asked about their other languages.

My going to the English Department at the University of London Institute of Education in 1976 coincided with the beginning of a remarkable project *Language and the Inner City*. Though it has been orchestrated by the English Department it has principally been an almost entirely unfunded collaborative under- taking by London teachers. From it have issued research papers, classroom materials and, more officially, the *Survey of Linguistic Diversity*, which is described in *Languages and Dialects of London Schoolchildren: An Investigation* by Harold Rosen and Tony Burgess. Besides introducing the 600 or so teacher and researcher participants to a range of work going on in London schools at twice-yearly conferences, this capacious network has encouraged investigations by particular groups and individuals. This book could be said to have come out of my involvement in that project.

I began, quite properly in my view, from a teacher's hunch: that children who were bilingual, and confidently so, did well in school. There is a good deal of research which supports that hunch, and some which does not. I have not set out to 'prove' that I am right, but to show why I might be. It would be easy to argue that I have concentrated on those – children and adults and well-known writers – for whom bilingualism does seem to have been an asset or one of their assets. It would not be difficult to find examples of people for whom bilingualism was one of their disadvantages. I do not apologise for my selectiveness, for I believe that these 'successes' have something to tell teachers about those pupils for whom the move towards English has been difficult.

Educational research which relies on testing large samples can be useful, no doubt, in certain areas. Yet those of us who are engaged in training teachers and in working with experienced teachers on in-service courses are daily reminded of the difficulties teachers have in making much sense in their own schools of research of that kind. Detailed and sensitive attention to the particular, as in books like Brian Jackson's *Starting School*, Peter Medway's *Finding a Language* and Michael Armstrong's *Closely Observed Children*, speaks powerfully to teachers, in my view, because teachers are able to recognise in these particular realities parallel contexts to their own, from which they can derive insights and develop practice. I have wanted to provide real voices, ones which teachers will recognise, and to draw from them the possibilities of new understandings and attitudes.

I have also wanted to put the descriptions people give of their own language capacities against those of linguists. This has made me reluctant to keep to firm definitions. A bilingual, for instance, is for me someone who operates during their everyday life in more than one language and does so with some degree of self-confidence. It will become clear from listening to 'my' bilinguals that terms like 'mother tongue', 'first language', 'main language', 'best language' and so on, are necessarily shifting concepts. Few, if any, bilinguals in this country maintain a perfect parity or balance between their languages, which will, inevitably, be used for different purposes at different times.

I have set my discussion and my proposals very firmly in

London, because that is where I teach and that is where most of my students teach. It would require, I know, very little modification for much of what I have to say to apply to other cities where there are mixed language communities. Yet each will be subtly different, just as each of the individuals and classrooms and schools which I know in London is different.

In suggesting ways in which teachers might make use of language diversity in the classroom I am making large claims for the centrality of this kind of work to the development of a multicultural curriculum. I shall hope, as I spell these out, to address objections that such an approach is sentimental, tokenist, even patronising. I do not see these proposals as compensatory ones or as attempts to mollify children who are either hostile to school or in difficulties there. Far from it. My arguments, which will be linguistic, pedagogic and political ones, are above all concerned with the possibilities of enriching the curriculum for all children. I believe that using linguistic diversity as a way of developing and understanding language provides a model for innovations in all aspects of the curriculum. My final chapter, where I look at writers who have used a second language, will suggest that these writers have discovered that in doing so their stance and focus as writers have been vitally transformed. Language is not simply an aspect of culture, its filter or its companion. It is the way in which we learn to make sense of experience and to represent it to ourselves and to other people.

1 The dimensions of bilingualism in London schools

Two poems to begin with, by children. The first one is written by a Navajo child in New Mexico. Ruth, who wrote the second one, spells her name with the first letter of each line. She used to live in Jamaica, but she goes to school in London now, and we will hear from her later. Both poems are about school and they are both about language too. Each of them is telling us that something is wrong.

> Our teachers come to class,
> And they talk and they talk
> Till their faces are like peaches.
> We don't;
> We just sit like cornstalks.[1]

And Ruth's poem:

> Reach school by 8.30
> Until the doors open I talk
> Then wait outside the classroom door
>   until teachers come along.
> Hurry to the hall where I lissen for so long.
> After that to lesson I go
> Learn a little fiction write one little code.
> Leave for my next lesson which is music.
> Every time I sit around and never learn a song.
> Next it's time to have a brake
>   Which isn't very long.

So what is wrong? In this first chapter I shall be trying to give body to that question and to begin a search for an answer to it. Both processes will need anecdotes, real voices, real experiences, as well as expert advice and opinion. I have set out to listen to people who know more than one language and people who have attachments to more than one culture. Some of them are children and some of them are adults, and there will be writers amongst them. Most of them believe that they are fortunate people, having that sort of knowledge and experience, and we may want to agree with them. Yet many children in the same position are treated as having problems in school. That is the enigma.

When I have told people that I am trying to write about bilingualism some of them have been concerned that I should devote myself to so marginal an issue at a time when education is under particular threat. I have become increasingly sure that bilingualism is not a marginal issue. This is not simply because we now know that something like fourteen per cent of London schoolchildren are bilingual.[2] Listening to these people, reading what they have to say, has convinced me that they are able to testify, in a uniquely revealing way, to experiences which are central to present-day British society and to the kind of education society provides for its children. It has confirmed for me the sense that language, first languages and subsequent or alternative languages, are inextricably a part of people's lives, their energy as learners and their sense of life's possibilities. Neither bilingualism nor the people I have talked to are marginal. Both have, in my view, something to tell us which may be central to learning and to people's lives.

Kulvinder is five and halfway through her first year of primary school. Her teacher sometimes feels concerned that Kulvinder doesn't speak at school, but she lets herself be reassured by the child's bright watchfulness and by the alacrity with which she always does what she is told. Besides, Kulvinder's mother and father are so keen for their daughter to speak good English that they have given up speaking Punjabi at home and speak only English now. Kulvinder doesn't say much at home either, but perhaps that will change when her parents have learned more English themselves.

Andreas lives in East London, and he goes to the nearest school, though his father worried at first about sending him there. He had heard that over half the children were black and that the school had gone downhill since it became comprehensive and some of the Jewish families round there began to send their sons to fee-paying schools. Andreas is tall for twelve, one of the tallest in the second year, and he seems to like school, though his father is never sure that he is learning anything. This week he has been teaching his class some Greek; in English lessons if you please. He began with the alphabet, writing it up on the board. Then he made the class work out the words 'West Ham for the Cup', which he had written in Greek letters. He could tell they'd got it when they jeered. His father has written a funny poem which Andreas will give them tomorrow. He will have to help them translate it. It's good the way Mr Orme lets the boys be teachers sometimes. They're learning all about the history of writing and alphabets with him. Andreas finds it strange that some people hate writing, can't see the point.

Michelle is twelve too. There was a lady in her English lesson today who asked them all what languages they knew. They all thought at first that she meant French, which they started in September with Mrs Brooke. But it turned out that she meant things like Indian and Brok French. Michelle was really surprised that apart from her there were five others in the class who spoke Brok French. She'd thought Nadia was Indian, but she speaks the sort of French they speak in Mauritius. By the end of the lesson they had discovered that besides English, which everybody speaks, there were children who knew Egyptian, Greek, Urdu, Spanish and Italian, as well as Jamaican language and French Creole. The lady said that their French teacher might be interested to know that six of her pupils spoke French patois. Michelle nearly told her that Mrs Brooke wasn't interested in anything much except getting your homework in on time.

Three voices, one of them inaudible, must be allowed to speak for themselves out of what is variously regarded as a Babel or a resource for teaching of unimaginable richness. The survey described by Rosen and Burgess (1980), in which 4,600 children in their first year at 28 London secondary schools were questioned about their languages and dialects, turned up 55 languages apart from English, and 65 overseas and home-based dialects of English. Among the 300 children in their first year at just one of those schools, 28 languages were spoken apart from English. London schools are often in the news for doing worst in tests set for the whole country, worse than Glasgow, worse than Belfast. It seems hard to believe now, but there was a time when researchers got used to urban children doing better than rural ones.[3] Children living in towns were expected to be better off, more ambitious and sophisticated. All that has changed, and London is suffering from that world-wide complaint, the inner-city crisis. It would be easy to blame it on all those languages, but mistaken. They are not spoken in the schools, after all. There are some English teachers, fewer than there used to be, who say that the children in their classes have too little language, not too much, and that what there is is usually bad, in every sense.

In Andreas's class they had a lesson last week from one of the boys, on Korean, and how you write it in different directions to show whether you're talking about the past or the future. That was amazing. Mr Orme did Ancient Greek when he was young and he wanted to find out whether that helps at all with Modern Greek. He's impressed by all the languages his pupils speak. One boy, who speaks Urdu, Punjabi and Hindi, can read and write in Urdu and Punjabi and is learning to read Hindi at after-school classes. It has taken him only four years to sound like a native Cockney speaker, and his writing is good too. Mr Orme is rare as a teacher. He has gone to the trouble of finding out what languages the boys speak at home; and because a lot of them are from Jamaican families he has learned to speak their language and can discuss in detail the differences between Kingston Jamaican, London Jamaican and the sort of English he speaks.

Some teachers think he is wasting his time, that he would have to agree that since these children live in England and will probably stay here for the rest of their lives, teaching them the sort of English which helps them to pass exams and get jobs is what he is there for. Mr Orme does agree, though he finds it harder and harder to be sure that he knows what sort of English that would actually be. When he was a boy he won a place at a grammar school in Durham. All the boys spoke with an accent, even used different words, but their teacher saw to it that they didn't speak 'sloppily' with him. For a long time Mr Orme believed that you couldn't expect even to spell properly if you didn't talk like the BBC. Wouldn't all those rules for doubling letters, spelling the *or* sound and silent *e*'s be much easier to get right if you talked posh? He remembered one of his mates saying that squeezing up the vowels and making a big thing of the consonants was the way to get on. Mr Orme's ideas have changed since then. He likes the way his pupils speak and he even likes his own accent now; still 'rough', as he thinks of it, after all these years in London.

4

When he talks about these things with his friends they think he's a bit sentimental or just making the best of a bad job. It is difficult enough to explain, let alone to justify, his conviction that his being interested in the languages his pupils speak does actually help them to write English of several sorts and to speak more confidently in class. It isn't as if he knew all those languages himself, though: Yoruba, Arabic, Cantonese, Gujarati. He often wishes he did when he is teaching his examination classes. He can't even find good dictionaries for most of the languages, let alone science textbooks or novels.

For a long time research into bilingualism operated within the assumption that bilingual children were likely to have problems at school. Welsh-speaking children in Wales and French-speaking children in Canada did less well than their monolingual (English-speaking) counterparts. In the way of so much of that kind of research, most of it had, by the early 1960s,[4] been queried and even contradicted on the grounds that the tests which were used to establish the inferior attainment of bilingual children ignored both the social factors underlying the bilingual ones and the effects on a child of speaking one language at home while learning (and being tested in) another one at school.

There had as well always been some people in Wales who were prepared to concede that knowing Welsh as well as English[5] might be seen as providing the benefits of a cheap classical education; benefits, by the way, which were not queried. This is one of the anomalies about attitudes to bilingualism. Whereas learning a foreign language and even one or two dead ones as well has always been the *sine qua non* of a 'good' education, and whereas a child who picks up fluent French and Italian, say, because her father has been posted abroad, is likely to be thought fortunate, at an advantage, even 'finished',[6] a child with two or three non-European languages, in some of which he may be literate, could be regarded as quite literally languageless when he arrives in an English school, where 'not a word of English' can often imply 'not a word'. Partly, this is a matter of the history which has made of English a lingua franca. I should want to suggest, however, that it also has a good deal to do with the view that English as a school subject is bound to concentrate on its written form.

It is not that there need be any argument with the tradition

5

which makes schools the promoters of literacy; but that the written form and its intimate relation, in many people's eyes, with Standard English speech can be made to exclude the realities of the language as it is spoken. Many children spend a larger proportion of their day in school on writing and listening than on reading or talking. Even tests which are intended to assess oral comprehension, reading competence and a response to literature are made to depend on the child's knowing how to write a certain sort of English prose. *That* is the sort of English Mr Orme *should* be teaching his pupils. It is not a form easily learned by anyone whose own speech is under suspicion. The best examples of expository or imaginative prose draw vitally upon the spoken language in ways which children should be helped to understand. The belief that a child can learn to produce even the most modest versions of such prose while his speech is dismissed, even perhaps excoriated, is likely to be doomed, and we can't, surely, be wanting children to 'talk like a book'.

To be genuinely multilingual or multidialectal in contemporary Britain is allowed, then, to be a drawback. It is still thought 'useful' to know some Latin, while knowledge of Standard Tamil, say, and one of its dialects, is thought 'confusing'. There is, of course, a special kind of usefulness in knowing something of a language from which English partly derives[7] and which has certainly mattered to English literature, just as there is another kind of usefulness in speaking your mother tongue.

Other claims have been made for the learning of a second language, however, beyond this sort of usefulness. One would be that another language embodies as it expresses another culture, and that another culture introduces the possibility of critical detachment about one's own. Another would be that there are aspects of the nature of language itself which are often more easily learned through an encounter with a second language.[8] Connected with this is the notion that the conscious mastery of a language is an intellectual discipline in itself. Recent research on some bilingual English/Hebrew children and some Spanish/English-speaking children by Ben-Zeev (1977a, 1977b) draws attention to those things which these children do better than their monolingual peers. The suggestion is that because they are earlier able to separate meaning from sound, they are also able to develop earlier what Margaret Donaldson (1978) has called a 'reflective awareness of . . . language as a symbolic system', which is a prerequisite for developing abstract thought. Perhaps because the learning of language has required more effort of them, these children are often more sensitive to the appropriateness of their speech and to the effect it produces on hearers of it. They also, it is claimed, become aware earlier than most children of the structures within one particular language system which contrast with those of the other one. Even at those points where one language might be expected to interfere with the other, to overlap or create confusion, possibilities for particular insights were noticed, so that fusion rather than confusion worked to produce at an earlier age a sense of what languages generally consist of, get up to, are used for.

What, it might be asked, is the hurry? Many monolingual children will develop that kind of awareness of language too, in time. But since learning to read depends on this ability to stand back from language, to hear it and watch it function, as it were, and since learning to read quickly and successfully can determine a child's whole school experience, it is important that teachers exploit what may be real advantages for the bilingual child. I shall want to suggest in a later chapter that there are other advantages for bilingual children: experiences of learning usefully, actively and collaboratively, which may be more crucial still as harbingers of successful schooling.

There are teachers who have seen the possibilities of exploiting pupils' bilingualism for the children themselves and for other people. A fifteen-year-old bilingual Turkish boy, for instance, was asked to translate into written English a story told by his mother in Turkish to her three-year-old daughter. He was able to discover for himself, and partly to solve, the problems of turning into written English an oral story in another language intended for a young child and told by a woman who was elaborating a narrative out of a real experience.

Then two thirteen-year-old Jamaican girls improvised a play in patois on videotape. Because they wanted to transcribe their play, in order to develop and improve it, they decided to transcribe its present version. They found themselves having to invent an orthography and a way of representing their own speech which would allow a reader to 'hear' it as far as possible. The exercise was useful on several counts, not the least important being that it

7

introduced one of the girls, who had barely been able to read and write until then, to the nature of written language and to the purposes there might be for her in learning to write. It is the kind of exercise which would be hard to match in a language for which conventional spelling already existed.[9] The improvising on tape, the passion of the chief performer and her extraordinary ability to switch between a wailing patois, a minister's Biblical rhetoric and a hectoring and controlling parental command, were qualities I should want to see as at least as important in the developing and appraising of language talents.

In one sense it is all quite simple. Where a child grows up speaking more than one language or dialect, and those languages or dialects have equivalent status in his own and in other people's eyes, and where the connections between those languages and their differences are made explicit, multilingualism can be an unqualified good. Mr Orme's pupil, Andreas, is in that rare position. He still visits Cyprus. English people know about Greek, even hear it spoken on their holidays. Andreas speaks Greek for most of the time at home, but other members of his family speak English too; and he is not aware of making conscious decisions about which language to speak to whom or where. He could read and write in Greek before he arrived in England,[10] and he learned English in a school where it was thought, rightly, that he was competent linguistically even if he didn't know English, and where they have come to rely on and to admire his success. He was lucky too to embark on the second of his languages before he was too old to do so easily and to learn it principally through using it with children of his own age.[11] As an example of a bilingual's advantages he is ideal, though hardly typical.

It is a characteristic irony that while the learning of languages can be an expensive business, nearly all those people in the world who grow up or become bilingual do so because their mother tongue or dialect has associations with poverty which make it likely to be thought inappropriate for education and some kinds of employment. Many of the people who have come to live in England during the last twenty-five years are in the position of speaking either a dialect of English or another language altogether, which they are encouraged, and in some cases are themselves all too ready, to relinquish. What will happen to Kulvinder between now and the first time she writes a letter applying for a job? Her parents' refusal to use their own language may have implications about their view of themselves which will go beyond the danger of depriving their daughter of a language which is hers as well as theirs. Kulvinder's watchfulness has something of the look which children acquire when they are brought up by deaf parents. Modern language teaching often makes good use of a temporary outlawing of the mother tongue. It is a strategy which assumes that sheer need to communicate is sure to power the acquisition of a new language, as it has been thought, simplistically, to power the acquisition of the first. For a child in Kulvinder's circumstances the refusal to speak Punjabi could be disastrous. Certainly she has proved that her need to communicate is not as powerful as all that.[12]

The variety of ways in which multilingualism is experienced by children is infinite, ranging from a kind of 'anomie' at one extreme to a quite special flexibility and effectiveness as a language user at the other. Somewhere between are all those children who leave their mother tongue at home and learn 'English' at school. This can produce a damaging dividedness, particularly when it is not discussed, shared or understood. A second language learned and used only in school can feel like a language of passivity, acceptance, attention, listening and Kulvinder's obedience. Its use will be constrained by rules and prohibitions, its vitalities and subtleties hidden. Similarly, the home language may be relegated to the terrain of childhood, interesting only as the expression of a vestigial folk culture.[13] The life of action and feeling, of first experiences and what is directly known, can become divorced from the world where language has become an instrument for generalisation, organisation and the assimilating of new ideas and knowledge. There is a danger of that happening to any child, but the danger is a much greater one if the two selves, so to speak, talk in different languages. Cultural values can be distorted and polarised into what is quaint and half extinguished, on the one hand, and what is practical, modern and remunerated, on the other.

Many children are marooned between languages and between cultures, forgetting one more rapidly than they acquire another; and meanwhile they may be regarded by teachers and by other children – ultimately, perhaps, by themselves – as bereft of all the things language stands for: intelligence, humour, daring, inven-

9

tiveness, enthusiasm, discrimination and curiosity. And without those qualities it is not easy to learn the new language which might enable you to regain them. A child's first sorting out of its impressions of the world, of its own place there, and of noises which are meaningful from noises which are not, came with a particular language, which is now forced underground, made inaudible, unintelligible. Learning a second language is bound to seem like a matter of attaching it to meanings which will always adhere in a special way to the first one. In fact this is a much more contentious issue than it might seem; and I shall consider it later. The confidence which allows us to use our language to make jokes and tell stories, however, let alone to answer a court charge or infer something of motive and intention from another person's speech, is not gained by dismissing as irrelevant the language which both produced and expressed the child's first thoughts.

Michelle's parents came to London from St Lucia before she was born. They still speak French patois at home, and though she thinks her parents' English absurd she herself knew some English by the time she was five and went to primary school. Most of the time she speaks like the other children in her class, a non-Standard London dialect. When she is with her West Indian friends she shifts into London Jamaican as they do. She says she has never spoken French patois outside her home and that 'most West Indian people say that patois is bad for young children to speak'. That may be part of the reason why her parents sent her to a school where there are relatively few West Indian children. That, at any rate, is what Michelle believes.

When Michelle recalls, and mimics, her first teacher at primary school telling her, 'You're talking bad language, bad English', she assumes that her teacher meant that there was something wrong with her accent. She is also able fiercely to say, 'You should be able to speak patois, Jamaican or English.' When Michelle assents to the disapproval her speech can elicit while defending her right to speak as she wants to and needs to, she is expressing the sort of ambivalence many dialect speakers grow up with. I am thinking, for instance, of a working-class woman in her sixties, who has lived in Fulham all her life. She is able to listen to an East End speaker and comment, 'I think I speak rough, but I don't speak like that', and even as she deplores her own 'roughness', to remind me that only the evening before she had been congratulated for a turn of phrase and an amusing anecdote. Brian Jackson (1979) quotes a Chinese woman defending her children's right to learn Chinese: 'I think there should be Chinese class in every town', and following this at once with a rebuke to the author, who had admired a Chinese girl in a photograph: 'How can you say Chinese girl is beautiful when there are English girls?' It is commonplace examples of this kind which remind us of the complexities involved in allegiance to language and culture.

Michelle's English teacher has no views about her language, except that her writing is 'weak in sentence structure'. Neither this comment nor that earlier one about 'bad language' have been substantiated or explained to Michelle. She speaks, in fact, three languages:[14] French patois, non-Standard English and London Jamaican. She is fluent and effective in all three, makes easy shifts between them, stylish use of the incongruities the shifts can produce,[15] and is able, as well, to do an excellent imitation of Mrs Thatcher. It is worth remembering, I think, that whereas all non-Standard English speakers are compelled to understand and sometimes to assume Standard speech patterns, Standard English speakers are rarely required to do the reverse.[16] Yet in spite of this rich language repertoire, Michelle, at twelve, has already been made aware that neither her speech nor her writing will quite do.

That many of the difficulties which exist for a multilingual child also exist for a multidialectal one is due to their being the product of attitudes to languages generally, and to particular languages, rather than to their being inherent in multilingualism itself. They are especially difficult attitudes to grapple with because they are about class and race and status, though they masquerade as value judgments about language and fine (even musical) discriminations.

There is nothing new about multilingualism, nor about the passions and the prejudices it provokes. Language has always been felt as a measure of identity, by individuals and by whole communities. It is this fundamental allegiance which has made it necessary to institute lingua francas, since language is for communication with some people, just as it is a way of avoiding communication with others. The certainties which have nearly wiped out Gaelic in the Scottish Highlands and have deplored Scots in the Lowlands have been relaxed, so that it is now respectable for plays on television to be in dialect and for novelists and poets to use the language of their childhood.

This makes it all the more surprising that no such welcome has been given by schools[17] to the mother tongues and dialects of children. This may be to do with the teacherly obsession with something called 'correct' language, and with correcting, in red ink, children's writing. It is an obsession which is encouraged and applauded by many people who would themselves find it hard to say what they meant by 'correct', as would we all. Children are famously less responsive to the thorough sub-editing job done by teachers on their writing – which can look at times like no more than a display of credentials – than to more positive ways of suggesting how a piece of written or spoken language might be made more effective, clear or truthful. This sort of approach, to be successful, relies on a sense of language being complex and diverse, and its 'correctness' being no more than one aspect of what children need to know about it. Official documents are circulated, it is true, which preach the virtues of 'mother-tongue maintenance'[18] without specifying how this might happen. Nor is it easy to imagine how more positive and useful language work could go on in school so long as examinations, which are allowed to validate all schooling and to determine the curriculum, continue to rely on a definition of English so exiguous as to exclude not just dialect but speech of any kind.

In America attention is focused at the moment on the predicament of Spanish-speaking and Indian children, and J.A. Fishman (1976) has presented some of the research and evaluation of particular schemes for introducing forms of bilingual education in America and elsewhere. There have been schemes to promote mother-tongue literacy before school and the use of the mother tongue as the language of instruction in school. These are brave moves, though it is not clear that they have managed to change the attitudes which have made them necessary and which still undermine them. In this country, where a request for a modest central government grant towards the funding of bilingual education in Wales can still produce angry letters to *The Times*, what little mother-tongue teaching goes on is undertaken for the most part by members of particular language communities,[19] and only in a handful of cases with help from schools or local authorities.[20] There have been a few successes, though all the schemes are on a small scale and necessarily dependent on a voluntary commitment to them. They may also encourage minorities to feel defensive

about cultures and languages which are plainly not valued by the
majority if they are excluded from school.

The tragedy is that schools themselves see their role here as so
confined, and the English language as so inflexibly unresilient, as
to reject the value of their pupils' languages to themselves, to the
curriculum and to the community to which the schools belong.
Kulvinder could be beginning an education which allows her to
feel proud of her language and of the special knowledge she brings
to the learning of English. She could as easily remain in a state of
profound bewilderment, fearful of having another language
snatched from her, struggling not towards an English which she
can take on positively as her own but towards something which, at
best, will enable her to spell her employer's letters correctly and,
at worst, will get her a job where speech, and indeed thought, are
not required of her.

Any normal child has mastered by the age of five an elaborate
symbolic system and internalised its rules. This is true for any child
learning any language. Through speech, and through learning to
read and write, the child will 'learn to turn language and thought in
upon themselves', as Margaret Donaldson (1978) has put it, so
that he can talk about language and think about thinking. Children
with more than one language may be especially well placed to do
this. Teachers in multilingual classrooms have at their disposal
resources for introducing all their pupils to the nature of language,
to the quality and the implications of linguistic and cultural
diversity, and, thereby, to an outlook on knowledge and to the
kind of relativism which can produce both intellectual rigour and
intellectual openness. The best teaching always moves from a
sensitive awareness of what the learner already knows to what is
new; and the best users of English, speakers and writers, plunder
the tensions and the variety which English has always so vigorously
incorporated.

If children are to become powerful users of language for their
own purposes, and responsive to the subtleties and excitement of
what has been done by others, and what can be done, teachers
would do well to begin from an appreciation of the strengths, the
highly developed social and linguistic skills, children bring with
them when they come to school. And that means all children.
There is more and more evidence that children like Michelle, who
are apparently 'weak in sentence structure' or possessed of 'limited

vocabularies', are encountered with a quite unusual frequency by some teachers and most researchers.[21] Perhaps it is because such teachers and researchers are the only people given to asking children questions to which they don't really want answers, and to engaging children in conversation about matters of interest to neither party. Those who have spent more time listening to children talking in their own language to their own friends about things they urgently want to talk about and find out about have come back with very different data.

It is time to make use of language diversity; not just the diversity as between one school and another, or between one child and another, but the diversity within each individual child and within the use of language itself. This respect for diversity would, after all, make of an examination or a letter of application no more than single items in a genuine language repertoire, one for use not one up for judgment. This does not mean that there are no possibilities of difficulty for a child growing up with more than one available language or dialect. I shall want to suggest, however, that a view of language as static and therefore describable, like a holding to monolingualism as the norm, may be partly responsible for such difficulties.

In this chapter I have tried to characterise the bilingual experience and to suggest that society and schools must make a response to it; not a remediating or a compensating response but a positive one. In the next chapters I will be discussing what twelve bilinguals, children and adults, have to say on the subject. Most of them are successful bilinguals, successful learners and successful people. Some of them feel confused and trapped by their position. Others feel exhilarated by their own achievement and by what they feel that they have, especially, to offer the world as knowledge and understanding. That there are important social, linguistic and pedagogic considerations in all this will only gradually be becoming apparent; and I shall not insist on these until we have heard from the bilingual speakers themselves. Later I hope to set what are personal and idiosyncratic accounts and impressions into a broader social, linguistic and educational context.

2 'So I think I'll stay halfway'

Have you ever hurt
    about baskets?
I have, seeing my grandmother weaving
    for a long time.
Have you ever hurt about work?
I have, because my father works too hard
    and he tells how he works.
Have you ever hurt about cattle?
I have, because my grandfather has been working
    on the cattle for a long time.
Have you ever hurt about school?
I have, because I learned a lot of words
    from school,
And they are not my words.[1]

In the next three chapters I shall concentrate on drawing out of some transcribed conversations the individual concerns and preoccupations of twelve bilingual speakers. There are recurring themes and issues which I shall point to, but I will keep the more general discussion of these to later chapters. There are difficulties in getting at people's experience of bilingualism, as these conversations show, and they are for the most part similar to the difficulties there are in getting almost anybody to focus on the language they use rather than on the use they make of it.

There is by now a vast and burgeoning literature on bilingualism, on its educational implications and its effects on or relation to cognitive development. There are treatments of the social and political dimensions, as well as of the linguistic and psychological ones. There have been large-scale, even international, research projects as well as detailed investigations of individual and group bilingual experience. I will be touching on relevant aspects of these in later chapters. What there has been much less of is testimony

15

from bilingual speakers themselves, though accounts of such experiences are to be found in literature and they have importantly affected the life and work of many writers.

This is by way of being an explanation of, and not an apology for, the transcripts of five taped conversations I had with twelve bilingual speakers, which form the substance of the next three chapters. The conversations themselves are often anecdotal, and my comments on them at this stage will be impressionistic. The speakers themselves are randomly chosen. There are ten young people who are still at school and two adults. All but one of the speakers were thrust into English because they, or their parents, came to live here. The twelfth case is a girl who learned French and English (and, briefly, Alsatian) simultaneously as a baby, because her father worked in Strasbourg. The length of exposure to English varies from one year to eighteen years (or a lifetime), and the levels of proficiency in English or other languages could be said to vary as greatly. Naturally, it is not going to be possible to generalise conclusively from these personal testimonies, and that is not what I wish or mean to do.

When I began my interviews with bilingual speakers it was with a somewhat unformulated expectation that they would exhibit a special awareness of language because they had operated in more than one language. I saw this awareness in terms of a sense of themselves as speakers and writers and a sense of language as a system and a resource, which came out of a sensitivity to what these languages had in common and where they differed. I also expected that this awareness might go with a recognition on their part that there were gaps and lacks in aspects of their languages, and that these might be attributable to the conditions of their acquiring their languages. I have not undermined these expectations, though it may be that as a starting point they have turned out to be crude and oversimplified. As I went on I was obliged to broaden out from these expectations and to hoist in the individual and shared concerns of the bilingual speakers themselves. These I shall group under three headings. The first is the time and age dimension. The second is awareness as a function of how the second language was learned or encountered. The third is the fact that most of these speakers saw the question of bilingualism in terms of biculturalism.

The only aspect of bilingualism which my small sample could be said genuinely to represent is its diversity. Not only were my speakers different in terms of age, sex and background, they had come to English by different routes and at different times. Some had grown up with access to English from the beginning. Others were now, or were once, learning it as a second or subsequent language, sometimes with formal instruction. Several of them testify to the withering of the first language and the consolidating of the second. In some cases the first language has been reclaimed as if it were a foreign language. For none of them are the two languages equal in terms of the people or the purposes for which they are used.

The question, therefore, of awareness of language and of attitudes to particular languages has, inevitably, a time scale. It may be, for instance, that those for whom bilingualism is still unstable, where one language is still being learned or another one is withering in its importance or use, are able to reflect more easily on the implications for them of operating in more than one language. Not all of these speakers sound like native speakers of English. Some do, and amongst those who do not there are those who give the impression that for them any conscious learning of English is completed. This in itself raises questions about when and why a speaker is able to feel that he is now proficient in the second language.

For all these speakers language is, for most of the time, transparent, a medium which they find hard to detach from their personal experience and their sense of straddling different cultures. They all express ambivalent attitudes to their languages, conflicting and changing loyalties, an unsettled view as to their proficiency in their languages, confidence alternating with uncertainty. For most people – though it may be possible to make an exception of writers, as users of language which is meant to draw attention to its own nature – language is transparent for most, but not all, of the time. So that, inevitably, my somewhat dogged insistence that my interlocutors keep to the subject of language was defeated time and time again. Only later did I realise that these speakers' evading of my questions about language in order to talk about immigration, culture, family conflict, social and political dilemmas, constituted, in fact, and significantly, answers to my questions.

My sample, and it may be useful to consider the implications of this, includes a majority of speakers who are, in fact, multilingual.

That is, what might be called a functional bilingualism has, in many cases, been preceded by the learning and knowledge of yet another language. This is obviously not always the case, though many people who come here from parts of Africa and the Indian sub-continent have grown up in communities which are multilingual, even where individuals may themselves be monolingual. It may be helpful to introduce at this point a view put by Ervin-Tripp (1973), which raises the issue of the optimum age or conditions for second-language learning:

> One way of looking at second-language learning is to assume that the first encounters with a second language will be handled by the apparatus of structure and process already available. But there is an additional factor to consider. An adult who has changed his linguistic system only in minor ways – by adding new vocabulary, for example – for many years may not have available ready strategies for change. An adult who has already learned other languages, or a child who is constantly in the process of reorganising his processing system and adding to his storage at all levels will have quite different approaches to new input. 'Learning to learn' is an established notion in psychology. The most adaptable, sensitive language learner we can find is a young child. Surely we can expect that his second language learning will reflect many of the same processes of development as he used to discover his first language. On the other hand, in the case of inexperienced adults we can expect the system to be most adaptable just at the point where it changes most readily in adult life – the lexicon. But we can expect the typical adult to be ready to process both the sounds and syntax of what he hears as if his usual processing devices were appropriate.

If we take from this the possibility that successful language learning may happen at different ages, but that whenever or however it happens it seems to involve the learner actively and consciously regarding himself as learning, this may throw light on the vexed question of what kinds of teaching or support are most helpful to learners. An acceptance of the fact of multilingualism, memories of learning a first or a second language, current involvement in the acquisition or even the losing of a language: all these may facilitate awareness of language and development in using it. The least experienced of my bilinguals, Fanis, is both the

18

most prone to confusions between his languages and the closest to the difficulties and the invitations they present him with. Similarly Jane, who has returned to what could be said to be her mother tongue, but as a foreign-language learner, is the most sharply aware of her own predicament in relation to her languages and of what that might imply about them.

At the moment I am speculating about these issues in relation to a sample of bilinguals which in most respects is not representative. Later I shall return to them through the work of linguists who have studied the terrain. In the case even of the most straightforwardly bilingual of the speakers there is evidence of gains in one language having involved losses in the other. An image which contrasts accretion with substitution may be helpful here, allowing for both processes to be going on, perhaps simultaneously.

A shared preoccupation for all these speakers is with the place in their own lives of formal language learning on the one hand and more informal acquisition. Several of them attribute their success in learning English to a formal grounding in the 'rules' and are, perhaps understandably, reluctant to see their proficiency as attributable to something a good deal less historically ascertainable than that. Clearly this raises issues of pedagogy, but it also reminds us of the difficulties we all have in recalling how we learned to read or to ride a bicycle, and more particularly how we are likely to confuse the mode of instruction with the process of learning itself.

Before moving from this intentionally superficial preamble to the transcripts themselves I want to quote a short extract from another taped conversation between three seventeen-year-olds in a North London school. They were discussing memories and the difficulties they had in writing them down. Sandhya, who is an English and Gujarati speaker, claimed to have no memory at all of her early childhood, which had been spent in East Africa. She said that she felt no sense of loss about this and then went on:

Me as an Indian girl; if I went to an Indian wedding party; it's completely different from what I do at school. It's two different parts of me; one is Indian and one is doing completely different things at school. It's difficult to connect things I do at home with the things I do at school, because they're very different. What I do, what I talk – different languages, everything.

This seems to me to be characteristic as testimony and as experience and to illustrate some recurring themes in the transcripts of my conversations with other bilingual speakers. In accounting for a sense of dividedness it begins with a cultural phenomenon and mentions language last. In the context of Sandhya's earlier remarks about her having and needing no history or past, and because of the context of her particular split life, her dividedness can be seen as intimately connected with her being an immigrant and a person growing up within and across several different and often conflicting cultures. It can, though, and this is what makes the nature of my enterprise so intractable, seem no more than a sharpened version of what all children know about and often admit to: a sometimes anxious sense of being dislocated and fragmented by the need to behave quite differently at school from the way they behave at home. This may be no more than an elaborate way of saying that the experiences I want to consider in these bilinguals' accounts of themselves could be paralleled at most points by the experiences of people who are either monolingual or at least bidialectal. It needs to be stressed that with each of these speakers bilingualism is just one feature of a life which has involved living in several countries and always, at some point, as a foreigner. It has involved disruption and change for them and for their parents, and often fluctuations in their economic and social status and in employment and way of life.

Fatima is eighteen and has lived in this country for four years. She comes from the Moroccan border with Algeria and she speaks French and Classical and Colloquial Arabic as well as English, and is literate in all three languages. She spent some time in a French school in Algeria and some time in an Arabic school in Morocco. She is now in the sixth form of a London girls' comprehensive school, studying for O levels in English, Russian, Arabic and two other subjects, as well as A level French. Her English is lively, fast and confident, though her accent would not be mistaken for a native speaker's and some of her structures and idioms are unstable. There is no doubt, however, of her ability to express her personality, humour and ideas in English, and she is much more than functionally multilingual.

Najat, also from Morocco, is seventeen and has lived in this country for three years. She speaks nearly native-like English with a slight non-Standard London accent. At the time of the interview she claimed to have forgotten most of her Arabic and she was never literate in it. At times she was reticent about herself during our conversation, though she can express herself passionately and with conviction. After we had talked I lent her a copy of *My Life* by Muhammed Elbaja,[2] which she read with enthusiasm. Later, she wrote a remarkable autobiographical story which was published with Elbaja's.[3] This appears to have affected her deeply; for since then she has re-arabised her name, returned for a holiday to Morocco and is relearning Arabic.

Maria, the third of the three girls, has Spanish parents who settled here when she was two. She is now seventeen. English is her main language, and she behaves and sounds like a native speaker of it. As well as keeping up Spanish as the language she uses at home she has now visited Spain on several occasions, has Spanish O and A level and is working towards English A level.

Fatima   I come from Morocco and I was brought up in the border between Arabic Morocco and Algeria itself and I have a slight different accent than Najat. I speak English. I've been learning for four years. I speak French, Arabic, Classical Arabic and Colloquial Arabic, because it's very difficult if you don't know Classical Arabic, you'd probably be lost in the Middle East if you don't know.... I can also help myself in Spanish. I can read and write in French and in Arabic. I mean if I go to Spain I won't be lost. My main hobby is just really languages.

J.M.   ...are you likely to stay?

Fatima   It's not that.... I don't really know. It depends on my parents. To me all I want is get the qualifications and leave as soon as I could. I would like to go to an Arab country, not particularly Morocco. Somewhere in the Middle East, about there.... When I came here I couldn't speak a word of English. I wasn't really planning to come to school. I thought it was too late. I was fourteen. I was an old woman and my father forced me to come, so I went to W..., that's the school. I started in the lower school and it was a disaster, people used to muck about and say, 'Ooh look at her, she can't speak English'... I had to work like mad, every night and day and in three months I started to sort of have a decent conversation and because of the teacher who was teaching English, she was, I admire her, she was fantastic, she was, it's Miss... and because she could speak a bit of French, she didn't have much difficulty with me because I could write already, because I was in full-time school in Morocco. When I was in Algeria, because that's where my family come from, I started

21

school in French as the first language, and after one year my father didn't like the idea so we went back to Morocco and they said 'No, the main language is Arabic', so I had to forget about French for about two years and did Arabic. And in Morocco you have to pass every subject to go to the next class, so in the third year of my education I started to do French and Arabic, and then after five years you go to college if you pass your exams and then three years in college and then you start English.

J.M.   I want you to think about when you'd rather speak French, when you'd rather speak Arabic, when you'd rather speak English. Who you do it to, what kinds of situation make you want to speak one rather than the other?

Fatima   The thing is when I'm in England I somehow, my mind turns into English, I've got a sort of English mind, 'cos full-time schooling you speak English all the time, so you get home you speak English all the time and you speak to your mother, of course, in Arabic, but somehow you're English, you're thinking in English, English, English. But last year I won a scholarship, and I was awarded to go to France for two months, one month in Avignon to the university to learn French and other month in a French family, and it was incredible. I just rushed to France and I forgot about English completely. It's not that I didn't know the language and all I could think was in French, speaking French, do French, and that happens as well when I go back home. I forget about French, I forget about English. I think about Arabic, I just speak Arabic, Arabic and it depends on the country I'm living in, atmosphere.

J.M.   Do you speak English to your family, your parents ever?

Fatima   No. It's just that you cut off English words in every way, you know. Myself anyway, I have this. An Arab spirit comes into me. I, all I speak is Arabic, Arabic as much as I can. And as soon as I leave Morocco Arabic is finished, English is for me and I don't know, that's how I feel.

J.M.   Are there things you talk about with your friends which are difficult to talk about in Arabic, which you'd rather talk about in English?

Fatima   When I'm speaking to my brothers in England we're speaking together in Arabic and suddenly automatically I find myself speaking English. It's when you talk about the things like schools, meetings, going to a disco or to a club or I see a friend of mine or you're going to see somewhere in London, something that concerns the English environment, and we somehow feel much better if you discuss it in English, but if I speak about the mosque or about religion, the Muslim religion, or I speak about Morocco, I, I feel much better if I speak it in Arabic.

J.M.   Are there times when you're in a slight muddle about which is the best language for this purpose?

Maria   That in general is in everything. You're between two societies, I

	think, between Spanish society and English. You can't make up your mind which one is best.
J.M.	Can you think of some situations where that happens?
Maria	When you come back from holidays. You step off the plane and it's terrible. It's awful, the first few months when you come back. It's really horrible, because everything's so different. You have to change again.
J.M.	If you're going to talk to your friends about what you've been doing in Spain, does that present a special problem?
Maria	Well, it just makes you homesick. I came here in 1963. I'm seventeen.
J.M.	So you were two and later you went into a primary school here. Have you any memories of learning English?
Maria	No. It's just sort of like my first language.
J.M.	Can you read and write Spanish?
Maria	Yes. I go to a Spanish school every afternoon. From 6.30 to 9.30. Every day. I'm preparing for the same exams they take in Spain. It's terrible. Two schools at the same time. Nine o'clock you start English school. You leave at four and then you have to go again at six and then till half-past nine in the evening. You can't do any homework. It's awful really.
J.M.	How is it that you've kept that up for so long? It was your parents who wanted you to do that, was it?
Maria	Yes, my parents and me and because I want to go and live in Spain as soon as I get my exams, good exam results. I mean if I go just with my English exams I won't go nowhere. I mean with just a few O levels in a foreign country.
Fatima	No, I mean they want you to have good qualifications in English, but before they ask you for that they say have you got any qualifications in Arabic? That's why I mean I did my O level without sort of going to school or anything, I just asked, 'Can I do my O level Arabic, Classical', and I got a B. And now I'm struggling by myself to do the A level. I haven't got any teachers or anything. There is no evening school. They haven't enough people and I'm just working alone for it.
J.M.	You've done your Spanish A, have you?
Maria	I did it mostly by myself.
Fatima	It was incredible. Last year about this time she hadn't started yet.
Maria	I didn't even read the books and I thought, Oh my God my exams are coming up. In the end I had a teacher for a few weeks and then she went and then, oh…
Fatima	I thought, if she gets, if Maria gets her A level, I admire her because it was about two weeks before the A level, she goes off to have a look at the Spanish books.
Maria	I got an A for the oral and a C for the written.
J.M.	So you've obviously not got many problems as a bilingual speaker and yet you say that it is quite painful at times. For

	instance, when you go back to Spain do you slip into Spanish quite easily?
Maria	For the first two weeks it's very hard to adapt to that society. Because you're sort of shyer and everyone's very loud. And everything's so different. And then you get used to it for a few weeks. And when you start getting used to it you have to come back here and it's like death.
Fatima	It's terrible, because you go there and you feel like a foreigner. Once you are out of your country, you're a foreigner in this world. You come to England they look at you differently.
Maria	When I go back to Spain...
Fatima	You go to Morocco, you're a foreigner and everywhere you go you look like a foreigner.
Maria	When I go back there they call me, 'Oh look the English girl.' Oh, I get annoyed. And when I come here, Oh look, Spanish girl. So I think I'll stay halfway...but you have to sort of sacrifice yourself.
J.M.	At home, with your parents, you speak Spanish?
Maria	Yes, with my parents, but I always speak English with my brother, always.
J.M.	Would you never speak English with your parents?
Maria	No. It depends. They don't usually speak English.
J.M.	Is it sometimes difficult using Spanish with your parents?
Maria	Yes it is, but I would say it in Spanish to them, you know. Explain it in my own way.
J.M.	Do you have to translate?
Maria	Yes. All the time. I think in an English way. I always think in English and I sort of translate my thoughts into Spanish and I find it sometimes a little bit difficult.
Fatima	It is hard. I mean the system is different, and you're speaking to your father in Arabic. 'I'm going to do the O level. I'm going to do the CSE', and he's going, 'What the hell is she talking about?' Because the system is different and then sometimes you go, you feel like, sometimes you feeling like forcing you to say it in English, but you know that if you say it in English your father will slap you.
J.M.	Really, he wouldn't like you to speak English to him?
Fatima	To him, no. I mean, the thing is, I mean I can understand that too, I really understand Maria, because she's been here for such a long time. I been here just four years and I find it hard, because, especially if you've got a little sister. My little sister was born here, and she's always speaking in English to me. Her Arabic, it's terrible. She doesn't know any..
J.M.	Are your parents going to try to get her to learn Arabic?
Fatima	My mother, my father, they never speak any English to her. It's always Arabic. But then there she is, answering them in English. She can understand, but to answer...
J.M.	You would talk to her in English, would you?

Fatima Yes, I don't know. I can't help it.

Najat I came from the same country as her. I came in 1975, so three years.

J.M. What languages do you speak?

Najat Colloquial Arabic, just, and English. Well I used to learn French for about five years but I forgot all about it and it's pretty hard for getting used to.

J.M. When you came here did you speak no English?

Najat Oh no, no. I had to start from scratch.

J.M. What about reading and writing in Arabic?

Najat Well I wouldn't say I'd got, you know, my writing excellent, but it's awful, I make lots of mistakes. I've got used to speaking English now. I find it hard to adopt to the old ways speaking Moroccan. I find it much easier speaking English nowadays. I speak English to my mother, to everyone. She doesn't mind really. She has a boyfriend, and he's half West Indian and she can only communicate with him in English.

J.M. So her English is pretty good too?

Najat No, it's not all that good.

J.M. And brothers and sisters, have you got? Oh yes you've got your twin sister...

Najat Oh yes, in this school.

J.M. She came before you?

Najat Yes, two years before me. My younger sister was born here, so she speaks English, so she can't speak in Arabic at all.

J.M. What d'you feel about that?

Najat Well I don't feel anything, because I'm not her, you see, I can't answer...

J.M. Are you pleased to have two languages?

Najat Yes, in a way I am, because you sort of communicate with other people who speak other languages beside English and there's a feeling inside you, it just feels marvellous.

J.M. I suppose what I want to know is how much you have to translate from one language to another and what things are hard to talk about in one language rather than the other. For instance, you're all living in a huge city. When you're in your other countries do you also live in cities?

Fatima I live in the capital of the, it's called the Isthmus of Morocco, but of course the main capital is Rabat and a place Oujda. That's quite a big city. There's Jewish, Algerians no doubt, French, Spanish and Moroccans.

Najat Well I was born in a town and I was brought up in the capital of Morocco, near the capital, called Sale. They're closely connected together in one place. I was brought up there.

J.M. Will you go back?

Najat No, I don't think so, because I live here, so I can't go back. I can't adopt to the old system. If I go back there I would feel like a foreigner. I would have to go to a lot of trouble to get used to

	their system, which I'm not intending to go into (laugh).
J.M.	Yet you've presumably got very clear memories of Morocco…
Najat	Oh yes. But I'm not really homesick, because I haven't been there for three years, I haven't been to Morocco.
Maria	I've never lived in Spain and I still feel homesick. We used to stay with relations, but now we stay in a house, in our own house, in a large village near the capital, it's eight miles…
Fatima	I think it's for the Europeans to live in another European country, it's quite all right. I mean it's not exactly all right, you do get homesick but it's not as painful as if you are from a completely different culture like me, for example. Different religion, different colour, everything different, completely separate, you know. My father took me from a world and put me in a completely different world, and when I get really homesick…. It's like last week. Last Saturday we had our festival and the Muslims kill the sheep, and of course we did it as well here, but somehow I remembered when we used to do it back home. You do it and everybody comes to see you, grandfather and grandmother and screaming and this and that and it was, you know, I just went to my bedroom and started to cry. Mum had to work and it's just like one of the other days and I thought um, nobody says Merry Christmas to me. It's very, very painful when it comes to feasts. It's terrible.
Najat	Yes, you know, this Christmas day, when it approaches you feel so excited to see people sacrificing the sheep and all that horrible image of it but you get sort of excited, you wanted to see it, but here you can't do that kind of thing, you can be arrested if they catch you, you know, sacrificing the sheep here.
Fatima	You have to go to a special place…. You are a Muslim in an English world. No, I had England all round, English people. It's got nothing to do with that. It's that I think I just came very late. I came grown up, if you see what I mean.
Maria	It doesn't matter, because I have been brought up here all my life and I still can't adapt to this place and I've never lived in Spain, never. I don't know, I just don't like it…. It's everything.
Fatima	I think the climate's more…
Najat	She's convincing herself, saying I'm Spanish, you must be a typical Spanish.
Fatima	…the more patriotic you get, that's what I think. And the climate is very hard to adapt to here and the people are kind of different, because when I used to live in Morocco sort of sit themselves…everyone was there, everyone from top to bottom and…here, my next-door neighbour, I've been living next to her three years, now, but I don't know her name. Sometimes I say hello, I really do my best to say hello to her.
Najat	That's because people here have lots of problems to think about, a lot of responsibilities…
Maria	That doesn't make them hostile…

26

Najat	They're not used to know other people and there's a bit of discrimination inside them. They might say well, they might show to be friendly to you, but actually there is a lot of prejudice taking place in this country, I must say.

Najat They're not used to know other people and there's a bit of discrimination inside them. They might say well, they might show to be friendly to you, but actually there is a lot of prejudice taking place in this country, I must say.

Fatima Prejudice all over the world. I mean take the Jewish in Morocco. I mean where I live.

Maria Because you'll always be said, 'Oh, she is still a foreigner.' I feel a foreigner here anyway, and in my own country as well.... I've never had many English friends.

Fatima I can't take people from just one, English friends or just Moroccan friends. I like to have one from each nation, sort of talk to them, see their minds working, what they think and everything. So if you see my friends, everyone is from different countries.

Najat I don't mind, whoever friends I have. I'm not sort of prejudiced against which country they come from.

J.M. Najat you've learned a great deal of English in three years. How did you do that?

Najat Well I just had to work hard, extremely hard, lots of exercises, pushing myself too hard, staying up late nights, waking up early in the morning.

J.M. You were mostly doing it from books, were you?

Najat Yes, and sometimes I used to speak to my sister and she used to help me sometimes.

Fatima That's a great help because she came and she found her family already being able to speak English. Well I came with my family, we all came together. Of course, my father was here, but my father's English is sort of broken English. We all were in my stage, and it was very hard, and almost incredible. And my big brother is twenty-one, it's very rarely that he speaks Arabic to me, because all his friends are foreigners. And when you've got foreign friends there's only one language that keeps you together, that's English. So he's English all the time, you know, and he comes home and translating things it's very, very hard. Like now, if I want to explain something to my parents and say – because my parents are very strict – if I say I want to go out somewhere and he said out where? I wouldn't dare to say it in Arabic. Because if you say it in Arabic it sounds such a, sort of a crime, something you're doing bad...

Najat It sounds rude.... If you explain something in English like love or something like this, which is all right in English but if you try to translate it into Arabic it sounds extremely awful...very rude.

J.M. Is this because in your own lives you were younger when you were speaking Arabic, therefore you haven't any experience as an Arabic speaker of talking about things like love or marriage or things that happen to people in their late teens? Or is it something to do with the culture which is part of the language?

Fatima It is certainly to do with the culture.

Najat   With culture, yes. They're embarrassed. Emotional feeling.

Fatima   It's like a taboo. I was talking to someone, a Moroccan girl. I did a project in my Social Studies when I was in the fifth year. It was about women in society and fifty per cent was about Moroccan women, and they all had the same problem as me, not exactly the same, but they all said, 'Oh yes.' I find it really easier to explain something like that in English to my father and Mum than in Arabic, because in Arabic it sounds so, you know it's like you're telling your father that I'm going to be a prostitute. That's how it sounds, you know. If you said to your father 'I'm going out with this boy.' If you say it in English it doesn't sound as bad as in Arabic, but if you say it in Arabic it's like I say I want to commit myself to be a prostitute, that's how your father would look at it, because they arrange marriages, they do so many things like that, and it's a scandal.

J.M.   What about him making sense of this? If you say it to him in English he knows that you don't mean that, does he?

Fatima   Yes, if I say, Oh, I've seen…. I can't talk to Mum and say, Oh I've seen that boy. He was so nice and everything, I'd probably mean as a friend or I love him or something. Because I've said it in English my father would think, Oh, it's a friend, just a friend, like a girlfriend, you know. But if I said it in Arabic it's like I had an affair with him.

J.M.   What about Spanish? Are there things you couldn't say?

Maria   No. But I don't usually talk to my father about those things, because he doesn't understand. It's not language, it's about personal understanding.

Fatima   I'd say it to my mother, but in Arabic. And if my father happens to listen to hear what I was saying I just shut up, but to me to go sort of straight, 'Dad, I want to tell you something', I never do that. Between us it's good morning and good night.

Maria   Yes, that's between my father and me….

Fatima   The only matter I speak to him is school…. I don't know whether it slipped for me in four years.

J.M.   Supposing I were to suggest your doing an imitation of you talking to your Dad. What language would you do it in?

Fatima   I'd want to do it in English because, as I've said, I don't feel in English in a dangerous state, but then I wouldn't dare to say it in English, so I'd just forget about it.

Maria   You just have to clam up and hold on.

J.M.   Do you think this is a cultural thing or do you think it's you and your Dad or d'you think it's men and women, or what?

Maria   For me I think it's me and my Dad.

Fatima   For me it's men and women and lots of it, I'm talking personally, is Dad and daughter. The way they look at women. You're a girl, shut up, you go and see what your Mum's doing.

J.M.   Do you think that's true of men in this country as well?

Fatima   No, as I've said, a girl from a different country coming to live in

28

England, very hard because you see all the girls have freedom and you see they want you to go to a club just to meet young people and talk, or go to your friend's birthday party or something and you come back on Monday and 'Oh Clare, what have you done?' 'Oh I've been there and there, the film was great.' 'Oh Maria, what have you done?' 'Nothing, I stayed at home.' The majority they all say...'and what have you done?' 'Saturday shopping, Sunday morning did the housework, the laundry. Afternoon stayed at home and did the homework.' And it's continually, every week-end, and you feel I'll have to go back to Morocco and live with the majority the same way I am. I wouldn't be anything.... With my hands folded like that, he'd be put out...

Maria You can't say it's the culture, 'cos that's definitely not it, it's just my father.

Fatima I'm saying it's the culture. It's incredible. Have you ever noticed? The way your hands behave in England. It's completely different from the way in Morocco.... My father is very strict, but somehow if I say I *want* to do that I might feel it, but once he's in Morocco he's absolutely a Moroccan person, if you see what I mean. He's totally against my opinion.

Najat The environment has an influence on you.

Fatima He becomes sort of a pain, you know.

J.M. Are there difficulties you have in explaining to your Mum what you want to do which you would say are cultural?

Najat Oh yes, I do have a lot of difficulties in explaining things to my mother sometimes in Moroccan because she keeps telling me you must speak Moroccan, but she doesn't sort of encourage me to speak it, she just sort of gives me good advice how to speak it, but when I try to speak it I make lots of mistakes, because I've got used to speak English at home and everywhere I go to, so when I don't explain it to her in Moroccan I find it extremely difficult, so I turn back to English. Then I explain it to her properly. But you know she doesn't sort of understand me when I'm speaking English. It would be better if I spoke to her in Moroccan. She'd understand more.

J.M. Do you get into difficulties about things like girls here being allowed to go to discos and so on?

Najat No, my mother gives me, does give me freedom to do whatever I want, so long as I protect myself from dangerous things, what they call dangerous, like having an affair with boys and bringing the family to disgust, and all that...which I don't believe anyway, and anyway I'm a very sensible girl (laughter).

J.M. What about arranged marriages? Do you think that that may happen to you?

Najat Oh no, no.

Fatima In 1976 I went back to Morocco, and there was a real mess. They said, 'You're going to be married, and someone's proposed for

29

it', so I thought I'll be crying a lot of the time, but I'm not going to stand for this. So I just stood up on my two feet and I shouted and I was completely against it and my father...my mother's very understanding, but somehow she can't do anything because she's a woman, and the father's the boss of the family. She's very understanding and I don't know what happened. She goes to him and...your daughter, and I said if you get me married to that person I wouldn't stay at home. And then they did it in the end. They said...something very silly, so they said it's up to you whether you want to get married. Since then I've completely changed my views, you know, towards marriage. I don't think I will ever get married. I really don't, because I've seen the Muslims' family. I know my parents are against me getting married to a European person. That's not my opinion, but I don't think I can ever leave home and marry. What I mean by a Moroccan, not just nationality Moroccan but if Moroccan culture is in him. If he's really Moroccan I wouldn't get married to him, because I'd rather have someone more European nationality, more liberal, more understanding.

Najat   But mind you, not all Moroccans are the same.

Fatima   You have the same in Morocco and you cannot tell me if you get five per cent of Moroccan men are understanding I'll admire him for that. Five per cent, they are all against women, believe me.

Najat   Is it fact? Have you got any proof of it? Because I don't think so.

Fatima   I'm speaking generally.... See how many arranged marriages happen in Morocco, see the divorce rate. Because of just fathers coming back and saying get married to this man. Next month you're divorced.

Najat   Arranged marriages nowadays in Morocco are decreasing.

Fatima   Of course they're decreasing.

Najat   Year by year.

J.M.   Do they still go on here, arranged marriages?

Najat   Just the ones who come from the very poor villages with traditional beliefs, carry on their beliefs, here or there, it's the same today.

Fatima   It's mostly the ones who have arranged marriages in England are the ones who actually lived in small villages...and had no education. I think education has some effect on you somehow. Not totally, but I think education has a little effect on you.

(At this point, I asked Fatima to read and then translate a passage of English into Arabic.)

J.M.   Where did you find most difficulties?

Fatima   No, it's not that I found difficulties. When I keep asking friends the English words I know, they say it like there...

Najat   Arabic is very difficult to speak because if you say why I'm

writing this story about my life and so on, you have to start the
other way round in Arabic, sort of, you know, the opposite to
our...

J.M.   So you've really got to look ahead a bit always.

Fatima   Yes, if you say a blue table, you say table blue.

J.M.   What did you think of her translation?

Najat   Marvellous. I couldn't understand most of the words she said.

J.M.   Why don't you have a go?

Najat   I don't think I can.

Fatima   Najat would do it in Colloquial Arabic. I do it into proper
Classical Arabic. That's why I had to get all the grammar
together.

J.M.   You do it in Moroccan.

Fatima   ...'Specially if you haven't spoken it for a long time...

Najat   Either way's very hard for me.

(Fatima translates the passage into Colloquial Arabic.)

J.M.   Any difficulties there? Any words or phrases?

Fatima   Not really, not as much as, you know, saying it in Classical.

J.M.   Now why is that?

Fatima   Yes, it's just the practice. I think I know just as much Colloquial
as, you know, pure Arabic, Classical, but it's just a matter of
practising. I've practised every night. I go home sometimes. This
year we've started speaking Arabic, haven't we?

J.M.   Do you do that for fun, or...?

Fatima   Fun, fun.

Najat   Just for fun.

J.M.   Is it nice sometimes having a language which teachers can't
understand and other girls?

Najat   Sometimes it's a bit rude to others. Sometimes, you know,
especially my sister, she can't or I can't, you want to say
something funny, not everyone can understand it, is speaking
your language...

Maria   ...what on earth did they say?

J.M.   Do you do that sometimes in Spanish? Do you use it as a
you-keep-out language?

Maria   No.... I used to do it when I was little, fourth year and the third
year, but I don't do it now.

(Maria translates the passage into Spanish – she gets stuck at one
point.)

J.M.   Tell me just what was difficult...

Maria   I have to read it first and then I have to sort of think. Some
words, yeah, some words, 'temperamental'...

31

Fatima   I think it was quite easy to translate into English language any European language because like in here you say 'avoided' and 'ignoramus' which is ignored in English. There are some similarities.

Maria   But you have to say, is it the same or is it different?

Fatima   In Arabic it is completely different.

Maria   'Cos many of the people in Spanish school, you know, they make mistakes like that 'cos, say like, 'importance', especially...*importancia*, you have to say is it the same as in English or is it a little bit different? You have to think a little bit.

J.M.   Can we come to a last point? The question, for instance, of examinations.... Did any of you find that if you were, say, doing an Arabic O level or a French A level and so on, that you were still expected to do it as though you were English, that is the translations to and from depended on the quality of your English as much as they depended on how good you were at Arabic...?

Fatima   No, I think it's really very unfair indeed, this system in England, because when I was asked in the fourth year to do my O level French, the teacher thought I was very good; I had no idea that English was involved. Because in Morocco if you get English it's got nothing to do with Arabic, it's just English, English, and I said OK and when they gave me the exam paper I found translation. I mean I could understand every single word that was there. O level French was nothing to me, so easy, but when they told me translate into English, good heavens how can I translate it into English if I didn't know any? It was about just one year that I started learning English, and the teacher said just do your best, what you can, and people will judge from your oral, your comprehension and your essay writing, and I really found it very unfair, because if you know a language, at the same time as they are testing your French they are testing your English as well.... Then on your certificate English is not mentioned in there. They just mention French O level and I had a B. I didn't exactly fail it. I did my A level French and I got an A for the oral and the written I just got an O level, and I think where I failed was the way I expressed myself in my literature. You can do it in French, but I thought I'll do it in English.

J.M.   What about you? Have you done any Arabic exams?

Najat   Yes I have, but I failed them both. I took two O levels. It was the Arabic. I found it extremely hard. I didn't have no teacher, mind you. I was just forgetting Arabic.

Maria   I did two Spanish O levels and I got an A in both of them and I did quite well in my A level. I'm taking a few more O levels and I want to do A level Art, and I'd like to do A level English Literature next year at college, and at Spanish school I'm doing quite well. I'm doing seven subjects, which is very good. And if I get some more O levels and the A level I could pass into university.

J.M.   And you'd like to go to university in Spain, and what would you like to do there?

Maria   I'd like to teach English to foreign students in Spain.

J.M.   So in a general way do you think that having these two languages has been a drawback or a good thing for you?

Maria   It's been a good thing, but you have to sacrifice a lot to get, to keep them both going. It's very difficult, but I suppose in the end it's.... Before I went to Spanish school my Dad used to make me write, you know just copy out a Spanish book and read it, but that wasn't very good. I didn't know anything about Spain. I didn't even know what Spain looked like. I imagined such silly things, what the houses looked like and the people. I thought they were sort of like Martians. I did, I did. But when I went to Spain I liked it a lot, so I thought. I just studied. I went to Spanish school for three years and I've gone to a very good level. So I'm quite pleased with myself.

J.M.   What about you, Fatima, then?

Fatima   My parents want me to go to university. I don't think I want to. I've just had enough learning. Because my education has been divided into so many sections and different countries and I think I've suffered enough and what I would like to do is...get my A level French, A level Arabic and probably get about seven O levels by this summer. I've got French and English and I'm doing English Literature, Language, Maths, Sociology and probably Russian. I'm not sure about that yet. The teacher thinks I'm very good 'cos I've picked up Russian so easily and quickly and she thinks I might be able to do the O level. I would like to work with the airlines. I just want to use languages. Because I've got such a wide experience and I love meeting people and I've travelled a lot already and I've been to Belgium, France, Spain, Morocco, Algeria, Wales, Scotland and you know, I think that's quite good for my age (laughter). I like travelling and I think the more I learn languages and meet more people the world is becoming my home, if you see what I mean. I'm not particularly concerned about Morocco and I've said already before now that I don't exactly want to go back to Morocco and live there, although I'd like to live in another Arab country and see how it works and then go to another country and live. And I love learning sort of classical languages. I'd love to go to the Far East or learn how to speak Greek or Chinese. I love those sorts of peculiar languages. Not peculiar really, they're quite nice, because people tend to learn European languages....

J.M.   Najat, what about you? Are there good things as well as bad ones about changing languages, having two languages?

Najat   I've got a country to support me. If I'm not wanted I can always go to another country. I'd like to become a journalist if I can. I have to go to university, which is very important for me to. I'm hoping to get there next year, hopefully, I'm in the upper sixth, so it's the seventh year. And I'm hoping to get some A levels next year and if I can't I can always go to a college. I don't want to go to a college because I find them pretty boring, just go straight to a university. I'll do my best. My sister wants to become a social worker. She wanted to use her languages and help people. She's had a lot of prejudice and so she feels she is responsible in a way to help people who might...

Fatima   She'd be a very good social worker because her experience is just incredible, that girl.

J.M.   She was here two years before you. So she had a different kind of experience from you, did she?

Najat   You see what happened actually, we're twins all right, but we were brought up in different families, and in different towns and places. We hadn't seen each other for eight years. I came here and met her here. Yes, because my mother had to divorce when we were about six, and the whole family just separated, it was just...completely. I don't like to talk about it.

Fatima   I think that Najat finds it hard to sort of translate into Arabic because she didn't have full education in Morocco. You didn't stop and suddenly come to England, you stopped for a while and then you came to England. To me I stopped today and the next morning I flew to England. I had to be transferred into England.

Najat   I didn't go to school for about five years and I stopped for about two years, which makes it seven, then I came here. And normally you have to be about six or seven to start school there. There's no primary schools like here, you just go straight away to school. I was six when I first went to school in Morocco.

J.M.   And then you did five years, that's eleven, and then you came here, thirteen, fourteen.

Najat   No, I stayed two years without going to school, I just had to stop. Because we had to change seatings and places and I found it very difficult to go to another school and get used to students and that, so I just stayed at home and my false brothers, the family that adopted me, no just fostered me, actually, well they used to give me some lessons in the house. I didn't need to go to school actually, so when I came here I was almost, approaching fifteen.

J.M.   So you had the shock of coming to school for the first time. What did it feel like, this place, can you remember?

Najat   Yes, I felt the whole place was sort of strange, and sort of imagining it to be something awful, something horrible to go to. But when I came here I started to get to know people and I'm the kind of person who makes friends so easily and knows so quickly, so I'm quite sociable and you know...

Fatima   ...Sometimes you try so hard, like me, sometimes I leave my home and say, 'Najat, you coming to do so some Arabic today?' you know, read that book or the newspaper, which I get daily, you know I try so hard to keep my own language. Some people like Najat they live sort of in a complete English atmosphere...they speak English all the time, you can't blame them. They've got someone who can't understand their language at home. I think it's quite good if you speak Arabic, you know.

Najat I don't actually speak Arabic at home, you know, because everybody speaks English. My mother doesn't speak all that proper English but still she can communicate in English. So there's no point for me to speak Arabic.

Fatima ...She's learning English and I think she's very good at it, but then at the same time you're losing your own language. That's the disadvantage of it.

Najat My mother doesn't mind. She thinks it's all right. She learns something from me because she needs to learn more English to communicate with her boyfriend.

Fatima My mother she's always pushing me to. 'Go on do some Arabic with your brothers, teach them.' Because my brother, he's twelve at the moment, he's doing O level Arabic and it's amazing because I've been teaching him all the time and he can't read a decent newspaper. He can read it and there's about seventy per cent he doesn't understand if it's Classical. If you write it how it's Colloquial he can understand it. He can speak it very well, but it's not Classical. He can only communicate with Moroccan people or Algerians because they speak similar to the Moroccans, the Eastern Moroccans, but speaking to people from other Arab countries he's lost, he wouldn't understand what they're talking about, and he can't write or read.

Najat I think that's because you have a different accent. Sometimes you say, you know, different words in Moroccan I don't understand. I have to ask, 'please could you explain that word?' I've never heard of it.

Fatima I didn't understand when I came, well I did, not about seventy per cent, thirty per cent I couldn't understand because they use Spanish words, like *cuccia*, all these Spanish words.

Maria But we've got some of the words in our dialect from you lot.

Fatima Some of them Arab, some from Spain. Where I live is they speak Arabic with a mixture of French.

Najat And where I live they speak Arabic with a mixture of Spanish.

J.M. Maria, what did you mean by your dialect?

Maria Well, you know in Spain there's four languages. Well we speak Castilian, but since the Arabs were there eight hundred years they left some traces of the culture behind. So we've got sort of an accent, sort of. I like it anyway. Some people don't but I do. Very patriotic, yeah. So we've got in Arabic, you know, some words, but it's still Castilian. Some people from the North, from Madrid....

(The girls have a discussion about translation, different versions, translating word-for-word. They also talk about writing their own life stories in English or their own language, or bilingually. They make plans to involve children of other nationalities in their scheme, and they talk about their multiracial school.)

Maria   If a member of the National Front came along here they'd have a heart attack.

Najat   We're all foreigners to this world, we all have to leave it and go to another one.

Maria   But you should preserve culture and the traditions.

Najat   But they have to obey the laws of the culture they're in.

Fatima   My father had a shop, a sort of clothes shop, then he was in trouble, not with the police or anything, but financially, trouble, and all he could think of was to sell his shop...so he came here to work. Some people deny it and say I came here for my education, but there's education everywhere, you know.

Najat   My mother started working here. She never worked in Morocco, because it's not a custom for a woman to go to work there. She worked in a hotel here, first she was a chambermaid, secondly she kept on working in a kitchen, washing dishes and that, and now she's helping the chef, you know preparing...

Fatima   My Mum works part-time in an office, just to help tidy up. My father is a chef.

Maria   My Mum wants to work but she doesn't work here. My Dad's a chef.

That is where the tape ended, but not the conversation. It is enough, perhaps, to suggest the complexities of these girls' lives and their ability to articulate what is peculiar to them and also common to many of the young people they have met at school and outside school.

In the comments on this transcript which follow I have first tried to understand what bilingualism looks like from the perspectives of these three girls. Later I shall want to winnow out from this those questions which are either more general or more abstract and in need, therefore, of analysis as well as speculation.

Fatima is a powerful talker in several ways, not least in her ability to take the floor and make use of what other people say as an invitation for her to speak. It is possible to feel that her effect on the other two girls is too often silencing; yet she is also able to goad or provoke them into some succinctly expressed replies and assertions. Since Fatima did dominate the conversation, however, I shall concentrate initially on what she had to say.

The first thing one might comment on is that her contribution, viewed as a whole, contains significant shifts in opinion and some contradictions. Her motives for learning English, for instance, include necessity, wanting to avoid mockery, the need to acquire qualifications which will be valid in North Africa and the Middle East, for fun, in order to please her father and in order to escape from him. Similarly, she can exult at her ability to get on with people from different cultures and feel as well that she is by now a foreigner everywhere. These are not really contradictions, but facets of the situation's complexity, and indeed they characterise not only a great deal of the talk in the transcripts but a large body of research into language and cultural attitudes and allegiances within minority groups. I will consider some of the reasons for this later, but there are some obvious and immediate explanations. The first is that most of these people had never been asked about the languages they spoke in quite this way before. Each of them had considered many aspects of their predicament, but it is possible that my approach, which combined a disconcerting mixture of puzzlement, admiration and curiosity, was unfamiliar to them. This unfamiliarity with the kind of question I was asking, combined with the territory they were considering – their histories, their present and future possibilities, their relations with their families – fraught often at this age anyway, and particularly so, as I want to show, when the children are better at English and more at ease in English life than their parents, must bear the responsibility for some of the contrariness and disorganised quality of the talk.

Fatima remembers learning English. Inspired by the mockery of her classmates, she says, she worked 'like mad', was well taught and in three months could 'sort of have a decent conversation'. Her experience of languages is described exuberantly. When she speaks English 'my mind turns into English'. Last year she went to France and 'all I could think of was in French, speaking French, do French', and in Morocco, 'I think about Arabic, I just speak Arabic, Arabic', and then, finally, 'it depends on the country I'm living in, atmosphere…'. When I asked her to translate a passage in English into Classical Arabic, Colloquial Arabic and then into French I had expected that there would be some confusions, hesitation, even interference. Her performance (and Najat's approval) suggested that she is remarkably sure of each of the systems, on their own and in relation to each other. She enjoys language and is proud of her achievement. It is possible to feel that she was urged into proficiency in English by a powerful need to communicate, make friends and have conversations, and that though both her French and her English are lively and expressive, there are signs that now that she has reached this level she no longer monitors her own language and is satisfied with it as it is. This is not meant as a criticism but as a description of her sense of herself as a language learner. 'Atmosphere' dictates which language she thinks and speaks in, but so do people. 'You speak to your mother, of course, in Arabic' and to your brothers and sisters until the subject turns to school and clubs and discos. You speak the language which will be best understood.

During the course of interviewing bilingual speakers I was struck by the frequency with which the conversations returned to the question of family life and to its particular vulnerability not only to the complexities of bilingualism but, of course, to the effects of immigration generally. Both Brian Jackson (1979) and Amrit Wilson (1978) in their case studies of, respectively, children and women, show how painful this can be and how subtle and ungeneralisable this sort of problem is. To look simply at the language issue is not enough, but I have an example which may illustrate one dimension of the dilemma. Some years ago a twelve-year-old Indian boy, a schoolfriend of my son's, spent the week-end with us. In his speech, behaviour and outlook he was simply a North London schoolboy. On one evening he telephoned his father, and with us in the room, and apparently unconsciously, his English became the sing-song of that caricatured accented Indian English which, I presumed, was the English of his parents. He also spoke slowly, haltingly and, it seemed to me, tenderly. Jack Richards (1978) has written about this:

Children of immigrant workers in Australia also have been observed to switch from a type of worker-pidgin when they speak to their parents to a dialect of English closer to standard Australian-English when speaking to their peers. Here the child would appear to be adjusting his or her speech in the case of child-adult talk, so as not to downgrade the parent's status by a demonstration of superior language ability, and to vary his or her speech repertoire toward standard English when speaking to a peer, so as not to downgrade the child's own status *vis-à-vis* a peer.

Most teachers will recognise something of this from parents' evenings when they meet, perhaps for the first time, the parents of second-language pupils with their offspring. Again, it could be said that this is no more than a version of what many children do with their language. I feel sure, however, that this kind of half-conscious language shift in young people tells us a great deal about the kind of stress undergone by families who have come to settle here recently.

Fatima, like the other girls, is certain that her English is better than her parents'; and this carries with it a sense of a wider, superior competence and knowledge, a belief that though she may belong nowhere she could also adapt to anywhere. In her opposition to her father's view of her educational and marriage possibilities she feels she has the weight of British society behind her. As Amrit Wilson has shown, though, that acceptance of the majority outlook sits uncomfortably with the knowledge that many parents increase their vigilance in this country for good reasons. They know how vulnerable their children can be. They also know that our notions about marriage, for instance, are no more the expression of love and concern for our children than theirs are. So that a girl like Fatima has a great deal to balance for herself: the mores of her contemporaries in this country, her difficulties with the ways in which her parents express their love for her, and her need to find a way of life which will reconcile these things and express her new and personal cultural experience. At the moment these conflicts make marriage seem impossible. She has a sense of cultural loss: of the excitements of festivals, of having a mother who was always at home and did not need to go to work, of the days when her father could be respected for his job and position, of a life where neighbours were known and friendly. Her younger sister does not speak Arabic, though she understands it. Fatima thinks this a great pity, and she is worried by Najat's apparent forgetting of her mother tongue. Fatima is also insistent in reminding us of the riches of her own culture and of the high standards and seriousness of the educational system in Morocco. What can seem like snobbery at times, when, for instance, she puts Najat down for not being literate in Arabic and speaking only a colloquial variety of it, she is also expressing pride in a culture which contains such elaborate and fine distinctions.

Both Maria and Fatima characterise their fathers as figures of

39

authority with whom they cannot easily talk or be straightforward. It is hard not to sympathise with these fathers, whose daughters have entered into cultures from which they themselves may feel excluded. Conflicts with parents are a part of both girls' sense of being divided, but these conflicts have also conferred confidence on them as people with alternatives. As Maria says, 'So I think I'll stay halfway – but you have to sort of sacrifice yourself.' I found myself wanting to say that many teenage daughters find it hard to discuss boyfriends, marriage, sex, with their fathers (and often with their mothers too). May there not be some advantages to a situation which allows them to blame such inhibitions on larger linguistic or cultural forces?

It might be thought that bilingual speakers have twice as many options as monolingual ones when it comes to range and subtleties of register. In practice it is not quite like that. These three girls are making up for the narrowness of their experiences in each language by having two of them. Yet because they use their two languages in broadly different contexts, it might seem to speakers within each language community that they are insensitive to some of the social demands contained in and reflected by notions of code. Fatima, at one point, says, 'I don't feel in English in a dangerous state', an ambiguous sentence, suggesting, I think, both dangerousness and vulnerability. Yet if there is frustration in all this there may also be security in the pretence or role-playing required by speaking a second language.

Many people are familiar with the feeling that in a foreign language we are not able to be quite ourselves, are too often inclined to say what we know how to say rather than what we want or mean to say. There may be, though, another side to this. If there is a reduction of sensitivity to nuance, register and context in speaking and responding to a language other than our mother tongue, there may also be a confidence which comes from a sense of the relative simplicity another language can seem to stand for. At university I acted in English, Russian and French. I was not a talented actress, but I was a more confident and successful one in Russian and French, because, I believe, so much of speaking another language does anyway involve acting, mimicry, behaving temporarily like a person for whom that language is natural. If our mother tongue allows us more scope it is also thornily redolent of our lives, personalities and relationships. This can be no more than speculation, but it has been my experience that the few native-like speakers of a second language I have known have also been, in several senses, actors. Jane, whom we will meet in Chapter 4, refers to this when she says, 'I didn't feel like an eighteen-year-old French girl, but I was making myself sound like it.' So that there may be a form of protection afforded by deliberate acting, and it may not be fanciful to link this with what Thom Gunn wrote about his youthful adaptation of Yeats's theory of masks to a theory of posing, based on the idea that 'everyone plays a part, whether he knows it or not, so he might as well deliberately design a part, or a series of parts, for himself'.

I shall return to this possibility in relation to ideas about 'interlanguage' in a later chapter. Meanwhile, I am speculating that the taking on of a new language importantly involves acting the role of a speaker of that language, and that, as in acting, this involves making broad simplifications about what such a person might be expected to think and feel. This can involve overgeneralisation, and it can also be disturbing, but it may afford a kind of protection. English provides Fatima with an escape from her father and from all the good and bad things he stands for. It also provides an escape from her subtler and more emotionally loaded involvement in her childhood and her past and present family life, embodied for her by Arabic. Arabic may be *dangerous* because it allows for greater clarity, sensitivity, knowledge than English, which is still for her an exciting, relatively simple and public language.

Maria is clear that her difficulties with her father are 'not language, it's about personal understanding'. Fatima feels that language is part of that, but it is also to do with cultural outlook, with her father's view of women and marriage and his hopes for her as a daughter. For her, though, the languages they speak are, at the very least, bound up with these things.

I have already mentioned my initial expectation that bilingual speakers would attribute the strengths or inadequacies of each of their languages to the times in their lives, their age, situation and development when a particular language was in the ascendency or relatively submerged. I shall want to attach some significance to the fact that only Jane could reflect on this idea and that that may be because of her present relation to her two languages. At eighteen this may be hard to grapple with in terms of your own life and history. Neither Fatima, Najat nor Maria were able to stand

41

back sufficiently from the languages they speak to consider whether either of them might be deficient for them because there were important experiences which were associated with, had been lived in, the other language. With these girls their first explicit contact with a world of teenagers and young adults, their first serious thoughts about love and sex and marriage and jobs have been in English. Arabic seems to Fatima and to Najat inadequate or inappropriate as a language for talking about such things. For them, it is beginning to be relegated, to some extent, to childhood preoccupations and relationships and to a remembered and quite different world, where their responsibilities were fewer.

This brings us to Najat, who had begun, at the time when I interviewed her, willingly to relinquish Arabic as the language of an appallingly disrupted and frightening childhood. She too is better at English than her mother is, in her own eyes; but English, now that her mother is living with a Trinidadian, is the lingua franca of the home as well as of the outside world. Like Mario, whom we will meet in the next chapter, she is now returning to her first language in an attempt to rediscover her own past and roots and, through them, her present identity. She, like Fatima and Maria, believes that her achievements as an English speaker are chiefly attributable to initial hard work and practice, mainly with writing. Najat was barely literate in Arabic, and had indeed virtually no schooling before arriving in London at fourteen. These last four years have represented relative peacefulness and security, reunion with her twin sister and with her mother and younger sister. She is a girl of tolerance and patience, whose moving into English and England has been positive, as has her attitude to school, if only by contrast with her earlier life. She has come to adulthood in English, and in the conversation she gives the impression of being pleased that as her English develops her Arabic withers, though, as it turned out, this was to change soon afterwards.

Where Fatima is a person who wants to take on the rich possibilities of diversity, both Najat and Maria see gain as involving necessary loss. Occupying both Spanish and English culture suggests pain and sacrifice to Maria, and a growing sense that though she is by now more English than Spanish she would prefer to be Spanish, but that she is regarded as English in Spain and, perhaps with less regret, as Spanish here.

In much of the current work on second-language learning, particularly amongst those who are exercised by the rival claims of 'contrastive' and 'error' analysis (approaches which I shall be considering in Chapter 6), the question of similarity and difference between the first and second language is given a good deal of attention. A second-language speaker's perception of the distances between the first and target languages does appear to influence their learning strategies and sometimes to affect their progress. Corder (1978a) puts it like this:

> Economy of effort suggests that we do not necessarily always have to strip down to bare essentials, but only so far as to reach a point at which the two languages begin to diverge structurally. In the case of such closely related languages as Danish this may not be very far down, but in the case of Chinese and English it may involve a good deal of simplification. It is one of the strategies of learning to find out just how far down the scale it is going to be necessary to go before starting to build up again.

Corder is anxious to suggest that the 'distance' between languages is as much a matter of the learner's perception as of the measurable linguistic features, but that this perception is bound to influence the way a learner approaches the task. The three girls touch interestingly on this point after Fatima has translated the English passage and they talk about the problems presented by public examinations in their mother tongues. Where Fatima is sure that the absence of perceptible similarities between English and Arabic makes it much harder for non-Europeans to learn English, Maria suggests that similarities present problems too: "Cos many of the people in the Spanish school, you know, they make mistakes like that 'cos, say like "importance"...you have to say, is it the same as in English or is it a little bit different? You have to think a little bit.' The question of distance between a speaker's languages or dialects may have educational implications for, for instance, English-based Creole speakers, who are moving towards written and Standard English. I shall consider later the possibility that their difficulties, compared with second-language learners, are connected with the fact that they already speak English and so have concentrated on similarities between their dialects rather than on the differences with which a second-language learner is instantly confronted.

I would want to claim that all three girls behave like language learners in Ervin-Tripp's sense (see p.18), actively working towards the new language and able to reflect on what they have learned and are learning, and that there are moments when they feel themselves to be possessed of advantages. When I asked Najat about this, she replied, 'Yes, in a way I am, because you sort of communicate with other people who speak other languages beside English and there's a feeling inside you, it just feels marvellous.' Fatima appreciates the cosmopolitan quality of the world she moves in, and Maria is proud of her sensitivity to variety within Spanish and within English. All three like their school for the range and mixture of cultures and languages it contains and for their own ability to know, understand and sympathise with people of so many nationalities and backgrounds. As Maria says, 'If a member of the National Front came along here they'd have a heart attack.' The quiet, philosophical Najat makes two moving remarks in response to this. 'We're all foreigners to this world, we all have to leave it and go to another one', and then, when Maria insists, 'But you should preserve culture and the traditions', Najat comes back with, 'But they have to obey the laws of the culture they're in.'

This part of the discussion could be seen as no more than a collective enumeration of some standard attitudes to cultures and to individuals' obligations, resistance and allegiances to features of them. I think that it points to something more complex and positive than that, something which some of the other transcripts point to as well. That is the sense of a new and intermediate culture, one to which all three girls actively and creatively belong. This might be defined by its difference from and relation to what can seem the oversimplified extremes represented by their home and their school. The possibilities of there being such a culture and of its including and manifesting their personal identity and experience is at once exciting and alarming. Piaget's remark (1964) could be taken as an indicator of what these girls share with many other people of their age and what they may have beyond that,'The adolescent...thanks to his budding personality, sees himself as equal to his elders, yet different from them...he wants to surpass and astound them by transforming the world.'

The issues raised by this four-cornered conversation are many and elusive. It was my first attempt to elicit from bilingual speakers their own sense of their advantages and their difficulties; and some of the richness of what they offered may even have been a consequence of my uncertainty about what I wanted to know and could expect to find out. Before going on to the other transcripts, which are, in many ways, simpler, I want to summarise what were important ideas for me in this discussion.

There is, first, the presence of contradiction, duality, ambivalence, which characterise the girls' experiences and attitudes and their accounts of them. Language meant for them the things they used it for, so that relationships, cultural differences, their efforts to bridge gaps between their own age group and their families, the past and the present and the future, were easier to talk about than language in isolation.

Second, there is the insight we might get from these girls as second-language learners. They seem agreed that their proficiency came from hard work, structured teaching, practice and writing. I shall want later to explore the extent to which it seems reasonable to trust simply to that account, and this will involve as well a return to the question of motive for the second-language learner and to fluency as a function of involvement with English speakers (native and non-native ones) and the learner's perception of particular communicative needs.

There is, third, the question of gain and loss and reconciliation, of accretion versus substitution, of what is sometimes known as 'semi-lingualism', and what has been called, in this context, 'language amnesia'.

Finally, entering English, the society, the culture and the language, has seemed to offer wonderful possibilities for them as individuals while, inevitably, bringing with it the possibility of friction, uncertainty and a kind of dislocation. It has taken courage, all this, but success in the second language has also come to stand for broader successes and has given them confidence as learners. How much, it might be said, monolinguals may miss of the lessons such patently useful, successful and rewarded learning can provide.

3   'Urdu has very deep manners'

A.B. was born thirty-two years ago into a wealthy Pakistani family and a tradition of multilingualism. He works as a solicitor in the Ministry of Employment and in a Southall law centre. He arrived here at fourteen in order to get treatment for his deteriorating eyesight, and was told that blindness was inevitable. Knowing almost no English, he set out to learn it and then to learn Braille, get O levels, A levels and finally go to Cambridge. There he got two Law degrees, taught for a while in the university and then moved to London. He is married to an English woman and has a small daughter. He has never seen English written down so has difficulties with spelling and is unable to read his North Indian languages now because he hasn't learned Braille in them.

A.B.'s mother's language was Urdu, his father's Punjabi, and before becoming totally blind he could speak, read and write in both these languages, can now do the same in English, speaks and understands Hindi (though he has never been literate in it) and learned Arabic and Persian at school. He seems never to have regarded the learning of languages as a problem, nor has he ever had any particular interest in the learning of them. He claims, for instance, that he learned English from the radio, and because doing so coincided with his becoming completely blind he learned Braille at the same time. He sees his mastering of English as powered by simple survival instinct and attributes his success to exposure to 'correct' English, which he set out to imitate. He maintains a clear-cut position on most topics, not least on how he learned English, why and what was involved, and on particular languages having somewhat inflexible characteristics which determine what the user can do with them. It could be said that the English he speaks still bears within it the traces of how it was learned. Selinker (1974) has a category of 'fossilised' items observable in advanced second-language speech which he attributes to what he calls 'the transfer of training'. A.B.'s English is precise, informative and explicit, with a formal, only slightly accented phonology and something of a dependence on rather old-fashioned idioms, learned, I suspect, from BBC sports commentators, but also from the students he spent time with at Cambridge, whom he characterises as 'public school'. There are occasional idiomatic confusions, 'it ticked', for instance, for 'it clicked', but on the whole he has perfected a succinct, businesslike, unemotional English which can be seen as determined by his motives for learning it, and as a tool fashioned for his role of superbly efficient and clear-headed lawyer. It was an English learned for survival and for professional purposes, though he has now married an English woman who speaks no other languages, and they have a child to whom he would like to teach Urdu, though he has not done so yet.

A.B. I can speak Urdu, Punjabi, a little bit of Hindi and a very little of Persian and Arabic. Urdu is my mother's language. Punjabi is my father's. I think it is probably fair to say that people who speak Urdu can understand Punjabi, but can't speak it. The same applies to Punjabi. Those who speak Punjabi can understand Urdu to some extent, but they can't speak it. Persian, we learned a little of it at school, and Arabic is almost like learning Latin for a Muslim. Hindi I can understand. I can't read it. With my clients here, when I help them, at the neighbourhood law centre in Southall. Hindi is, in fact, an exaggeration or development, because of the Independence in India, from Urdu, Punjabi and Persian, but written in a very different way. I can't read Hindi, but I can read the other four.

J.M. So you spoke Urdu and Punjabi from the word go, and both of them?

A.B. Yes.

J.M. Were both your parents able to speak both those languages?

A.B. My mother only spoke Urdu and my father could speak both.

J.M. And was one of those languages the language of instruction at school?

A.B. Urdu was taught, yes. I started on Persian at the age of ten, I think. Arabic right from the beginning, from the age of six or seven.

J.M. Spoken and written language?

A.B. Yes. Not very well understood. I've got out of practice.

J.M. At which point did you come to England, and at which point did you learn English?

A.B. I did start learning English from the age of twelve, I think. I came to England at the age of fourteen. There was a subject called English from the age of twelve onwards.

47

J.M.   You come from where, exactly?

A.B.   Rawalpindi. My parents moved when the partition took place in 1947, but that's the year when I was born. When I came here no school would have me. I went to the polytechnic in the evenings.

J.M.   Why would no school have you, because you didn't speak English?

A.B.   Not fluently, no. For the first year and a half I learnt English on my own. I just listened to Radio Four, Home Service I think it was, and that was enough then. And then at the age of 15½ or 16 I went to South East London, a place called Kennington College, in the evenings. I did 6 O levels and then the A levels. And then I did three A levels from Camden Town College, which is now the Polytechnic of the North, also in the evenings, and then I did my entrance exams for Oxbridge, and then I did Law at Cambridge.

J.M.   And you've been operating principally in English since then?

A.B.   Yes, but when I do the Southall neighbourhood law centre I speak Hindi, Punjabi and Urdu because the people who come there clearly can't communicate in English their legal problems.

J.M.   Are there ever areas of things that happen to you which you would rather talk about in a language other than English? Is English a totally satisfactory language for you at this stage?

A.B.   To express, you mean? Well I think it is fair to say that English is all I use, most of the time, but when I take instructions in another language, languages, I just have to translate them and present the problem in English. It gives me no problems. Whether I would prefer to express myself in Urdu, Punjabi or English depends really on who I'm talking to. If I'm talking to my Pakistani friends then I would quite happily switch over to Punjabi, because it's a bit more expressive, and a bit more ruthless. Urdu is a bit poetic and a somewhat aristocratic language. As I say, if I'm drinking with my countrymen I probably hardly use English. I would say that with my own people Urdu and Punjabi are more expressive languages than English, really.

J.M.   And you feel it is the language itself which is more or less expressive rather than your connection with it?

A.B.   Yes. I would say it's the language itself.

J.M.   It seems clear, doesn't it, that a language you've spoken as a child can have a special quality for you when you're grown up, even though you may actually be better in the other language. Is there any loss for you, do you think, in not having spoken English as a child?

A.B.   No, that wouldn't be so. As I say I find that if you're talking to your countrymen I find my own language to be more deep than the English language. Whereas when I meet my contemporaries, English people, I just talk in English and it's equally good. My own language is very colourful. Punjabi itself has a very humorous aspect to it. I would say that my humour in Punjabi is probably better than my humour in English or Urdu, but if I'm talking on literature my Urdu is better than anything else. Urdu has very deep manners, deep-rooted manners really, it's got words to respect a person who's even a few days older than yourself. You would say *Ap*, meaning, well in English, for instance, the person you is you, whereas in Urdu it can be *Ap*, it can be *tum*, it can be *tu*, depending on are you talking to a younger person, older person or the same age person.

J.M.   Is it based on familiarity or age?

A.B.   Age and familiarity as well. I wouldn't use *tum* for anyone who is a bit older than me. In any case it doesn't matter how familiar, how well I know him or her.... If I'm talking in English it would be very seldom that I would talk about Urdu literature, unless I'm explaining it to you. It depends on who you're talking to.

J.M.   What about thinking and dreaming and remembering, and so on?

A.B.   I dream in all languages, depending who I'm talking to in my dreams, yes. My wife says I often mutter in a language unknown to her.

J.M.   Does your wife speak any of these languages?

A.B.   No.

J.M.   So you communicate totally in English? If there's a mixed group, let's say, your wife and somebody to whom you would normally speak in Punjabi or Urdu?

A.B.   No, wait. In that case my manners would prevail and I would speak in the language common to all.

J.M.   Supposing there wasn't one? Has that ever happened?

A.B.   Yes, with my mother here recently, it did. She wouldn't speak any English, so I found myself translating here and there and then confining my conversation with her to Urdu.

J.M.   Are you aware of any strains or confusions when you are doing that?

A.B.   Sometimes, yes. I'm aware that I'm not conveying myself very well in Urdu, sometimes, to my mother, but that problem only arises when, for instance, she asked me, 'Why do the couples snog openly? It's so embarrassing.' It was very difficult to explain why. They are cultural difficulties.

J.M.   Either because it would be unusual to discuss that in a particular language, or, would you say, because the language isn't equipped to discuss such an issue, or thirdly, that you yourself have never in fact discussed it in that particular language?

A.B.   It is the second one. It is outside their culture. It's also abhorrent to their thinking, even my parents won't kiss each other in my presence. You can express it but you wouldn't want to express it. So the difficulty is not expression. The difficulty is simply that you would be shocking the other person.

J.M.   And yourself?

A.B.   No, I wouldn't be shocking myself. You're not at ease. To my own age group I can say exactly what I want to say, sexual or otherwise. In any language, but I wouldn't be able to say it to girls, well they'll get away with anything behind the veil, but to talk about it openly is not on.

J.M.   Presumably you have to make shifts from English when you are discussing English law?

A.B.   When I'm being consulted I explain the principle to them, an English principle of negligence, or contract or tort. That presents no problems. I may use X, Y and Z instead of Ali, Be and Ke. But if I'm pushed to use Ali, Be, etc., I'll use that as well.

J.M.   The three languages in which you have operated seriously in your life are Urdu, Punjabi and English, I suppose. Are those languages equal, both in terms of how good you feel you are at them and how much they matter to you?

A.B.   Subject to what I said, yes. That culturally, depending whom I'm talking to, a certain language would be more expressive than the other.

J.M.   Do you have any special feeling for Urdu, as your first language, your mother tongue?

A.B.   Emotionally, my only feeling is that I can't read in it any more, because I haven't learnt Braille in it. I can write it with my own hand, if I want to write to my mother, I can write it to her. I learnt Braille as a blind person in this country. I learnt Braille exactly at the same time as I was learning English, really. I learnt it ABC and then I listened to the radio and it all ticked. It's very strange, as I say, my.... I haven't had any training in English language at all. My first concentration was try to understand it and speak it in the way it was being spoken, and Radio Four was a tremendous help, there were always discussions and plays. I was very interested in plays. And I tried to develop an accent which was really a non-accent, represented nothing, not even BBC. Simply as clear as possible. And that really I learnt from the Home Service. People like Holmes and people like Phillips. They were the old news readers. They had no accent. And it was Snagge, John Snagge. Now I can notice that BBC has had a shift, a considerable shift, towards regional accents, and even the news readers are a bit sloppy. I personally am probably a bit old-fashioned in that I don't like it. There has been a considerable shift. But I'm glad it wasn't there when I learnt English. I just listened to it continuously. As a blind person I was on my own. I didn't go out very much. Coming from a family which was enormously rich I was facing poverty. Poverty in the sense that I didn't have any servants to look after me. I had to do everything. I didn't like using the white stick, and I was stuck at home most of the time, or in the flat, and I listened to the radio.... I came here on my own. I was sent here for treatment at Harley Street, and they told me quite bluntly that I had no chance of regaining my sight, and would I like to learn to live as a blind person? Well it was not a matter of would I like, just a matter of you do or you don't. So I decided to do that, instead of going back where I'd have ended up with four wives and three servants, or whatever it is and a regular income. It is quite common amongst blind there. You become priests or beggars or just landlords. Those are the three fields open to them.

J.M. And you feel pleased with the choice you made?

A.B. Well, it's just the choice you make, really. It's hard. You feel pleased that you did it yourself. But as I say you are probably talking to a person who has learnt English simply because it really was imposed on them. And there was no help coming from any school, or any local authority. And it's just a matter of listening to the radio, and I did have some, a rudimentary knowledge of, English, so that I was not utterly new to it. I mean I could say 'a cat sat on a mat', but that's how it extended at the time. My daughter, for instance, whenever I speak to her she looks at my face and says, 'What are you saying?' She is two and a half, and when I pray with her in Arabic, for instance, she says that's difficult. But you see a child is brought up by the mother mostly, and when I go home I'm too tired to concentrate on talking to her in Urdu.

J.M. Do you think that knowing several languages already when you started to learn English was a help?

A.B. Not really. At school I never had any interest in any academic subject, let alone languages. I was too keen on cricket, which has no language, apart from 'How's that?' And shooting. So really I can't...no I was never interested in languages. When I learnt English it was a matter of life and death. I had to survive. I had to float in this part of the world. It was sheer bloody-mindedness. I said to myself well, look, I've got to float. Until the age of sixteen or fifteen and a half I didn't even know blind people could read and write here. It was only the Royal Institute for the Blind told me that I could learn Braille, then they said, which comes first, language or Braille? It was only really meeting a blind solicitor in a pub, who told me – I was living amongst the Irish and I got into bad habits – it was only he who told me that I, a blind person, can be a physiotherapist or a social worker or a solicitor. So then I decided that perhaps I ought to choose one of those, and see what I'd do about it, and then, that's when I approached schools, and they wouldn't have me. Well it's funny really, I had a test, which has always confused me to this date. There's a very good public school for the blind in Worcester, and I went there and they gave me a test in Maths and they gave me a test in English. And one of the questions they asked me for English. They said, 'How do you spell ship?' So I said that would be s h i p. They said, 'How would you spell shipped?' I said with a double p, e d. They said, 'Why a double p?' I said, God

51

knows. Would an ordinary English person know? He said, I'm not concerned with an ordinary English person, I'm concerned with you. I said, 'In that case I don't know.' And they failed me for that. And then the Maths chap said, 'What's two and two?' And I thought he was bloody joking. So I said twenty-two. I thought there was a catch in it. They probably thought I was cheeky or that I didn't know what two and two was. So that was the end of it. I'm glad, because in the long run it may have, the way I did my Os and As, made me very hard, and the As they were offering there, which they didn't think of at the time, they were Geography, History and something, but I managed As which I wanted to do. They were Economics, Politics and History. And I was interested in Politics, so that made me go into the field, and I was interested in Economics, it ticked, and when I was doing A levels they wouldn't let me fill UCCA forms with Cambridge or Oxford in it, mind you I didn't.... I was just told they were good universities, so I just put them down, and they laughed at me. They said, 'You won't even make it to the university, let alone Oxford or Cambridge.' Probably they were right, because they said that never in the history of the Polytechnic of the North did anyone make it to Cambridge or Oxford. I went to Downing. 1968–72. I did two degrees there: Law and International Law.

J.M.   And by that time you felt perfectly at home in English?

A.B.   Yes, by that time, really, life had become too frivolous. Getting up at eleven. The only thing I had ever done consistently throughout, since I came to this country, was studying four hours a day. It doesn't matter what else I did in life, during the day or during the night, as long as I worked four hours a day in my studies I felt perfectly at ease and I could really go out and enjoy myself. And I did that at Cambridge too. I drank. There was only one thing, well there were other things, I got into a public schoolboy circle, who were very shy with girls, which I never understood. Their language was slightly different. The first morning I was there my teacher asked a neighbour to look after me and show me around, because I didn't know the college set-up. And he came up to me and said, 'Hello, old chap. Have you had your brekkers?' And I had no idea what he was saying, because there I was doing A levels among cockneys and taxi drivers, and here it was a different class altogether. I liked them. Probably by that time I was twenty, two years older than those public schoolboys, I had had the rough wear and tear at London. I could take my drink, but they would giggle after three and I had to get them home. And that was the advantage I had on them really, that's how I settled down very quickly, and I could work consistently, the others couldn't. Some of them were very bright, as I say. They could get a first by just working in the third term.

J.M.   Have you been back to Rawalpindi?

A.B.   Yes. I used to go every summer because my parents would send me a ticket. Instead of doing nothing, why don't you come and see us? It was always very boring because the lifestyle changed altogether. And there were plenty of restrictions. I couldn't go out dancing. So I had to tell them I was going to a friend. I had to lie. And they said, 'Will you be back by ten?' Well then one morning I turned up at nine-thirty next morning. And I tried to wriggle out of it legally by saying, Well, it is before ten. It did become increasingly difficult. There are more restrictions there. When you are here from fourteen or fifteen you forget. A certain part of your culture, which restricts you doing outrageous things like dancing.

J.M.   And what about going back to the language?

A.B.   No, that was no problem. As soon as I'd landed at Karachi I just walked into it. I didn't speak any English there.

J.M.   All that seems remarkable to those of us who had, painstakingly, to learn languages in school...

A.B.   But I think your style of learning languages is very different, you see. It's not imposed on them, is it? You never find yourself sinking in a different culture. This is it, I have not learnt languages in that way.

J.M.   I want to come back to the first language question. The learning of the first language is not a matter, after all, of matching language with language, but language with reality. Thereafter, is it a matter of matching language with language? I suppose I'm looking for gaps in your language, gaps attributable to the time in your life when you spoke them.

A.B.   My vocabulary is a bit poor in Urdu now. Technically, it would be poor. Sometimes it is increasingly refined, which is a thing which surprises me. That has always surprised me that I would read or meet a very cultured Urdu writer, for instance, and suddenly I would be speaking words which I haven't spoken and only heard in the past.

J.M.   There is a little period where the Urdu was not developing, and so you had to kind of leap over it back to something that was earlier than that. Is that right?

A.B.   Yes.

J.M.   And are you ever bereft in English for that sort of reason?

A.B.   Yes, Shakespeare still confuses me, but that's because it's old English he uses. I don't understand this 'thou' and 'thee' and all that sort of thing.

J.M.   Well nor do a lot of English people. Some of us get 'taken through it'...

A.B.   Yes that's right. I didn't do English literature. Because of that I found that part of language particularly difficult to get into. The reason why there is a gap in English literature in my life is because I was pressed for time, and I had to get on, I was getting

53

old, and I kept saying to myself, 'Well I've got to earn my own living and then perhaps I'll go into literature', but now, finally, the only literature I really like is biographies or autobiographies or books on politics and economics. Shakespeare is grossly left out or Wordsworth. Poetry I've no time for because I associate poetry with emotion. And I try to detach emotion from my own physical make-up. This is it. Life, I've seen very hard days, and if one were to be emotional then I often found myself crying and breaking down, so I got that system out of me altogether. I was very cruel to myself. I said, well, no crying, no emotions. Stiff upper lip, and that's why those gaps in literature have been left. Another great gap really, that simply stems from blindness really, that's spelling. I only spell the way I listen to things, unless I'm told. My exam papers were a great laugh to everybody. Because I spell phonetically. They never corrected it. It's strange, in Cambridge, they will never correct it. They didn't mind it. When you're doing graduate or postgraduate work literature in Braille was very little, so I taped a lot, a hell of a lot. I got people to come and read.

J.M.   What I'm getting at, I suppose, is that you have operated in English since fourteen, but the whole of you until that time was expressed in other languages. Has this ever been cause for feeling even mildly at a loss or uncomfortable, do you think?

A.B.   No, not really. I would love to talk to my daughter in Urdu, because I would like her to know some of it, some of my culture. I do believe that although I've come to England and settled here I would like to retain something of my past, very distinctly. That's why she doesn't call me Daddy, she calls me Abba, which is, you know, in Arabic, father. And she's seen other people saying Daddy, and she's understood it now that I'm Abba-Daddy, though she doesn't call me Abba-Daddy. She can correct other people, she says, 'Yes he is my daddy but he's called Abba.' And I used to go to church with my wife – she's a very profound Catholic – whereas I am not. I've now stopped going, because I don't want to associate myself with it, the Catholic or any other church. From silence, from abstinence I like my child to know that I'm a bit different. But when I talk to her I never feel that I can't communicate things to her in English which I would be at ease to convey to her in Urdu. I mean I've got books in Braille and I'll read her things and she'll follow on the page, because the Braille is just embossed in the same colours as pictures. But she understood until I got these Braille books that I couldn't read. She had been reconciled that I was illiterate until these books arrived. Now she knows I only read with fingers. Well, you see, that's my curious circumstances, really. Had I been sighted I probably might have taught her Urdu, yes I probably would. But not now, I can't. Talking. This is it. When my parents came here she was very shy of my mother, she would seldom go to her, because she realised that my mother couldn't speak any English. Whereas she'd go to my father, who does.

J.M.   If languages are equivalent, they aren't necessarily so for any individual. I'm thinking of what you said about Punjabi being colourful and Urdu being poetic.

A.B.   Punjabi, you see, one sentence can have so many meanings. You have to be careful. If I am talking to a Sikh I have to be very careful. They're great learners, and that's their mother language, Sikhs. And I have to be extra careful what I say.

J.M.   But you sound like a native Punjabi speaker to them, do you?

A.B.   Yes, yes. Simply, even if I have to say that the interview must come to an end, because I'm running late. One sentence can mean so many things. Ethically, I have to be very polite to start with. I feel that when I speak that sentence I may not be polite. So there is an extra effort.

J.M.   If you were teaching English now to a Punjabi speaker, what pitfalls about politeness would you want to point out to him?

A.B.   That example is probably easier to give...in Pakistan if you're lost on your way you say, 'Hey, there. Where is such and such?' Whereas if I was teaching him here I would simply say, first of all you say, 'Excuse me. I need some help. Could you tell me where is such and such?'

J.M.   Yes, those forms aren't linguistically institutionalised in English as they are in most other languages. Are there rules you could offer for those sorts of soft-soaping exercise?

A.B.   Yes, first of all you'd say that this is a country where you are all equal. You'd start from the premise, leave alone the class system, which I've noticed is very deep in this country. The class system in my country is between rich and poor, whereas here that's not the system. Class means aristocracy and class means upper middle class and lower middle class and working class. A person has only to open his mouth he conveys his class. Here, but not there. There, you see, the concept is that you're not equals. That's why you have this ruthlessness in asking someone to shut the door. It depends who you're talking to there. To your father or mother you wouldn't say it, 'shut the door'. You wouldn't, you'd just go and do it yourself. To your older brother or sister you wouldn't say it. Children who are born here will probably not have those manners unless they're very vigorously taught at home. You'll also find, which I find in Southall, when there were these murders – there were two murders, a Sikh was stabbed and then a Sikh stabbed an Englishman – I also found that a youth who has been brought up here from the age of five or earlier is very conscious of his rights. I was trying to reconcile the community leaders with the police. The elders were very mild. Their attitudes were, we have our backs up to the wall. We have no place to go so we'd better be careful and make peace

55

here. Whereas the youngsters were saying, you can bloody well go and jump in the river. We were born here and we are as equal as the next-door Englishman. So the politeness, the cultural politeness was definitely missing. Let me give you an example which came to me. A Sikh was murdered by the father, because she kept going out with someone. She was prepared to take the stand and she met her death. So youngsters are blending into the culture here, which is quite obscene to their parents. But that's transitional. And I think you'll come to a point in twenty years' time, in my case, when they will probably ask me to shut the door. They will. They will. If I'm going out and they want the door to be shut they'll simply say, 'Dad, shut the door.'

J.M. If a younger person than you said, 'Shut the door', would you feel affronted?

A.B. No, I wouldn't, no. No, as an accepted saying here.

J.M. There must be lots of affronting things about English behaviour. What about English language behaviour?

A.B. No, I'm not really. Well I used to be by this public school bluntness, but then I got used to it. When they say, 'What?' Very seldom would they say, 'Pardon', 'Excuse me', 'Can you repeat that?' No, they'll just say, 'What!' Even I started saying it. You just got used to it. You can't say 'What' in Urdu. It would be considered extremely rude.

J.M. What about your exact contemporaries and equals in your own country?

A.B. They find me quite rude, actually, they find me rude, not because of the language, now that's another thing, because I'm so true spoken. In the Indian culture, if somebody wants your advice and asks for it, you try to say politely and indirectly what he should be doing. I find that my friends say, 'Look, we want to go to Europe.' I'm just giving you an example. And when I tell them the truth to what is the set-up, what is law and all that, then they find that hurtful, it was put so bluntly. Whereas I feel that I'm only telling them what the position is. There is this naiveness in their minds at not facing the reality straight away.

J.M. Are you suggesting that you have learned that bluntness via English and England?

A.B. Oh yes. People aren't offended by bluntness here.

(I tell him about a television programme where an Indian offends a post office clerk and his interviewers, by what seems like bluntness, even rudeness.)

The only thing really I've experienced from the English – but really that's nothing to do with language – you see, especially for those people who come here from the ex-colonies have this tremendous barrier to break with the colonialists, that they are as good. That, I find a very strongly prevailing attitude here. That is more strong in the Civil Service than in the outside world. But nevertheless, people over forty, and probably people under forty influenced by the over-forties, feel that way. That these chaps who come from outside; we've ruled over them for several hundred years, so they must be inferior. That is a very strong barrier. I feel that increasingly. In fact, I've learned quite a few things. Until A levels I was amongst the rough and tough, and amongst the working class I had no problems. I took their girls out, and even if they disappeared for the night there was very little problem with those. Then at university level everybody was incredibly kind, very helpful, provided you didn't integrate in that class. If I took a girl out who belonged to the middle class, a Chinese wall would be built around it, round the family, and you really would be disliked. But to any other extent they were polite, they were very helpful. Then you come into open competition, you came to compete with them finding jobs; because of the economic atmosphere and because of this colonial mind I found that there was once again a barrier which I couldn't break through, which was very difficult to break. There was quite an utter shock sometimes. I find that sometimes in my capacity as a blind person, as a foreigner, you have to be twice as qualified, work twice as hard probably, to say that you're doing as much as an Englishman next door. But then you see I can understand that. I can rationalise that, but nevertheless that's there. Socially, the middle class would be difficult if you tried to integrate, and economically, if you compete with the Englishman you'll have plenty of difficulty. But you can't associate that with language. Partly language would be a difficulty because I suppose the foreigner is not conveying himself as highfalutinly or as precisely as the Englishman would. Take this telephone conversation (which I overheard), for instance. I had to tell the person who was calling me, I had to tell him in one sentence, 'Is this what you're asking me?' And I don't know whether he would have liked that. People can waffle on, and it is from that waffling that I have to sum up in one sentence and I ask him whether, 'Look, all right, I heard you, but is this what you're asking?' He hadn't made up his mind what he was asking, to start with. As I say, he had to be told, 'Is this your problem?'

J.M. Do you see this as characteristic of your job or of your nature?

A.B. I do precisely like to know what I'm being asked. Otherwise, you end up giving advice which is in all directions. And you have to pin them down. Probably in law it's necessary, that's OK.

J.M. But you don't think that perhaps it's characteristically English...?

A.B. It is. Well it's probably more Civil Service. In private practice, yes, I would say in private practice when a client came I had to

57

be polite to a client because he was paying for the time. When you put the clock on and charge him £20 an hour, and I tried to help him to minimise the waffle by saying, by listening to the story and saying, Look. You get to know the trick, to know the problem. And you say, 'Well, is this your problem?' 'Well yes, that's it.' 'Well I'll see what I can do.' And you can terminate the interview. With orientals, if you want to draw a comparison, they don't like to be told that this is the problem. They'd be embarrassed to come to a problem. Say a divorce problem. They'll come to me and say, 'This has happened, this is happening and that is happening', and I'm rather in two minds. You see with an Englishman I'd say, 'Well look, I know what is the problem. Is this the problem?' They'd say, 'Yes, that's it, you've put your finger on it.' With an oriental I have to think, how do I cut him short? Because I've got six others waiting outside, and that becomes a problem and then I have to be very diplomatic, say, 'Look, I can see this is the problem and I'll see what I can do.'

J.M. Aren't you suggesting that both groups are offended, but for different reasons?

A.B. It's easier with one group. It's easier with the English, I think, to tell them. They don't like it coming from a non-English, do you see what I mean? That's the aspect they don't like. But an Indian would simply be offended because I cut him short.

A.B. holds simultaneously two views of his multilingualism, and they are views which might be thought incompatible, though they sit together comfortably for him, as for many another multilingual speaker. The first view is that languages are interchangeable media for him, equivalent in their communicative capacities; so that people, settings, needs, simply trigger off speech in the appropriate language. The second view is that languages are in themselves significantly different from each other, and those differences (which he suggests are embedded in structure, sound, the range of register possibilities, syntax, inflection and vocabulary) affect the cultural outlook and the intellectual and emotional development and expression of their speakers. If this suggests that multilingual speakers like A.B. must necessarily have chameleon qualities of character, learning to don and slough off the cultural trappings encoded by the different languages they speak, in the manner of professional impersonators, then A.B. and other people in his position seem not to see this as either difficult or damaging on the whole. It has also to be said that a version of this is familiar to monolingual speakers too.

58

A.B. differentiates clearly between Punjabi and Urdu. Punjabi for him is an expressive, ruthless language, colourful, humorous and dangerous in its ambiguities and in its invitations to offend, get things wrong. Urdu, for A.B., is poetic and aristocratic, literary, redolent of respect and of 'deep manners'. This distinction seems to me, though not to him, to have as much to do with the contexts in which he has used his two languages as with their intrinsic potential or constraints. Punjabi is his father's language, used now principally with male friends, in an atmosphere of relaxation and drinking and pubs. Urdu is his mother's language. He uses it now less than Punjabi and mainly with female relatives. When he did, in the past, read poetry, it was Urdu poetry, and that was before he went blind. Since he cannot read Urdu in Braille he no longer reads in Urdu, as he once did, so that its literariness is something he remembers with nostalgia and feels he has lost. He admits too to having read almost no poetry in other languages.

When A.B. remembers the only recent occasion of difficulty, which occurred when he was asked by his mother to explain something about European sexual mores, and to do so in Urdu, he seems to be expressing a double difficulty: the impossibility of talking to his mother about anything on which he and she would think very differently and the impossibility of his doing so in Urdu, which he has not used in any way for that part of his life. To say that he has a temperamental need to detach the cultural and linguistic differences he perceives so entirely from his own biography and to place them squarely as inherent in the languages and cultures themselves, is not, of course, to suggest that he is wrong. It is, rather, a matter of emphasis. There may, as well, be a confusion for him between the sense of languages as bearers of very particular cultural messages and his own experience that moving between them is merely a matter of finding new words for single meanings.

A.B. sees English as efficient and unexpressive, and this goes, I believe, with his admission that he has read almost no English literature, something he regrets but does not apologise for, since, as he says, 'I have been pressed for time' from the moment he started his education here. He dreams, though, in all four of his main languages and claims to have no difficulty switching between them. He began by representing his multilingualism as something easy for him to negotiate, so that I was tempted to see him in terms of Weinreich's (1953) compound/coordinate distinction (an idea which will get more attention in Chapter 6) as a compound bilingual, so used to the notion of having more than one language at his disposal that he saw the learning of a new one as simply a matter of attaching new language to stable concepts which adhered to no particular language. Clearly, however, this does not match his equally strong belief that his languages mirror as well as determine the thinking, feeling and behaving of those who speak them in a powerfully Whorfian[1] way. The fossilisation of his English has occurred at a level of extreme competence (and it is likely, after all, that I was witness to only a part of that competence), but it does involve the invoking of some crude, if workable, generalisations about English behaviour as it is expressed in language. These cultural generalisations and oversimplifications could be said to resemble the sorts of linguistic short-cuts made by second-language learners in the areas of phonology, syntax and structure.

In another interesting passage A.B. talks about polite forms in Urdu, Punjabi and English, which suggests that he is sensitive to fine distinctions and their implications for social and class relationships and control. While admitting to a sense of there being differences of a cultural and linguistic kind between his languages and the cultures they represent, he has also brought to English an expectation of uniformity and rule dependence, which has as much to do with his own needs and the languages he has come from as with the reality of the kinds of spoken English he has encountered. For instance, he speaks confidently of getting on well with working-class students at his further education college, and disparagingly of what he believes to be a move in the BBC towards using speakers with regional accents. So that it is not easy to believe that he would be receptive to certain kinds of expressiveness in English if he heard them. Language for A.B. is a tool on the one hand and a shared cultural determinant on the other. It is available to the individual, but not in itself the way by which the individual perceives and understands the world and himself.

A.B. also illustrates the way the learner of a second language may arrive at a particular notion of the target language he is aiming for: what kinds of English will serve, perhaps temporarily, as model and objective? Most children coming into London schools and acquiring English there will be confronted by a bewildering number of models. There will be forms of Standard and of dialect, both spoken in a variety of accents; and these may derive from school or the media or the community he lives in. There will be the non-Standard varieties and the patois of his peers and the kinds of English spoken by members of his family and his mother-tongue community. In the case of children coming here from the Indian sub-continent, for instance, there may well be a familiarity with English as it is spoken there. I shall want to suggest later that schools have a responsibility to all their pupils for making such variety and the social implications of language choice explicit and understood. This will involve an understanding of the relation of written language to kinds of spoken language just as it will mean enabling second-language English learners to approach English as inevitably various and changing.

A.B. is an exceptionally gifted and successful person, who has dealt with blindness and with dislocation on a scale which would defeat most of us. He cannot be considered typical of more than a tiny minority of bilingual speakers; but he does, for me, highlight some aspects of bilingualism and some of the problems I have had in attempting to understand even my very small sample of such people.

What seems something of a miracle to me is, it seems, commonplace for him. The multiplicity of his linguistic talents is such that, though he is prepared to pronounce on each of his languages, he has had so little difficulty as a learner of them that he has rarely been forced, or chosen, to reflect in detail on his own strategies for accommodating to them. Multilingualism, for successful multilinguals, is often taken for granted by them as an achievement, and as with so many of those things which we learned out of school and easily the learning process is forgotten or idealised. And yet such learning success may be one of a collection of successful learning processes, and while it is often attributed by the successful to hard work, or 'good' teaching and carefully organised practice, its quality, the kind of bilingual fluency achieved, is inevitably beyond what anyone could simply teach anyone else. It may be that there is more to be learned, not only from writers but from people who are still aware of themselves as learners and who believe that they have a considerable distance to go towards the sort of fluency in their target language which would be satisfactory to them as well as serviceable.

It is possible to see in what A.B. has to say a conflict between his account of his own experience as a language learner and his views, developed retrospectively, of what that process actually involves. There are contradictions of a revealing kind about language equivalences and about the individual's use of them. It is also possible to speculate about the ways in which motives for second-language, and informal and formal strategies of learning, interact to establish the nature of the learner's target language and his ultimate approximation to such a target. Some of that process will remain visible as fossilisations in even the most competent bilingualism.

Mario Jerome is twenty-nine and a history teacher in Brent. He came here from Mauritius when he was eleven, speaking Mauritian Creole, French, in which he was literate, and having done a little English in school. He went first to a school in North London, then to a school in Newport in Wales and finally to Sussex University. He differs from the rest of the sample in a number of ways; he has considered the political implications of language, which he sees as critical to racial and cultural identity, and his hard-won and determined optimism about the advantages of the culturally diverse experience he has had is something he wants to share with the children he teaches.

J.M. Do you see yourself as bilingual?

M.J. Yes I do, yes. I think it once came as a very great surprise to me that I actually no longer thought in Creole, actually was thinking in English. I don't know, I must have been about fourteen years old or something like that and then it really surprised me, but by that time I think I'd forgotten Creole almost entirely, only remnants of it, what my parents spoke.

J.M. You're really talking about being trilingual, aren't you? What about metropolitan French?

M.J. Well I am in that sense, well I speak French as well, but I don't see French as being my most important language, that's Creole. That is much more important than French.

J.M. More important than English?

M.J. No, not more important than English.

J.M. So what you're saying is that when you started to think in English, English became your more important language?

M.J. Yes it did, and it was only much later when I think I was about eighteen, or seventeen, that I was deliberately looking for a way of learning Creole again. By that time language was as much part of finding my identity in British society. And also, kind of finding out more about where my parents had come from. For me I think it was a kind of search for where I'd come from because when I was in Newport I was very isolated, both from the West Indian society and also isolated from kind of my own friends at school as well, so in a way I was forced back on myself, and also at the time I was reading a lot of black literature, English black, American black. And then I was deliberately looking for Mauritius, where I come from and I think that must have been in a way back to Africa, or back to Mauritius, as far as I was concerned.

J.M.   How old were you when you came?

M.J.   Eleven. I spoke French Creole. I spoke French. Some English. Smattering of English. Very kind of book English, if you like.

J.M.   Between eleven and fourteen in Newport you were presumably talking Creole at home?

M.J.   No, I think after about a year of having been to England, both me and my sisters spoke English between ourselves. Then eventually even with my father and mother, but they possibly asked questions in Creole, we answered in English, and it was like that. But even now it's very rare that we actually speak Creole. I deliberately now have to force the fact that I want to speak Creole, my sisters don't.

J.M.   Your parents do to each other?

M.J.   Yes.

J.M.   Was it a deliberate decision to move towards English when you came here?

M.J.   No, I think it's just one of those things. I mean everyone spoke English so we spoke English. And also in a way also it was losing the kind of authority and discipline of my parents, because they spoke Creole. We spoke English. And we understood much more of what was happening then in British society than they did, and in a way we tended to see them as not understanding what was going on. And in a way we thought we were smarter than they were. I think that that was unconscious but I think it's true.

J.M.   It's very common for people at some point in their lives to see English, the host language as it were, as modern, technological, all those things. But then you had a wish to revert?

M.J.   When I went back to Mauritius in 1973–4. Before I went to university I understood very little Creole. I couldn't speak it, I could understand it and it was from there that I actually learnt the words. I actually learnt Creole in about two years again, just picked up the main usage of the language, and I deliberately wanted to learn it because for me it was a means of belonging. A means of belonging to Mauritian culture, to Mauritian people. And it took another three years to work that out, you know. At university by that time all I wanted to be was to become a Mauritian. And then over those three years you work out what's

63

good about and bad about this. The good thing about a Creole language is that it unites the people of Mauritius because they're very disunited as Mauritians. There's Asians, there are Africans, people of African background, Europeans, the French Colons, the Chinese, and the only thing unites them is the language. Everything else divides them.

J.M.   But they don't actually learn Creole in school, do they?

M.J.   No they don't, but Creole had been looked down on for a long, long time, still is in a way, partly because French and English is the language of culture, and Mauritian culture tends now, it's only now, that the young people in Mauritius are beginning to see it as a unifying force, the language as a unifying force and they're writing its grammar, for the first time.

J.M.   Is there a literature in French Mauritian Creole?

M.J.   Yes, there is, now. Newspapers are coming out. Over the last ten years politics have developed towards some kind of ideology, some kind of philosophy. They're not so much on a racial basis as they were before. If you were Asian Indian you'd vote for Ramgoolam. If you were Creole Chinese you'd vote for Duval, he's a Catholic, he's Creole. Now that's changed, now you're voting according to what your language policy is, and that's good, and part of that has been the need to use Creole as a language, use it as a unifying force amongst people, not to downgrade it, as not being important, because it is Creole society, Mauritian society. I think that when I deliberately wanted to learn Creole at the time I didn't want it through my parents, because as far as I could see they represented the kind of authority, the discipline, the rigid hierarchical even racist society that Mauritius was, but get beyond that and find something else.

J.M.   The whole business of authority embodied in a language is very complicated, isn't it, because I can see that your parents stood for authoritativeness in Creole and Mauritius, but then by resisting that, of course, you enter another hierarchical and authoritative language and culture, don't you...? Did the process of learning English, turning your back on...?

M.J.   Yes, I think it was. I think it did that. I think I was lucky though, because I wanted to find out. My sisters never had a longing to find out where we actually came from. I mean as far as Mauritius is concerned they washed their hands of it, don't want to know about it. They've both been to Mauritius, and they're Welsh girls, as Welsh as you could get, you know. As far as I can see by the time I was seventeen, eighteen, it wasn't just Mauritian culture, it was, if you like, a black identity, although, if I thought about it very hard, my identity with the West Indians was based on very little, as was my identity with the kids I went to school with, the white kids. So as a means of finding out in some way where I came from....

J.M.   ...Your business about West Indians seems to me must be
         replicated all over the place. That is, OK you join them for
         blackness, but, in fact, there is no reason why you should have
         any more in common with them culturally, linguistically or in any
         other way than other people brought up in Newport. So is it a
         matter of what comes first, and is language to do with it? I mean
         what, for instance, about French patois-speaking West Indians?
         Do they seem no nearer, no further than Jamaicans?

M.J.   Yes, I think that is the basis at the moment, as far as I can see.
         They identify according to those colour lines, not language lines.
         I would say that when I was in school there was very little
         recognition that some of the kids didn't come from the same side
         of Newport, and I suspect that because of that I wanted to find
         out where they did come from. I was part of the whole kind of
         third world, exploited masses, immigrants coming to Britain,
         etc., etc. That's how I saw it. There were constant problems,
         even though I didn't identify very much with the black kids in
         Newport. Very few black kids in the school, and I think I was
         one of the lucky ones. My class did O levels, and I was the only
         black kid in the class, and that in a way pushed me aside from the
         black kids who were mostly in kind of lower classes, left school
         by the time they were fifteen, and who saw me, they really
         thought I was bright. I really hated that, you know. You go back
         there and they say, 'Oh you're smashing to have got those O
         levels, you know, you must really be bright.' I still go back and
         still those kids will say, 'Cor, what are you doing now then? You
         were always bright', you know, kind of business, but I identified
         myself and a lot of people identified me with West Indian
         society. I think they still do. I mean most people who see me
         don't think twice, they probably think, 'You must be West
         Indian.'

J.M.   Does that present problems to you, now?

M.J.   No, I rather enjoy it now, actually, but it's very different. But
         they make terrible mistakes. People think I'm Spanish,
         Brazilian, Algerian, which I can understand, fair enough, there
         was one other, really funny, Moroccan, and Iranian. It must
         have been Iranian, and obviously I can't understand a word
         they're saying. But most people I would say think I'm West
         Indian. I expect that.

J.M.   What about this business of being thought bright and being
         divided off from other black kids?

M.J.   Yes, in a way it did. I wanted to be with the black kids. I made a
         special effort. I went to Reggae parties Saturday nights. After a
         few weeks I got fed up with it, draining of energy, not much
         going on anyway. At the same time I was working out for me, I
         think I was a pretty nasty kid then, I was really angry and mad,
         you know, because I think the teachers were well aware that they
         couldn't quite speak to me, so they didn't. I shut them off, I

65

deliberately shut them off, not wanting to know any white teachers, whatsoever.

J.M. Was this going on simultaneously with your rejection of Mauritian-ness through your parents?

M.J. Yes. I needed to reconcile it, in some way. I think that's why I went to Mauritius, and I managed to get enough money to go. It became like a real paradise, but when I went there I didn't see anything actually. I just saw Mauritius, and it was there and it was great. And it was only when I actually got to university and met other Mauritians and actually thought about it...what I saw was totally impressionistic. I was there, I mean with people, and people are really wonderful there, friendly and welcoming and you tend not to see the bad things that you want to, you know, racism amongst the Creoles, racism amongst the Indians, amongst themselves and the caste system amongst the Asians, then the colour thing to do with Creoles. If you are a little bit darker, if you marry a girl who is a little bit darker you're going down. If you marry someone who's a little bit whiter you're rising in Creole structural life, and I didn't see any of that. I just had a great time, great, five weeks, I think it was.

J.M. Then you said you met Mauritians here....

M.J. Well, I think they pulled the rug from under my feet, really, and they started painting a picture that is not so clear. First of all the Creole society. When I met Mauritians I met Asian Mauritians at university, there were very few Creoles. I was the only one in there, and there was one Chinese boy there and most of us, I think all of us, wanted to go back to some type of work, and we became a bit more politicised about what is going on in Mauritius and I tended to lose that illusion that Mauritius is a kind of paradise.

J.M. You call yourself a Creole. Do you mean by that a mixture or a particular mixture?

M.J. A particular mixture of African and, it must have been, white, must have been some kind of Asian. Must also have been Chinese. But Mauritian Creoles, the way that the Creoles themselves see themselves, as being African. African plus all the others, but the lighter you are the better you are. Even within that. So it's very kind of contradictory in a way, and they seem to live with it, and they all say things like 'A good Creole family'. But Creole stands for that particular kind of people.

J.M. Coming here and learning English. Have you any memories of that and how it went?

M.J. No. I think it must have been very easy. I don't see any problems. I can't remember them anyway. I went to school in Holloway, in North London, for two years, and then went to Newport, and I remember the first day at school. I couldn't understand a word they said and I thought that was English, you know. Partly because the accent, they were all cockney kids. It took, I think, well, it must have been about a year or so. I was in a fairly good class as far as I can remember, something like 2B, or something like that, instead of 2A, which was the top class as far as I can remember. I don't remember having any confusions about English whatsoever. I think, though, that possibly Mauritian education is very, very good, in terms of grammar, you learnt everything so that you don't make mistakes…you learned the basics, the basics of English.

J.M. You learnt English as a second language?

M.J. Yes. The language of instruction was, I think, in French. Even if they were English. I must have done about five years of English. From about five years old. English is a lingua franca of the island. It's an official language. It's the official language, and French is the language of culture. Teachers speak English, all teachers speak English. They have learned English, though we do have ex-pats.

J.M. So in a sense everyone is being shifted towards another language. I wonder whether that has anything to do with the ease of your transition.

M.J. Could have done. My sisters had no difficulties either. I think we were fairly young, so…

J.M. So you were used to operating in several languages and being taught in a language which wasn't necessarily the mother tongue of the pupils? Would you not like it if I talked to you in French?

M.J. No, it's not that I wouldn't like that. I think I'd find it a little bit difficult. I don't speak French very well. I can understand it exactly what's going on. I can. I can read it. I can write it. I was very clever at school when we did French. I was a wonderful speaker, you know, the accent, no problem. I used to kind of play the field a bit. But I had problems with the grammar, couldn't quite work out the grammar, that was the main fault, but what I used to do I used to translate from Creole into French. No problems. How would you say that in Creole – translate it into French. And I knew it near or near about…. My Mum would much prefer to speak French when people come than Creole.

J.M. You've actually plumped then for the language which came third, is that right?

M.J. Yes, English came third.

J.M. Do you ever feel now that you have any difficulties with English?

M.J. No, no problems whatsoever.

J.M. And if I asked you to translate something English into either French or Creole. Would that present difficulties?

M.J. No. It might a bit perhaps in French.

J.M. Did you know other Mauritians when you were growing up in Newport?

M.J. Well we did know one family, but there was a lot of trouble between the Mauritian families. My father has a nephew and he didn't get on with him at all well before, so that stopped any kind of relationship there.

J.M. Would you be able to pinpoint any conflicts in school, cultural ones, religious ones, behaviour ones, speech ones?

M.J. Well in the later years, say up to A level, first year A level, it was cultural conflict mostly, because it was a white/black conflict as far as I could see. I remember George Jackson's book, and he'd been in prison, I think, 1968, *Soledad Brother*, I remember reading that, and for me it was on the level of black and white. And the ironic thing is that my friends at the time were white. Two friends and I used to go to a club called Polly Pill. Both of them were much older than me, late twenties and early thirties, and in a way they never sort of said anything about this, they let me get on with it, which was very good of them actually, when I think about it. They never interrupted the way I was thinking. I actually wrote something about it. I wrote something about Frantz Fanon. I scribbled everything he said, you know. I wrote something about the black people being exploited, both in British society and around the world, and I copied most of it out of Fanon. That's the way I felt at the time, really anti anything that was white, anything I read about, and that's the way I felt at the time and it was on that level, which in a way had nothing to do with school. And school I felt had nothing to give me, they could give me the A levels at the end of it, at the same time I played football for a club. All the kids in it were white, and I got on with them fantastic, you know, but I still kind of had this thing going.

J.M. When you wanted to identify yourself as a black person your family was not the place you looked to for support?

M.J. No, I felt that they couldn't quite understand what I was going through. They couldn't give me any support in that area. They were possibly...they had conflicts of their own, in that first of all, I was getting further and further away, certainly from my Dad, for whom I think I lost almost complete respect. I was very close to my Mum, but I knew that they couldn't understand, first, they couldn't understand British culture, British society. My Mum actually.... My Dad is really staunchly Mauritian, anything Mauritian is good.

J.M. And yet you didn't sympathise with that, did you?

M.J. Not at all, no. My Mum actually learned English. She made more effort to understand what we went through. I think that's perhaps what mothers do.

J.M. They may be less competitive with their offspring?

M.J. I think my Dad wanted us to be Mauritians, and then we decided it was just impossible.

J.M. And yet it was partly what you wanted.... Did his wanting you to be Mauritian entail his talking to you in Creole?

M.J. No. I don't think he ever spoke at all in that time. I don't think I ever understood my Dad until I went to Mauritius in 1976 and he was there, actually saw him within his own culture. He was a totally different person. It was amazing.

J.M.   Was that upsetting?

M.J.   No, it opened my eyes. I think he feels now, even now, that he's wasted his life, or wasted many years actually. I think he thinks that. He would have been better off even in Mauritius, even though possibly we wouldn't have had as good an education or as many opportunities as here, but I think he still feels that. He still goes back there, now and again.... I don't know if I can explain it, but my sisters, one's older than me, Pat, and Linda, much younger, both of them, first Pat, the oldest sister, she's twenty-eight, she's got a baby. She's an unmarried mother, she...won't have any part of them, so that's resolved in some way. And that created a lot of conflict within the family circle. My Dad wouldn't have anything to do with us. He actually decided that he wanted to go back to Mauritius and not have to face it. And he did, and my Mum and both sisters have raised the baby. In a way they act as a kind of trio, supporting each other, raising this child. Pat is, I'm not sure really what she is, she has very few friends, she's only got one friend, a West Indian girl, who lives in London, and at school they tended in some weird way to put a lot of black kids, black girls especially, into nursing. I don't know why, but it seemed that way, as if they were gravitating towards nursing, and my sister ended up in this. But she never liked nursing. She managed to get her SRN, and left. And Linda went to a convent school and I think she failed school or school failed her, and she tends to sit round and watch the telly. They're Welsh girls. I mean if you get them on the phone now you'd never believe they were anything but Welsh girls, totally Newport accents. And at that moment that's the situation. My two sisters, my Mum, and my Dad has just gone back.

J.M.   Did they feel sympathy with your turning back to Mauritius and with your anger?

M.J.   Yeah, I think they did, particularly Pat does. Because of her boyfriend, a West Indian friend she's got at the moment, very, very anti-men and I can't blame her, but she used to feel very strongly black, in a way, very strongly black, but she no longer feels that. She feels you have to accept people as they are, and a lot of black are probably worse than white people, etc., etc., it's not on those lines.

J.M.   The dimension which has come out of this which is very interesting is your possibly being forced to identify with West Indian people who may not necessarily be any closer to you. I mean that that is insisting on the blackness, which may at certain periods in your life be the thing you want insisted on, at other times may seem highly irrelevant. And that maybe what you were looking for was Mauritians, and you say that in fact when you met Mauritians who'd had an English experience at university that that was particularly important. It opened your eyes to something special. When you look at groups of West Indian kids in schools there is this sort of Jamaican dominance on the whole, the language, the music, the culture. So that even blacks I've come across from Algeria actually start sounding like Jamaicans. It's worth thinking about the problems that may arise for people who've actually grown up in a different island. After all, Trinidad has a very different sort of social structure, in some ways; then there are the French-speaking islands. And then you have a place like Mauritius, which must be enormously different. Do you feel, for instance, that Mauritius is very African? Supposing you'd been identified with people from some parts of Africa. Would that too have seemed inappropriate?

M.J. No, it wouldn't seem inappropriate, but Mauritius is not Africa. It certainly is not that. If you put it in the West Indies it would kind of mix in fairly well, actually, but just to think about that a minute. Actually, it wouldn't. It's got a very Asiatic atmosphere, which I think conflicts with the very black atmosphere in the West Indies.

J.M. There must be a lot of children growing up in England now who are being forced into crude categories. To be called 'Asian' must be bizarre.

M.J. I don't think so. I do that in school, partly because there are kids within the classroom not from one part. They may be Indian, Pakistani, Bangladeshi, etc., etc. So in a way my word for it is Asian, but they don't see it in that way at all. I think I wanted to belong to a black category, but there was no such thing, there was only a West Indian category which you could belong to, and after a while I didn't particularly want to belong to that, because in a way it's a bit of a trap. But I think a lot of kids in school now are in that situation. It's very strong in my school, the West Indian culture is very strong. But at the moment it's very negative. The way it is manifested is very negative.

J.M. A great number of children, not just black children, develop a culture for themselves, don't they, which can seem extremely negative to adults.

M.J. Yes, but it helps them to survive.

J.M. Did you find that this West Indian group which, in a sense, you were slightly moved towards, was welcoming to you?

M.J. It's very easy to get into that particular culture. But the main problem there is that I can't speak West Indian dialect, you know, to save my life, and I tried, but I couldn't. It was all I could do to understand words. I gave up, though I didn't want to.

J.M. Was that very important?

M.J. Yes it was. You were in. There's a boy from the West Indies called Gary Morgan, from Jamaica, and he used to be called the

English boy, and he hated it. When he came back – he was a really nice boy – and he was all over the place when he came back. Really messed up by that atmosphere, by that experience. And it took him a long time to sort himself out. I think it destroyed him in a way.

J.M. Do you think a time is going to come, when you have children, for instance, when it is going to be possible to be a black inhabitant of Newport, full-stop?

M.J. I used to use that at university. They used to say, 'Where are you from?' And I used to say, 'From Newport, South Wales.' I deliberately was Welsh, I had a flag. I used to put it on my door. And when they came to the room, surprise, surprise, you know. But I was very proud of the fact I came from Newport when I went to university. Particularly Pill, because there were some very nice people there, the community was very strong then, and it's the dock area of Newport, you see, the oldest area, and also the old Welsh people are there, and all the immigrants, the Irish are there. Then there are the West Indians, the Asians and a smattering of other people. It was a very thriving, colourful, tight community. I was very proud of the fact I came from Newport, and I think by that time I was willing to accept that I came from Newport, that my background comes from Newport, also all the way back to Mauritius, and *all* of that makes me. And I went to the university with that idea. And when I was with Mauritians I didn't speak English, deliberately. Because there's one thing in university, you have to speak Creole. Because when you take on the language you take on the culture. You speak the culture, you know, it's all part of it. So if I want to break that I start speaking in English. It's gone.

J.M. Would there be a need for that in a genuinely multicultural society? Has there ever been such a society?

M.J. I think a lot of immigrants feel that way. I'm sure that they probably feel that they are not accepted. If you talk to anybody from overseas who's got a black skin, eventually you will ask, where do you come from originally? And even those that have been born here, you will probably find that he will talk about his parents from so and so that he would like to visit. But at the moment, as yet, the kids' culture, black culture, still comes from the West Indies, still going back to it, and the parents are still going back to it. And even if they may say we are going to stay in England to work; at the back of their minds, one day maybe, you know.

J.M. If we were to feel that it was important to know that somebody who came from Jamaica had a very different cultural badge on them from somebody who came from Mauritius, does that make it more difficult for them to feel that they are black Britishers?

M.J. I do know that my two sisters, for them they find it impossible to go back and live in Mauritius now. And I think that possibly a lot

71

of people who have either been brought up here or born here would find it impossible to go back to their former island because we have all learned to cope with it and we've all learned how it's worked out and in a way that's the culture we've been brought up with.

J.M.   So you've got this culture which is yours, which is both Newport and Sussex and Mauritius and all those things?

M.J.   Exactly.

J.M.   And you've developed, in fact, a new culture. I mean it's not a matter of taking on ours or keeping your own. It's a mixture. If we are educating for a multicultural society, this might mean, I suppose, on the one hand valuing diversity, and saying we are potentially rather a terrific society because we've got all these resources. But that, maybe, has its sentimental and difficult sides to it. Because it may be that a child growing up here and being black and feeling, none the less, that he's got to go to a London school, from the word go, that for him to be seen as part of that diversity may present him with problems. Again, one might want to answer that by saying that even before black people came here we were full of diversity. We always have been. There's a hideously elaborate class structure anyway, and to talk about a mainstream culture at any moment in our history would have been crude. It may be that by putting a value on diversity, which I would want to do, we may be putting pressure on individual children who want things to be simpler, not more complicated.

M.J.   My sisters also feel that they don't belong here either.

J.M.   Is it hard for people to accept diversity as a fact about themselves and other people? Do they, in fact, want to be united on some simple level?

M.J.   It seems that way. I enjoy the fact that I come from Mauritius and I enjoy the fact that I come from Newport too. In a way that's possibly where I'd like most immigrants in this country to come to, that they enjoy the fact that this is where I've come from, at the same time I come from this place across the seas, and it has this, this and this to offer. And all of that is part of me.

J.M.   In terms of school and the education system you've been a success. Has that been an important element in allowing you to be what you wanted to be?

M.J.   Well school gave me the opportunity first of all to go to university, that I'm glad of, I think. University opened various resources, libraries, etc., and the fact that you meet a lot of different people from all over the world. It gave me an opportunity to use those resources, to find out things for myself. And of course it valued the fact that I am Mauritian and the fact that I grew up in Newport. That, for me, means something, coming from Newport. The most important thing at university is the social education. That's what I went for, and I was fortunate enough to be with a good bunch of people. Everything else I think comes afterwards.

J.M.   What sort of confidence do children need to have to combat and resist racism?

M.J.   Throughout the time from when I was about sixteen I've been wanting to know why, why have all these things happened in this particular way. And then in the end you resolve it. It's certainly taken a long time for me. When I was a kid I hated being black, partly that was the Mauritian bit. Then I hated whites, then you mix the two together, and somewhere on the way you find out what's going wrong, and to actually come to the level of knowing exactly what is going wrong in this particular society took a very long time and also to actually accept a few things on my part. Actually I don't really hate anyone, that the reasons people do things are this, this, this and this. And it's an emotional feeling, and to actually explain this and get kids to see that is very difficult. If you're actually on the receiving end (of racism) you want to know why. Black kids are often more aware of the dynamics of racism than white kids are. And I think possibly that stems from there. Some kids just want to lash out and not know why, and then unfortunately you've got the great big divide. Nobody actually telling them what's going on. There are kids who actually want to know what is happening, and I think I was a bit like that. I wanted to know what was going on.

J.M.   As a teacher, would you tackle this subject with a class? How would you respond to a racist remark made by a child?

M.J.   Actually I can't do that. Usually the kind of remarks are not black versus white, it's usually black versus Pakistani or black versus Irish, and I tend to get very nasty about it. I say, 'what d'you mean by that?' And bring it out into the open, because I get so fed up with it. Having an argument. 'Cos it's ironic, it's absolutely incredible. I'm not sure that that solves the problem. As far as I can see it's a game, which doesn't actually mean anything. They see it that way, though it isn't that way. A lot of what they talk, ugh, 'You don't eat curry, do you?'

A large part of what Mario has to say turns on his adolescence and his isolation as a child in a town where his family had quarrelled with the only other Mauritians they knew, and where his blackness caused him to be regarded as Jamaican, from whom in some ways he felt as different as from all the other groups in the town. It is interesting that this particular sense of difference should focus on language, when he says of the Jamaican youngsters of his own age, 'It's very easy to get into that particular culture. But the main problem there is that I can't speak West Indian dialect, you know, to save my life, and I tried, but I couldn't. It was all I could do to understand words. I gave up, though I didn't want to.' Whether this was a matter of inability or of constraint may be academic.

He drew away from his father, losing all respect for him and feeling at odds with his Catholic and authoritarian outlook. During his teens this also involved the rejection of Creole, or at least the forgetting of it, and of Mauritius. And by that time the 'book English' he'd arrived with had become the language he thought in, learned in and used for most of the time. His abandoning of Creole he now sees as having been 'a way of losing the kind of authority and discipline of my parents, because they spoke Creole'. In retrospect, I think, Mario, ten years older than the girls in the first transcript, is able to describe what may be a common kind of confusion for adolescent bilinguals. He goes on, 'We [he and his two sisters] spoke English. And we understood much more of what was happening then in British society than they did, and in a way we tended to see them as not understanding what was going on. And in a way we thought we were smarter than they were. I think that that was unconscious but I think it's true.' Later, he visited Mauritius and started to relearn Creole, and yet it was important that this relearning was done independently of his parents and as part of a discovery of Mauritius, something that was accelerated by his friendship with several Mauritians of Asian background whom he met at Sussex University.

Mario is conscious of there being ironies in his refinding of Mauritius and of Creole, since the identity he discovered for himself via those two things was one located, even embedded, in a strongly hierarchical society, where Creole has been allowed to represent the inequities of the old regime, within which he would have been no kind of beneficiary. Yet by returning to Creole, and temporarily to Mauritius, he also discovered people like himself, uprooted, cosmopolitan people, for whom Creole could be a unifying force in a multiracial society; and he discovered that a Creole grammar was being written for the first time and that some newspapers in Mauritius were now published in Creole. Then, by the age of eighteen, he had become involved, rather solitarily, in black writing and had identified with a somewhat generalised blackness and black experience. On its own, though, this seemed inadequate. It was necessary to combine and modify this new awareness with something much more particular to his own experience: the place where he had grown up, the place he had left and the language which he had temporarily abandoned. He also needed to rejoin society through what was special to him, being the only black child in an O level class, for instance, and the language and religion of his parents.

Mario is less clear about his learning of English than he is about his losing and regaining of Creole; and his sense of his capacities as a French speaker is muddled too. The status of French and English in Mauritius is complex. While the language of instruction is French, whether the teacher has French as a mother tongue or not, English is the island's lingua franca. Mario's mother would prefer visitors to talk French rather than Creole, however. French was his second language in Mauritius, but has now become his third. Though he attributes some of the rapidity with which he learned English to his Mauritian education, which 'is very, very good, in terms of grammar, you learnt everything so that you don't make mistakes...you learned the basics, the basics of English', his account of his French is rather different, though I suspect that this is a consequence of his conflating his early years with the present time. It is grammar and speaking he finds difficult in French, though he can read it and write it and suggests that he has an ear for it.

Mario's return to Creole and to Mauritius has not brought about a reconciliation with his father, though having seen his father in Mauritius, where 'he was a totally different person', he feels he understands him better now. One aspect of the immigrant experience seems well illustrated by what Mario has to say. A common colour, religion, family background, these are not enough for most young people growing up here now. In drawing away from the identity provided by their families, they need something more specific than such an alternative seems to offer. His present self-confidence comes from understanding his own predicament in the context of a broader picture of social and cultural diversity and change. He is proud of having come from both Newport and Mauritius and of evading stereotypes offered to him or imposed upon him. There is nothing marginal to him about his position. Indeed, he sees that this country will depend more and more on people like him, people who relish their own mixtures of culture and background and language as giving them scope to create and sustain capacious new definitions. For him, languages are not simply necessary tools, but agents of both social cohesion and conflict. An experience of isolation, rebellion and educational success has allowed him to confront the dilemmas of people in his position: racism, family disruption, limiting and damaging expectations. He is able to articulate possibilities which transcend conciliatory models of assimilation or benignly accepted separation.

4 'It's a positioning of the self within the language'

Jane Taubman is eighteen and has just done her A levels in French, English and Biology. She was born in Strasbourg of Scottish parents, and had an older brother and sister who had been born here. For a time, between the ages of one and two and a half, she was looked after by an Alsatian girl, so that she learned to speak English, French and Alsatian simultaneously. Since she now has no memory of speaking Alsatian we only discussed her experiences in the other two languages. Since the age of eight, when she left France and returned to Scotland, French has been a school subject, and one in which Jane, quite naturally, excelled. Perhaps the two most interesting aspects of what Jane has to say are, first, her sense of both losing a language and regaining it, and second, her experience of having known a language both 'naturally' and 'artificially'.

J.M.   Do you have any memories of muddles?

J.T.   There's one I have in particular, which was that actually in school, in the French school that is, where I was speaking French, and it was very much enforced to speak French there, but I remember coming out with the wrong French word. It was more a variation on the French word, or rather I think it was an English influence on the French word. We were going to have the school photograph taken, and I was talking about...I was talking about...and I think I said *le photographier* or something like that for the man who takes the photograph, and people were rather surprised that I said that. I was seven or eight years old. It was nearly the end of my time there. It wasn't that it was an inability to speak French at that point, but it was a mix-up. I remember feeling very embarrassed that I'd done that mistake, mainly because of the people's reaction, but that was a mistake or muddle which was made in the context of the French, within a French school, which surprised me and surprises me now that I think back on it, because at school there was no problem. French was what was spoken and I spoke it and there wasn't any confusion about the roles or anything, which language belongs where. Not when I was at home either, but I'd have thought, looking backing on it, that if muddles were to happen anywhere it would seem more likely at home, because we spoke English with our parents and French amongst us, the children. The thing was that the language that was spoken was not in fact English, even though I say it was English with the parents, it was *Franglais*, which was now, I can't actually remember, but I have a feeling it was probably more French with quite a lot of English words in it.

J.M.   School language took over, did it? There was a time when you felt that French was your...?

J.T.   Very much so. Because I remember coming over to this country and seeing my relations and being asked by them, by those aunts, did I think I could speak English or French better. I mean it's French that I spoke better. There was no question in my mind, at that point, and I must have been somewhere between six and eight.

J.M.   And at that point, presumably, you could read and write in French? Not in English?

J.T.   I think I could read English. I couldn't write it. We had simple books, English books, fairy tales. French certainly was the language that I felt was mine. English belonged to various places and certain people like parents and all...this country in the summer. I never spoke French with my cousins and no French words came out, I don't think.

J.M.   Do you remember being clear in your head that there were people to whom you ought...

J.T.   I don't remember making a distinction, not consciously, no. But I may have done. I don't remember either way. I certainly don't remember deciding that these people I would speak English to, these I would speak French to. It was not like that, it was more what everyone else was speaking.

J.M.   Most children who are bilingual actually are conscious in some way that French is one system and English is another, though they're not conscious of what is involved in moving from one to another. But they seem to remain within one system. Your example of *le photographier* is memorable to you presumably because it was something you didn't do much?

J.T.   Yes, especially in the context of the school, which was completely French to me. It was a French school and you spoke French there. It wasn't as if a mistake or muddle could have been made. Also because English was very much a status symbol, and at one point I was asked to teach English to my school friends. Their parents wanted them to learn English, and we didn't have English at that point. And I became sort of a teacher at the age of seven or something. I remember feeling I couldn't do it. Because I had no idea what they wanted to learn. I mean we did things like I taught them the English words to French songs and the English versions that I knew. English numbers. Things like that. I used to show off about it. I remember how we used to have these sessions and sit around and talk and sing and stuff, and these songs, it's the songs I remember doing. I think it was 'She'll be coming round the mountain when she comes', and so I'd sing it in English, feeling very proud because I was using this foreign language and they would then sing it in French, I mean it was not that I didn't know the French version. But it was slightly different in that school as well because so many people had another language, and it happened that my little group of friends, most of them were French and didn't have a second language. I had a Dutch friend and an Italian friend and they each had a second language. I remember once talking with them all, with my Dutch friend and us both talking about the fact that we couldn't write in the language which we spoke at home.

J.M.   You talked just now of your home language as a foreign language.

J.T.   I don't think that I considered it a foreign language, because it was too much part of us. It was very much the language that belonged to the home and was different.

J.M.   Were there ever difficulties about things which happened at school which you wanted to talk about at home and vice versa?

J.T.   No, I don't think that the fact of having two languages did ever create a communication barrier. There was the language, you might say, of the mind and the actual speaking.

J.M.   Do you think that you thought, that you dreamed in French?

J.T.   Yes. I remember thinking that and saying that.

J.M.   Was talking English, living in it, attended by any strain? Were there any limitations to it as a language?

J.T.   No, I don't remember feeling that at all. But I remember one thing, for instance, that I didn't like it when my mother came to the school and spoke English to us, and I wanted her to speak French when she was at the school picking me up, because I didn't want the distinction to be made. I didn't want to seem different, I suppose. But I also remember that I refused to speak French to her, which in a way now seems strange, because we used so many French words within the English that, for instance, she wanted us at one point to call her Maman, and it just seemed completely wrong. I couldn't, it just wasn't on at all, I couldn't even begin to start. Because that would have meant that we were bringing the French into the part of our lives that didn't feel French at all. It felt very foreign. I've a feeling that that sort of problem (i.e. talking about subjects contextualised by one language rather than the other) wasn't dependent on the language...but the actual idea of the language comes last on the list, that is of the differences between home and school. I think that does come into it, but you don't take it as a consideration of the actual way you're living. I was eight and a half when we went to live in Edinburgh. We had, during the summer of 1969 and throughout that summer, we as the children were taught to write, because we couldn't write. In order to get into school we were going to have to show we could and so we had, we were taught by Mum and Dad, we had lessons, every day, little spelling books, and I remember that very clearly as an experience, actually having to learn how to write these things. It wasn't a horrible experience at all. It was kind of a chore. We all sat down and we had these spelling tests.

J.M.   You could all do it in French at that point?

J.T.   These words, yes.

J.M.   This is a hard thing to ask, but do you think you used your knowledge of French spelling, your knowledge of how language operates to learn to read English?

J.T.   I don't think so, because I don't think I ever felt the need to put accents on in English.

J.M.   Let me put it better. There seems to be some evidence that children learning English as a second language, who have been literate in their first language, have less difficulty moving towards English in school.

J.T.   I think this was slightly different because I already felt very familiar with English. It wasn't that I was learning it as a second language. It was really learning how to write these words which I already could say and was very familiar with the meaning of. I find it very difficult to remember because it was too close for me, the two languages were too close. I did learn them nearly simultaneously. It happened that I learned one – I felt more confident in one than the other – but I did really learn English and French together from babyhood, and I remember reading English in France. I remember reading *Peter Pan* in English.

J.M.   Were you ever taught to read in English?

J.T.   No, but we used to read it at home. Dad used to read us stories in English, and then we had fairy tales read to us, as English children do, bedtime stories.

J.M.   So you don't remember having any particular problem learning to read in English?

J.T.   Not reading, no. It's the writing I remember. I don't now quite know why it should have made a difference, really, but I suppose I hadn't ever needed to write English before, as we didn't do English at school and I suppose I didn't write letters. And suddenly coming over there was the necessity actually to write these words, which I had been reading and speaking. But it's not quite like learning the writing system, that's what I mean. It's too close. It was only lack of practice, you might say. I also remember with the Dutch girl, us both saying and being aware of and talking about the fact that we couldn't write our second language. Where I think we almost didn't consider it a second language, because she was exactly in the same position as I was, in that she spoke Dutch when she was at home, though I think she spoke French with her sister. The thing about writing which I also remember: feeling the pressure on me to know these things. I remember once in the class not being able to spell 'eight', and asking the teacher and being laughed at by one of the pupils because I couldn't spell it, and the teacher defending me and saying, well she's only been here six months or something, and so I was always being defended and had very much that behind me always. So I didn't ever feel guilty about not knowing these things.

J.M.   What about now? I suppose you feel easier reading and writing in English now, though you have been learning French and are obviously very good at it. Can you remember French becoming a subordinate language?

J.T.   I can't actually, but I do know it happened very, very fast, because I got very homesick at one point, when we were still living in Edinburgh. So it must have been a year after we'd moved, and I went back to stay with some school friends, and I was ten then, and already by then I couldn't, I'd forgotten, I couldn't. I didn't feel confident in speaking it. When I went over there I felt very much as I feel now when I go over there.

J.M.   Did it get better?

J.T.   Yes it did.

J.M.   Did it ever get to the point of your feeling it was your language again?

J.T.   No it didn't. I certainly was a lot better at it after the three weeks, but I also remember the very last day I was there saying, to Nancy it was, and I said, I was talking about my school, and I said about my school, '*l'école que j'étais dedans*', and Nancy went absolutely mad and she said, 'Oh no, you've been here three weeks and you are absolutely translating. It's awful and you haven't learned anything.' And again I felt very embarrassed and stupid. At the same time I'd obviously been translating English. It was very obvious, and English was still therefore the language I was probably thinking in. Well it's strange. I never feel French as a first language when I read and write in it, but I know I feel more confident in French now than I did, for instance, when I was ten and went back, because I feel I've learnt it through the school now. Through the English school system, I've learnt it as a foreign language, and so I wouldn't ever make a mistake like *l'école que j'étais dedans* now. I wouldn't ever say that because it would seem completely wrong, and I couldn't say it. I would know that it was the wrong thing to say. I don't know if I would know what the right thing to say was.

J.M.   Your knowledge that that is the wrong thing to say comes from a different....

J.T.   Source, yes. Because I think it wrong now because I've learned it as a foreign language at school and I know through my knowledge of learning the grammar that that's not how you say it.

J.M.   None the less, you're probably better at French than most people in your class?

J.T.   I'm more colloquial, I suppose. I can, I can use, I've got a feeling of the language, about how you say things and how you don't say things, but I almost think that has developed since I've been over here. I mean I don't feel that just because of the fact that I wasn't, I didn't at the age of eight think of French, I didn't think of it as a language, and what I was saying and the way I was putting it together, as I do now with English, and yet now I feel I can make use of the fact that I did speak it, and I feel I've got something there which I can make use of now.

J.M.   Do you know what that something is?

J.T.   Well, it's almost a memory of the knowledge of it, it seems to me, it's almost knowing how I spoke it, and now realising what it is and everything, and therefore being able to remember it much better.

J.M.   When you think about Strasbourg are those memories and thoughts ever in French?

J.T.   No, I don't think so. The thought process and the memory are two completely different things, I'd have said. It's strange, because I used to speak French quite a lot to Cassandra [her cat, now dead], and it seemed quite easy to do that. That's the only time I can think of spontaneously saying something in French. As you got older and became more aware of the language part of it, the actual structure, that you were able almost to use the resource that you had of having been able to speak it at one point, and use that familiarity with it, to be able to speak it better than people who'd learned it.

J.M.   I don't know whether you've read Beckett. It seems to me that when you read him in English he has a fineness of ear for phrases, colloquialisms, idiom, cliché, kinds of language like the language of marriage, if you like, or the language of bureaucracy. When I read him in French – French after all released him, it was a language he knew very well, but very much as a foreign language when he went there. The language did something for him; it separated him from his childhood in ways that he liked – yet when you go back to him in English the language of childhood is very much there. What I know I can't do is tell whether it is there in French, or whether, as I suspect, his French somehow has less of that texture that you have when the language of your childhood is there. You had a French and an English childhood, though there were divisions, friends and home, for instance.

J.T.   Except the children who came in the school, other English children. I was often called up as the English speaker to be a translator.

J.M.   Some people who have moved into another language later than you did feel that there's something missing, what could be called the language of childhood, the language of first learning. Certain children who learn English extremely well at school have some difficulty with the idiomatic texture of the language. They might find that when reading literature....

J.T.   I think that that probably didn't happen because we were learning English with our parents. So that that sort of child's English, the basis I think you're talking about, came with that because we were learning English as other English children do, from their parents, but at the same time we were also learning French as French children do. The family thing and the school thing were about half and half in importance to me, and also we did spend the summer holidays in an English-speaking country and with English-speaking people. In that context there was no question as to which language I was speaking. I did feel very much that I did belong to that. My cousins were my cousins, and I felt close to them in that way. I didn't feel at all a foreigner to them. I knew them as I feel I'd have known them if I'd grown up with them.

J.M.   Some memories might have involved conversations in French.

J.T.   I think I don't remember whether I spoke them in French or in English. Now that I think and speak in English, memories are, I suppose, English. I think it's difficult to tell because if I was speaking to, say, someone who was there, the other person I was talking to when the French conversation took place, I think I might remember it in French, and remember what I'd said. I've often remembered things I've read and possibly things I've said and not known which language it was I'd said it in, and had to remember the context and work it out as to what was most likely.

J.M.   Have you worked it out because you wanted to or because it seemed important to get it straight?

J.T.   It depended on the thing. I haven't gone back to all my memories and tried to remember which language I spoke them in. I have always done it by the context.

J.M.   Have you ever dreamed in French?

J.T.   No, I don't think so.

J.M.   What about reading French and writing French? How does that feel nowadays?

J.T.   It feels like a foreign language, but one that I'm familiar with. Writing certainly does, writing. I make the same grammatical errors that English children do, and I think Alison [her older sister] is better at French grammar than I am, and I've come to the conclusion that that's to do with the ages we were when we left France. That because she had had two more years in the French education system she knew more French grammar than I did. So that writing French to me doesn't come naturally. Reading is much easier. I feel I can read French, though in fact when I go through it word by word there are lots of words I don't know the meaning of. Words I didn't use when I was there, big words.

J.M.   After all, you had the fundamental vocabulary of any child of eight...

J.T.   Yes, and I think that's about where it stayed.

J.M.   So learning French as a foreign language doesn't simply help you fill in the bits you didn't know?

J.T.   No, because the thing which now makes it feel like a foreign language to me is the fact that I feel I wouldn't be able to have a spontaneous conversation with a French person.

J.M.   Particularly not at your present intellectual...?

J.T.   Yes, because the things I would be saying I would very likely not know the words for, the things I'd be wanting to say, now, just because of the things I'd be likely to have a conversation about. Because I'm going to Strasbourg in the summer one of the things, I'm not dreading it, but I know that I'm going to find embarrassing, is if I do meet people who I knew up to the age of eight. I will be embarrassed now being eighteen and not being able to talk to them. And before, when I was eight, I could say, I could talk to them spontaneously, without thinking about it, and without any difficulty at all.

J.M.   Here you are, with probably a well-preserved eight-year-old's French, overlaid with the development of ten years in English and having learnt French as a foreign language.

J.T.   The thing is, I suppose I feel it's not an eight-year-old's French, it's not simply an eight-year-old's French that I know. I feel very much, as I was saying, I've grafted on that knowledge of French, that eight-year-old knowledge of French to my learning of the foreign language at school, and that's what made me good at French, because I've been able to use that familiarity with the language with learning it grammatically as a foreigner. And the two together have made me better at French than my co-pupils, but not a French speaker. But it's also been a bit of a challenge, really, all to do with the status symbol, with the fact that French has been a useful language to know, and the younger I was the more impressed I could make people (laughter). As far as last year (a visit to Paris) I remember really wanting those French people not to know I was English. And quite often it worked. I was very pleased about that. But I know it only worked because those French people, who were surprised when I did actually tell them I was English, were people, say, in the shops. So I only had a very limited conversation with them, like two to three minutes at the most, and it was very simple French, shop French, which I was able to make sound like real colloquial French because of my accent. I didn't feel like an eighteen-year-old French girl but I was making myself sound like it. That's where the grafting of the eight-year-old French to the language I learnt at school comes into its own, because I know, not just from the school but as I've grown up I've become more aware of the kinds of thing you say in a shop in France, which....

We couldn't in fact call her Maman without sounding completely foreign, and a wrong thing to say, in fact among ourselves we did say things like *Maman a dit ça*. That's what makes me think now, looking back on it, that the whole of the language thing, you know English or French, was more a means to an end, you so much weren't conscious, I remember so much not thinking about these things, about what language I was using, and using whichever language was appropriate, how I could communicate best with whatever person it was. It is, or very much was, a means to an end. I couldn't quite work out, though I was rather pleased, what the fuss was about, and I liked people thinking I was in an advantageous position, and to me, in fact, it made no difference whatsoever, really. It's the fact that I've got so few memories, that I can remember so little about it, makes me think how little in fact it was a thing that was talked about. Actually, when I was using it I was made aware by other people.

J.M.   Are there things you actually feel you couldn't talk about in French?

J.T.   Yes, lots. Anything that is complicated really, anything with a specialised vocabulary, which I just haven't heard. I couldn't talk about music. I couldn't have a conversation about politics, or industrial action. I listen to the French news and French radio. I can understand it and I enjoy listening to it, but there are a lot of words, I think, that I don't understand. I can't actually tell you any, but there are some slightly more specialised words that I'm not used to hearing in general conversation, in school conversation. They are not words I know the meaning of. Whereas in English, just because I'm living there; I definitely have a general understanding of what those people are saying on the radio, in particular, but they have these awful French radio programmes. I remember listening a couple of weeks ago to one, and it was about Jeremy Thorpe and the whole Liberal thing and I could understand it all because I knew what they were saying. At the same time I know that there were a lot of words I didn't know.

J.M.   Do you find now that you have an awareness of French as a language?

J.T.   I don't think I was (with the Jeremy Thorpe programme) focusing on the way they were saying things. I don't think I was translating. I was very much taking the language in and understanding it without translating it into English. Like now I couldn't tell you what they said word for word, either in French or English. I just know what the subject was, which makes me think that I absorbed it in the way I would with a language I was

85

familiar with. But I know I wouldn't be able to say those things as they were saying them. I would be speaking in a foreign language. I feel very vulnerable in French, a sort of vulnerability which I don't feel in English. I'm much more easily lost for words in French. Inability to speak.

J.M.   I suppose I can understand a good deal of French, but I'm aware of not being rooted in French, having to translate, having no ear, as I have in English, for nuances and associations.

J.T.   I've a feeling that I'm not really in a different position from someone who has just learnt to speak French really well. I have an advantage and an ease with the language, if you like, in those very things; jokes and things like that, but I've a feeling that's to do with having spent a French childhood, schoolboy jokes, that kind of thing, I really do have an understanding, a feeling for.

I think that's one of the things I find most crippling about it. I feel as though I'm understanding French people when I'm talking to them and their gestures and what they're saying, and then there's the sense of humour, and I feel I understand that. And yet, I can't respond to that feeling, because I feel I've got one part of it, which necessitates the other part, and yet that is the part which seems foreign to me. The understanding isn't a problem, but...I think that's what I meant about going to Strasbourg and meeting these people. I feel that I ought to be able to talk to them as I'm talking to you, and yet I know I won't be able to feel the same way, because the actual process of speaking is going to be the thing that's occupying my mind and not the thoughts. I think that's what makes me feel I'm not a French speaker, not bilingual, now. Because the difficulty is with the speaking.

J.M.   And you feel that not just as a loss or absence, but as something you once had and no longer have?

J.T.   I know I didn't feel like that when I lived in France. I know I spoke French, not as well as I speak English now, but just because I was eight then. I wasn't thinking of language, I didn't think of either of them as a foreign language then, and I know I feel French is a foreign language to me now and I feel that as a loss, because it always feels artificial. It doesn't feel a part of me, the actual speaking. That's what I mean, I was trying to con these French people into believing I was French. It was pretence. I don't feel French, and yet I was very pleased when they thought I was. But I felt pleased in the way, I would imagine, that someone who has learnt a foreign language and is mistaken for a person of that country.... I feel, maybe, that I'm able to recognise or relate to a certain Frenchness in French people. I suppose I don't know how people see French people who haven't lived in France. For instance last time when I was there and I was on the metro and a man decided that he would talk to me, and he was just a very nice, funny French man, and everybody was standing there looking very forlorn, and he cheered everybody up. You know, he had a very loud voice and he was asking me all about my life and I ended up telling him and the whole of the rest of the carriage about my life. And I very much felt at that point, I didn't feel foreign at that point at all. I felt anyway that I was the same as he was, in a French sort of way, and yet I was also very much aware of the fact that I didn't feel comfortable in speaking French. I feel I have a feeling for French custom, way of life, whatever. I'm not sure that it's to do with language. I feel homesick at times for forms of French life. I feel it is, or has been, part of me, and I don't feel I can deny that feeling.

J.M.   I suppose, very crudely, there are two views people have about their languages: first, that languages are equivalent, and that in principle there is nothing that can be said in one that could not be said in another. And second, that languages develop to mirror particular experience and then themselves shape and determine that experience. That *is* crude, but what I'm getting at is whether people who speak two languages have difficulties transferring from one politeness system, say, or tense system, to another.

J.T.   I think that once you become aware of the use another language is making of certain elements, say, that your own language has...I'm thinking of Tolstoy in *Anna Karenina*. He says several times about the Russian *vous* form. It would be too forward, so Anna calls Karenin, speaks to him in French. He does say several times about it not being satisfactory in Russian...and they speak several languages, but the difficulties come with politeness. There are certain degrees of politeness which are more appropriate. But the thing is it's always in the society, in the people, the levels of politeness. They're making use of these levels of politeness accessible to them in the different languages. But it is almost as though he's saying that Russian isn't large enough to incorporate....

J.M.   Is it a fundamental difference between languages, or is it, as it was in his case, that Russian was the language children of his class learnt from the servants and that they moved into French for grown-up life?

J.T.   He doesn't give you the impression, I think, that the Russian isn't good enough from the point of view of the social thing, so much as the *vous* form is too formal.

J.M.   *Ti–*, which is the *tu* form, would in his case be used to servants and to other children. When writers in Russia in the middle of the nineteenth century felt it very important to resurrect Russian as much more than that sort of a language, the language of peasants and servants and children – which it was, after all, perfectly capable of being, a real literary language – but clearly, therefore, *vi*, which is the *vous* form, had special connotations for them, which were different from the *tu* and *vous*.

J.T.   You see, when French people I've spoken to recently, and it

87

didn't happen to me when I was a child, because it was much simpler, but I find now that the sort of difficulty I might have in not being sure when I call – say, like the French *assistant* from school – I didn't know whether to call him *tu* or *vous*. And I find now that French people are very much aware that there is this use and they would say, very early on in your relationship…they'll invite you to *tutoyer*. It's much more formal.

J.M.   In a sense there aren't equivalents in English, are there? Supposing you wanted to teach a French person about the difference between formal and informal in English…

J.T.   It almost seems as though that very restriction, in that there is only one term, allows almost greater possibilities, in that we've got other elements, it's not just a case of a word. I'm often uncomfortable calling somebody 'you'. It seemed odd, with teachers, for instance. I suppose you make up for it with other words you use. In French, it seems to me, you have a much more specific use of the language, in that you have these words available to you, which are there for that purpose, words like *vous* and *tu*, and *monsieur* and *madame*, and you have almost role-playing words, which have very, very specific uses, and you can only really use them in one context.

J.M.   Suppose a French friend was staying with you and addressed your parents as Sir and Madam at breakfast, how could you put her right? Explain why those are inappropriate forms of address.

J.T.   I suppose I would suggest calling them by their names, and I mean their surnames with Mr and Mrs. Or in another context, rather than worrying about addressing them personally, which is a thing which I think French does a lot more than English, is rather get on to the next bit which is, 'How are you this morning?' and that sort of thing.

J.M.   This is important, isn't it? Because one of the objections people make about people coming to live in this country is that they are rude or have bad ways of addressing you. These are things which are very hard for people to learn. You find it very hard, as I'd expect you to, to say what being polite in English *is*. I'd want to say that it is not necessarily any more difficult in English than in French, but it is marked in different ways.

J.T.   I'd have thought that wasn't true. In French you have these words with certain specific meanings and uses, which are always used like that, and you can get away with using these words and only these words and conveying the feeling that you want to convey.

J.M.   Let me give you an example. Our Italian lady, who takes our house in the summer, is a kind, considerate person and she writes good English most of the time. In her last letter, though, she put, 'Take note, please, that we'll be arriving on the 28th and not the 30th.' And I bristled. What would you want to tell her was wrong with that? What might she have written instead?

J.T.   I think I'd want to say that there is a slight difference in the position you're putting yourself in, as the speaker, *vis-à-vis* the person you're speaking to, rather than directing it at the person, reflecting it on yourself, saying, you know, I would be very grateful if, or. Making it almost self-deprecating. There you see that having these specific uses of these words provides you with that form of politeness almost in a formula, which isn't there in English, and that's what makes it easier in a language like French, in that you are able to use that formula, and it will be understood by the person you're talking to, while in English you are having to use a sense of yourself in relation to the person you're talking to, which is in the actual language you're using.

J.M.   Does that mean that languages actually do mirror and contain different...?·

J.T.   It used to be said that if you learn a second language after a first one, in learning a second language you're going to be made aware of a different culture. I don't ever remember feeling that I was dealing with two different cultures, not consciously ever. So I may have been able to say the right things to the right people at the right time without actually being aware of the differences, just because I'd learned both languages in the same way.

J.M.   Very good English speakers can cause offence, and it may be that that is one of the territories which it is very hard to teach formally. It may even be that your sense of French being simpler in this respect is because French was a school language for you and English a home one.

J.T.   It still seems different to me. In French, there are certain words, specific words, which render that meaning, whereas in English, there's no one specific formula like...it's a positioning of the self within the language.

J.M.   This is often the hardest bit of a new language, isn't it, the formalities and greetings, things which don't mean very much but send the most powerful messages about relationships. Your sense that it's all very simple in French. I don't think that English people learning French would agree with you.

J.T.   But then I don't feel it in English, and that's the strange thing. In trying to explain, like you asked me to, I found it very difficult, since I find it more difficult to explain in English than in French, and yet I don't make the same howlers in English that I make in French and so it should seem as simple as it does in French. And, in fact, I think I would probably instinctively get it right. Actually to try to find what it is about, it seems to me more complicated in English.

J.M.   I don't think I'm denying that that may be so...though presumably it's not harder for English people to learn.

J.T.   Maybe it's to do with a way of thought.

J.M.   Yes. Suppose it is much easier for French people to learn their forms than it is for English people to learn theirs, would that, d'you think, suggest that we have actually much more complicated views about superiority and inferiority and where formality is due and where it isn't?

J.T.   I think it might. Well there's the tradition of the language, and language development, the use of that language, the very same language.

J.M. Some people would say that language actually carries within it, in its use, political attitudes. I mean France had a revolution, and as you probably know more than half the population of France in the middle of the nineteenth century didn't speak French as their mother tongue, therefore schooling in French was, in a sense, teaching a second language and therefore it was formalised. Certainly the history of French as a school subject in France has been different from the history of English as a school subject in England. Here, after all, there's been a version of that, where everybody is taught to speak their language rather differently from the way they did speak it. But one of the things which happened as a result of taking people out of their mother tongue and into French was the actual formalising in books of what French consisted of.

J.T.   But don't you get with dialects and so on the same thing anyway? The uses of English, like, say, the Bristol use of 'l', which is the Bristolian dialect but is wrong by a generally accepted English.

There can be little doubt that Jane has a quite exceptional awareness of language for a person of her age. She remembers French as being her stronger language until she was eight years old. She was, for a start, literate in it. She spoke it all the time at school and with her brother and sister, though she also talks of using a kind of *Franglais* at home as well. She was proud of knowing English at school, and was occasionally asked to teach children some English, though she 'had no idea what they wanted to learn'. Her one memory of confusion indicates that she had very few difficulties with her two languages, though her reluctance to call her mother *Maman* and her embarrassment if her mother spoke English to her on the school premises, suggest that it was important that the languages keep their place. Throughout our discussion she talks about things 'feeling French' or 'feeling English', and at one point says, 'There was the language, you might say, of the mind and the actual speaking...'.

What is particularly interesting about Jane as a bilingual is that she has surprisingly clear memories of being what has been called a 'coordinate bilingual', and it is against that memory that she measures her progress towards becoming a 'compound bilingual'.[1] This is not, in fact, an uncommon experience, though it is, for obvious reasons, less likely to happen with people who have moved permanently to another country. Leopold (1954), whose classic study of his own bilingual child will be considered in the next chapter, describes several such moves, or possible moves, in both directions between languages.

It is not impossible that this double experience of bilingualism and the problems it has posed for Jane over quite a long period as a language learner are responsible in part for the very detailed awareness she has of what is involved linguistically in having two languages.

When Jane went to live in Edinburgh at eight years old she believes that she could more or less read in English but not write, and that her parents prepared the children for school by teaching them English spelling. Her language awareness and her language abilities are impressive. Yet oddly, and perhaps coincidentally, she is bad at spelling in both her languages and has found none of the formal aspects of writing in either language easy. She believes that her older sister, who did more formal school work in French, is better than she is at French grammar. *Grammar* is used here to mean, I take it, both accepted forms and idiom. Moving from a bilingualism which felt 'natural' to a conscious manipulating of two languages encouraged a self-consciousness and an expectation, perhaps, that rules would solve her confusions.

The second half of the transcript deals with her experience of 'losing' French and partly regaining it through studying it as a school subject and holidays in France. On her first return to France two years after coming to live in Scotland she was made aware that she was translating from English into French and making very un-French mistakes. *L'école que j'étais dedans* is something she would not say now after many years of school French, which has taught her to recognise anglicisms, even where it has not always supplied her with better alternatives. She now has a sense that two things operate for her French. One of them is a knowledge about the system and a knowledge about language generally. The other is harder for her to define: 'Well it's almost a memory of the knowledge of it, it seems to me, it's almost knowing how I spoke it, and now realising what it is, and everything, and therefore being able to remember it much better.' Knowing about

91

French and remembering how to speak it seem to her separate: 'The thought process and the memory are two completely different things.' Ervin-Tripp (1973) and others have conducted studies on bilinguals who have groped in the same way towards a definition of these different ways of 'knowing' a language. It is a definition which is sometimes expressed in terms of a tension between their productive and receptive capacities or between being able to speak a language but not think or remember in it. Jane is working towards something even more difficult to articulate, I think: a distinction between operating within a language or from outside with access to it. Bringing her 'thought process' to bear on her 'memory' of French sometimes works. Doing that with written language in French or in English appears to confuse her.

Her account of reading French and listening to bulletins on French radio is revealing. She behaves like a native user of French, to the extent that she goes for meaning and context, and, for the most part, ignores what she doesn't know in the lexis. Yet she says that she would find it hard to reproduce what she's heard in French and to a lesser extent would find it hard to do that in English too. This partly connects with two other questions Jane raises. One is her sense that there is a stretch of her life experience, between the ages of eight and eighteen, which has not been in French and which leaves her vulnerable as a French speaker. The other is that her receptivity to French is possibly more sophisticated than her production of it. Her particular bilingual experience has made for her demanding a very high standard for herself as a French speaker. It is not adequate for her to be taken for a French girl after a minute or two talking formalities in a shop. She has memories of 'being' a French girl, and knowing French as well as English has conferred a kind of status on her, it has impressed people. Her feeling that this is now 'a con', a pretence and artificial, dependent on her accent mainly and on her ability to manage formal interchange of a sort which does not expose her, goes with her belief that the things which have occupied and interested her, have mattered to her during that ten-year gap, would be beyond her French. She understands French easily and without translating it for herself, and she feels in tune with French people and sympathetic to them, able to appreciate their humour and their conversational approach. So she can 'feel' French and yet feel crippled by her inability to express herself in French.

It was Jane's contribution which brought out most clearly for me the quality of acting in second-language use when she said, 'I didn't feel like an eighteen-year-old French girl, but I was making myself sound like it.' It may be this ability to 'act', and Jane certainly has it for some of the time, which constitutes that rare native-like second-language speech. That is, it seems to involve seeing yourself as a native speaker of the language with all that that entails in non-verbal behaviour and style; finding the language you need from within a posture or role which triggers it off. Later, when Jane and I were discussing polite forms in the two languages – and I shall be returning to this point – she says of English manners that 'it's a positioning of the self within the language', a superb description, it seems to me, not only of how polite forms come to convey attitude and to express perceived relationships, but as an account of the way we make language work for us by both resisting and yielding to its constraints in many forms of spoken and written discourse.

Our discussion about polite forms, in which Jane argues that the marking of the 'you' forms and other conventions makes the learning of such items much easier in French than in English, raises fascinating questions about the way language incorporates attitudes to class and status and what is hard or difficult about language learning.[2] At one level it is easy to agree with Jane that there are in French useful formulae for greeting, thanking, asking, signing off and so on. Formulae, that is, which can be taught, learned and broadly adapted to particular situations. Yet most people who have had experience of living in France would also recognise that for a good deal of the time these rules are subtly and significantly adapted in ways governed by things like class, age, sex, context, relationship and so on. What I am getting at here is the difference between what may be easily teachable and what is easy because it has been 'naturally' learned. What we find easy is often particularly difficult to teach, to derive rules from or to systematise, which is not the same thing as saying that it is hard to learn. This brings me back to the intractable heart of my inquiries, to the problem of getting people to account for their own language use and attitudes, from their midst, so to speak. Jane's unusual sensitivity to these things comes, I want to maintain, from her experience of having occupied two languages, 'naturally' at times, 'artificially' at other times.

In the last section of this transcript Jane and I talk about various aspects of bilingualism which arise out of literary examples. She makes an interesting point about Anna in *Anna Karenina* using French to talk to her husband, partly because the Russian *vous* and *tu* forms strike the wrong note: either too redolent of social status or of a childlike and trusting intimacy. For Tolstoy and contemporaries of his class, Russian was their first language and the language which was being forged into a literary language during the first half of the nineteenth century. None the less, Russian was also for many of these writers a family language, used almost exclusively for talking with peasants and servants and children, so that the polite forms it embodies, which may be linguistically parallel or equivalent to the French ones, have associations which are to do with childhood relationships. Notions of age, respect, superiority and so on are bound to be differently perceived by children and by adults. Children could be said to enter these conversations with a limited range of roles. Where another language intervenes in childhood or adolescence the conventions in the new language will necessarily include an individual's acquiring new perceptions of himself and his relationships with other people. The child may come to see herself as a woman, a girlfriend, an employee, perhaps even an employer, and, generally, as someone involved in an expanding variety of contractual relations with other people – and this may happen in a second language. Jane's sense of the simplicity of these conventions in French, and of their complexity in English, may be connected with two biographical factors. The first is that her sense of their simplicity in French is associated with the fact that they really were simple for her as a child, while in English she has become a young woman and has moved into more complicated and protean relations with other people.

The second factor I have already referred to as the difficulty we all have of systematising and describing those things we do by now naturally. This might be seen as analogous to the difficulty Raymond Williams suggests we have in getting at the 'structure of feeling' of any moment in cultural history, either because we are inside it and take its manifestations for granted, or because we are outside it and are therefore likely to be insensitive to its most significant signals. Jane, for instance, is adamant that as a child she did not feel she was 'dealing with two different cultures'. Now she feels that she is, but is not able to pinpoint the differences beyond her 'feelings' about them. I shall hope to discuss in a future chapter what appear to me to be some of the educational implications of this, and to ask whether there are aspects of language and of our own language that children should know about in order to make awareness work for them productively. Patrice Higonnet (1978) has written about the way in which school French was imposed on a population in the nineteenth century, for half of whom it was a second language. His account of how French developed as a subject, with an explicitness about its system, usage and ideal forms, provides an interesting contrast with the confusions in this country, where English is simply assumed to be everybody's mother tongue. Questions of register, standard forms versus dialect ones and the relation of spoken to written language are often left undiscussed and certainly unexplained. It is interesting to speculate whether the always higher success rate in literacy in Scotland has anything to do with teachers being able to assume a common dialect amongst their pupils and, therefore, a common shift towards standard forms and written English.

Certain themes which have run through my conversations with other bilinguals were highlighted here by Jane's particular experience of learning and relearning a language: the role of acting in second-language use, questions about how aspects of language are best learned, problems of polite forms and what they suggest about the cultural determinants built into languages. There are implications for school, I think, in the kind of awareness of language which Jane has developed. Her linguistic biography has its parallels, I suggest, in the experience of most people who grow up using more than one language or dialect. The two languages will change in their relation to each other and in their significance for the speaker as viable and valid ways of organising and representing different kinds of experience.

This final transcript represents just a small part of the morning's conversation I had with six bilingual youngsters. For several reasons I taped only small portions of it, and the occasion was arranged as much in order to try out some materials with the group from the booklet *Languages* (Raleigh and Miller, 1979) as to find out about their bilingualism. What I shall have to say, therefore, relies as much on my impressions and on what the speakers had to say to each other as on the transcript itself.

Arina Patel is fourteen and speaks Gujarati, having started learning English at five. She thinks of Gujarati as her main language, has attended classes in it in England and also spent the years between seven and eleven in India, where she learned most of her English in a Christian school. She values English as a lingua franca in India but is clearly more attached to Gujarati. She admits to having gaps in both languages and is better, she says, at writing in English. She found English difficult to learn, she says, and did so initially as a foreign language.

Dan Lam is also fourteen. His family came here from Hong Kong, and he was born here and started English when he started school at five. He speaks a rather racy non-Standard London English and appears to read and write with equal facility in English and in Chinese. He attends classes in Chinese and regards it as his 'main' language.

Maria Ferrary is fourteen and the third of the straightforwardly bilingual children. She speaks Spanish and English, which she began when she started school here at five. Her family came here from Gibraltar, where she has spent several holidays. Though she is now learning Spanish at school and still speaks it for a good deal of the time with her parents she likes English better. 'I can't express what I'm trying to tell people in Spanish. I can in English.' She is pleased to be learning Spanish as a school subject, both because she feels she should be able to read and write in it and because it is the language she speaks with her grandparents.

The other three speakers might be called beginner bilinguals.

Eyal Batt is thirteen and has been in this country for a year, though he started to learn English three years ago in Israel. He says that he never thinks in English and still doesn't 'find the right words'. He describes Hebrew as his main language, but English as 'my important language...because Hebrew is spoken only in Israel and English is spoken all over the world'. He testifies to occasionally confusing the languages, though he can say so in very elegant and confident English: 'When I first came to school, I found myself talking Hebrew to a friend of mine.' He is already aware of the contrasts between his two languages: 'There are some words like "day off school", something with off and on, that I can't translate, because there are no words for on and off, you just

96

say....' Even from the few examples of his speech in the transcript it is possible to detect an intriguing 'interlanguage', full of instabilities as well as sophistications, and of overgeneralisations of learned idioms and structures of the kind Ben-Zeev (1977a) has described. There is a sense that this is a learner who is still consciously learning the language all the time, reflecting on his progress and monitoring his own errors in the light of a clearly perceived target of successful English.

Jazenco Prolic is from Yugoslavia and is twelve years old. He came here two years ago. He too sees the importance of English as an international lingua franca, but, since he will be returning to Yugoslavia soon, believes that his own language is much more important for him. He had an assured and amusing explanation of the 'you' forms in his language. 'The "you" thing. We've got three kinds. Two kinds. To animals and to grand people.' His own English fluctuates between something uncertain and more formal than he intends and something which sounds very like his native-speaking peers' English, full of 'and everything', and difficult constructions like, 'It's harder for me to talk English.'

Fanis Sarafides is fourteen and Greek and has been here and learning English for only a year. In some ways he was the most impressive of them all as a learner, able already to joke in English and follow everything said by the others (though not always by me). Interestingly, though, he became confused whenever I asked him to contrast his two languages, completely muddled one task and produced his wildest structures at those moments when he was being asked to reflect on questions of language generally and of differences between Greek and English particularly.

(The first six statements were prepared by the speakers from written notes.)

A.P. I speak English at school to friends and teachers and Gujarati at home with parents and my sisters and brothers. And I speak English to my brothers and sisters, but not to my parents. Gujarati is my main language.

F.S. I speak English at school with my friends and my teachers, some English with my brother at home. And I speak Greek with my parents. My most important language is Greek.

J.M. I'm right, aren't I, in thinking that for all of you English was the second language you learned? (Assent.)

J.P.   Well I speak Yugoslavian at home, and I speak English in the English school here at Holland Park. I always speak Yugoslavian with my parents, but with my brother I mainly speak English. My most important language is Yugoslavian, then comes English, because I'm returning to Yugoslavia, so it will be the most important.

D.L.   I speak English at school and with my brothers and sister. And I speak Chinese when I go to Chinese school. I speak Chinese with my parents at home. Chinese is my main one.

E.B.   I speak Hebrew with my family and friends, everywhere and any time. I speak English at school and to English or foreign friends. My main language is Hebrew and my important language is English, because Hebrew is spoken only in Israel and English is spoken all over the world.

M.F.   Well I speak English at school. I speak English and Spanish with my parents and my brothers. I mainly speak English with my brothers and my main language is English.

J.M.   What do you all mean by 'main'? Is it the one you're best at?

J.P.   The most important.

J.M.   Is that Eyat's idea of importance?

J.P. &
F.S.   Yes.

J.P.   Because it's used all over the world.

J.M.   Arina, would you find it hard swapping over languages? Doing your lessons in Gujarati and talking at home in English?

A.P.   No, it wouldn't make any difference.

D.L.   I wouldn't mind if I never spoke it again.

J.M.   Which? Chinese?

D.L.   Oh yes, I'd mind that.

(Some conversation amongst themselves about the differences between using one language rather than another. There is a general sense that it doesn't make much difference.)

J.M.   Are there any difficulties?

E.B.   Sometimes I don't find the right words in English. I've been learning it for three years. But I've been here only one year.

J.M.   Do you think in English?

E.B.   No, never.

(They agree that translating goes on a lot.)

F.S.   You don't realise you're thinking in English.

J.P.   When my parents have some guests I don't know whether they're Yugoslavian or English so sometimes they don't say they're coming. I talk English. I always go English because they're bound to know English if they live in England.

M.F.   My Spanish isn't as good as my English. I can't express what I'm trying to tell people in Spanish. I can in English. I dunno, it's just that it's always been like that. Everybody can understand me if I'm speaking in English to them, and they can't when I speak in Spanish.

J.M.   How many of you remember learning English?

A.P.   I do. It was very difficult.

F.S.   It was difficult at the beginning, but after a few weeks...

J.P.   The first few months were difficult, the first four or five months...

E.B.   I didn't learn English at school. I did learn English but I had a trouble, a lot of teachers, because I knew that I'm going to go to England, and I want to speak more English than at school, so I got....

J.M.   When did you start to feel at home in English?

E.B.   Only last year.

J.M.   Did any of you learn English very young?

M.F.   I did, when I was five. When I went to school. It didn't take very long. It was difficult, though, but it didn't take very long. I didn't like school, so that's probably why I found it difficult.

A.P.   Well I learnt English in my country. Well I was born here and I went to school when I was five. And then at seven I went to India and I stayed there and came back at eleven, so most of my English was done in India. I went to a school run by Christians.

J.M.   And is there no difference for you between your languages?

A.P.   No.

J.M.   What about reading and writing?

A.P.   I'd rather write in English.

J.M.   Have any of you ever spoken the wrong language to the wrong person?

E.B.   Yes, when I first came to school I found myself talking Hebrew to a friend of mine.

A.P.   I know sometimes a word in English and not in Gujarati. Sometimes the other way round.

J.M.   Are there sometimes things you can say in one language which you can't say in another?

(A chorus of assent.)

F.S.   The most times some word which you can't explain...

(At this point I tried to get examples from them of what they could say only in one language. The attempt was scuppered by Dan Lam, who immediately thought of how to say 'bunking off' in Chinese.)

E.B. There isn't a special word for bunking but you use other words, similar.

J.M. It isn't really a question, is it, of one language being better than another for talking about this or that, but of what you have used it for. Another thing which is different in different languages is politeness talk....

J.P. The 'you' thing. We've got three kinds. Two kinds. To animals and to grand people.

D.L. They speak it different there.

J.M. How would you explain to someone who had just arrived from the country where your first language is spoken how they should greet your parents in the morning?

All Good morning.

E.B. May I have a cup of tea please?

A.P. Just, tea please.

J.M. Is there anything you'd tell them not to say, because it's rude?

J.P. Give me two eggs.

F.S. Tell them not to say, 'Yack.'

M.F. They should say, 'No, thank you.'

A.P. No, thank you, I don't like them.

J.M. Let's look at that 'you' thing you mentioned.

M.F. When you're talking to adults you say *usted* and when you're talking to someone of your age you say *tu*.

A.P. If it's someone say your age or younger it's *tu* and if it's someone older *tumi*.

E.B. In Hebrew 'you' is the same.

F.S. In Greek it's different. We've got two different 'you', one for when you're talking to your friends and one.... (He couldn't say what they were.) I've forgot them.

(We used an idea from the *Languages* booklet at this point: collecting words for 'mother', 'father', 'school', 'family', 'happy'. One or two of them found it hard to produce words on demand like this. They claimed that they were unused to using their own languages with people who do not understand them.

Each of them told us something about their day in their own language and then translated it for the group. I asked them to write it in their own language as well and to make an English translation.)

E.B. This doesn't seem right, just translating, because there are some uses of words I can't translate.

D.L. It is difficult to say those things because in your country you've never had experience of those things before, you never did it. Like 'bunking off'.

E.B. There are some words like 'day off school'. Something with 'off' and 'on', that I can't translate, because there are no words for on and off, you just say….

J.M. Are there subjects which you have never talked about in one of your languages?

A.P. I would find History difficult in Gujarati, because of the dates and names.

D.L. Yes, I'd find that very difficult. So many centuries and kings and emperors and that. It's hard to remember.

J.M. What about other things? Are Maths and Science hard for you to talk about in Chinese?

D.L. No. They're very easy.

J.M. If your parents ask you about what you were doing at school in Biology or Cookery?

D.L. No, we just say it was good or bad. Sometimes it would be hard to say much because we ain't done it.

M.F. We speak half a sentence in English and half in Spanish anyway, so if we don't know what a word in Spanish is we just say it in English.

J.M. What about things to do with religion?

D.L. I have to talk in Chinese. There aren't English words for things, because they're not known to English.

E.B. No. There would be a few words you can't translate into English, but most of them you could. Almost all.

F.S. There are some names, you can't translate them in English.

A.P. Well I could talk about it in both languages, but I'd prefer to speak Gujarati about religion.

J.P. When I talk English I don't talk it with ease, like when I talk Yugoslavian I talk it with ease. It's harder for me to talk English, because I can't find expressions.

J.M. How many of you are carrying on with lessons in your own language?

M.F. I do Spanish at school.

A.P. I do Gujarati at Wembley, at a school up there. It's run by people there.

E.B. No, I don't really, because I'm here only one year and I don't think I'll forget it.

F.S. I do but they've stopped now, you know, the Greek school's stopped now so I don't do any more.

D.L. Yes. It's a kind of club, you know. It's different from English school. You have to pass these tests to go on to a higher standard class, and if you don't pass them you stay in the same class. I spend two and a half hours each week this year, but last year we had two days, Saturday and Sunday. In my class there's about eleven people. Some of them are seventeen. I don't like it at the time.

J.P. I'm staying here a year, a year and a half. It's going to be very difficult for me to get jobs if I don't go here somewhere.

M.F. It's good because I didn't know how to read or write before. If I

101

can speak the language I want to know how to read and write it
as well.

(There was a general feeling that keeping up your language was a
good thing. They all said that they had opportunities to read books
in their own language.)

D.L.   Down in Gerrard Street. There's loads, a whole street of
Chinese restaurants…. There's places where we can buy
newspapers.

J.P.   I think it's a great advantage to speak English. I'm really happy I
can speak English. All the places I'll be able to ask people
where, you know. It's one of the most important languages in the
world.

E.B.   When I come back after one year I go to junior school and then
in the end of the four years in junior school I have some exams,
and English is one of the most important subjects in that exam.

F.S.   I think it's very important, a great advantage. When I came here
and didn't speak any English and I wanted to go back to Greece.
The school helped me, when I came to school I found I could
speak.

A.P.   Well it's nice to know English because sometimes your Indian
friends might not know your language and you could speak to
them in English. I know just a little bit of another one, Hindi,
but I'm not very good at it.

M.F.   If I couldn't speak English I'd feel lost. Because English, I think,
is my main language. I wouldn't mind so much if I couldn't speak
Spanish, but I think English is a very important language. I
couldn't talk to my grandparents.

A.P.   Because your grandparents can't speak English if they're living
in our country all the time, and if we go there we just need
Gujarati to be able to talk to them at all.

J.M.   Dan, what would you miss if you couldn't speak Chinese?

D.L.   Not a lot. I'd miss the chance to talk to…

F.S.   I'd miss books, comics.

D.L.   I'd miss books as well. I suppose I read and write best in English.
In Chinese I got a high standard. I'm in the highest class.

J.M.   Have any of you got ideas about what you want to do when you
leave school?

J.P.   I'd like to live in my country. I am going back anyway, and I like
my country very much.

D.L.   I want to go back to my country. My parents were born in Hong
Kong and I was born here. I've been to Hong Kong, but I've
never been to China. I wouldn't mind which.

M.F.   I'd like to stay here or go off to America. I don't come from
Spain, I don't think I could live in a place like Gibraltar after
being brought up in England, because Gibraltar's so small and

just not like London. I don't think I could live in that place.

A.P.   I'd like to go back.

J.M.   Let's hear what you find strange and different about England.

J.P.   I find the people here are very polite and everything. It is really different than in Yugoslavia. It's hard to say it. What I tell them (Yugoslavs) is if you come here to go to school and everything...well I'd tell them it's a bit less strict. I think they're good schools, friendly teachers and everything. Friendly people. They help you. I'd tell them about the buses and everything. Tell them about London. Show them about.

J.M.   What's difficult for people arriving here for the first time?

J.P.   The language, and the town is very big.

(Sound of breaking glass.)

D.L.   That sort of thing.

J.P.   If somebody was there they'd have a nice open head.

F.S.   Somebody's come to do the windows, come to take them out. There's something which is not in Greece so much, the parks, the green. The weather is not so nice like in Greece.

D.L.   It's all kinds of thing. One minute it's sunny, one minute it's raining.

F.S.   In England you can't realise the weather from the morning. In Greece if it is a sunny day from the morning, it is a sunny day all the day. In England if it is a sunny day in the morning, after five minutes it will be raining, cloudy, you know.

M.F.   The weather, and the people are not as friendly in London as they would be in Gibraltar. This is so big and in Gibraltar everyone knows everyone else, and over here nobody could care about the next person.

J.P.   How big is the country?

M.F.   About 3.5 square miles. It's not very big. It's at the bottom of Spain but it's not Spanish.

The transcript does give some flavour of the conversation I had with these six London schoolchildren, though it barely scratches the surface of their individual lives or the cultural experiences, conflicts as well as accommodations, which are likely to underlie what they have to say about being or becoming bilingual. There was, however, a particular usefulness for me in working with this group of children in this way. They attend a school which, according to the survey described by Rosen and Burgess (1980), contained the largest number of languages spoken by first-year pupils in their sample. I taught in that school for several years, and at one point in the early 1970s we calculated that there were at

103

least seventy languages spoken there. The population is diverse in other ways. There is a large number of children who speak dialects deriving from other parts of the country as well as forms of English which are American, Australian, African and Caribbean. Amongst the bilingual children are some who are here for a limited period because their parents are on diplomatic missions or business assignments. Many more are the children of families, European, Asian and African, who have settled here for what is likely to be the rest of their lives, though some of them hope to return one day to the countries where they were born.

My group of six children was mixed too as to age, sex, class and educational aspiration. In their normal school day they work in classes where monolingual native London children are usually in the minority, and where some notion of a target English, Standard or otherwise, is hard to hold to. These children will have broken into English in many cases via the English of children who have had relatively little experience of the language themselves, and yet, and extraordinarily, there were moments during my conversation with these children when their talk with each other and with me sounded like any group of native English-speaking schoolchildren in any London classroom. I have been struck at other times by a discrepancy between the fluent English children like these will speak to each other compared to the difficulties they can seem to be having with the language in a formal English lesson intended for learners of English as a second or foreign language.

Talking with these children on their own helped me to focus on some of the skills as well as the difficulties which may be submerged by the normal bustle of the classroom: their ability to distinguish between different institutions, linguistic and social ones, their facility with translation, their philosophical acceptance of different kinds of behaviour and different teaching styles.

The children feel differently about the importance of keeping up their mother tongues. Maria at fourteen is beginning to return to Spanish, having allowed it, even wanted it, to lapse. Eyat and Jazenco and Fanis expect to return to their own countries and their own languages, and they are pleased to have learned English as a second language. Dan is pulled both ways, proudly asserting the value of Chinese, the high standards maintained by Chinese schools in this country, the richness of resources provided by and for the Chinese community here. It is possible to sense, I think, that he may well assert similar strengths in the London and English culture which his bilingualism allows him to enter and understand in ways he may feel his parents cannot. Arina has moved during her life between her languages, and this had made her able to see English as a useful language in India just as Gujarati is a language spoken by people living here.

Many teachers can produce examples of pupils who insist that now that they know English they don't want to speak their home language any more. There is considerable evidence that this changes, and that at fifteen or so many young people begin to look for the language they may once have possessed, as part of the identity they are looking for. Probably a majority of children whose parents came from the West Indies, and who are growing up here, will move away from the patois or Creole which their parents have spoken to them in childhood towards a London English barely marked by Creole features. They will often do so with parental encouragement. Yet in a large number of cases they will consciously and deliberately move towards a form of London Jamaican dialect during their teens. Often this will be true too for children originating from other Caribbean islands. Multilingual and multidialectal children often take this fact about themselves for granted, so that only a very persistent questioner will discover the full extent of their language competences and their own valuing of them.

David came here with his family from Burma when he was a small boy. His speech is barely distinguishable from that of the rest of his first-year class in a Hackney secondary school. Here he is talking with one of his teachers:

D. I've forgotten my own language, sir, because I went....
T. I thought you spoke Burmese.
D. No, sir, forgot it, sir, then I came....
T. Yeah.
D. Then I came to this country and I did know a lot, I didn't know a lot of English...a bit of words. Then I watch, my Dad didn't send me to school, I started watching the television and them things, then I got a bit better at English, then I went to school and I learnt English there, sir.
T. So you...so your Dad...you've forgotten your Burmese completely...you don't speak it to your Dad at all.
D. My Dad speaks Burman and my two brothers and my big sister. They start talking about me but...don't know what they're saying.

> T. And they speak Burmese sometimes, but you don't speak it to them, and...well, obviously, your Burmese stories are just stories that people have told you, you haven't got books about them, or have you got some books in English?
>
> D. I think that there are some books at Burma, but, if my Dad goes again, I'll ask him to bring some.
>
> T. Yes, that would be interesting. Would you like to learn to speak Burmese?
>
> D. No, sir.
>
> T. There's probably a Burmese school on Saturday mornings, somewhere, isn't there?
>
> D. I think so sir, but I don't like to learn Burmese. I like to learn English sir...and French and German. But I already know three languages. I know English, Urdu and Gujarati.
>
> T. Ah, you speak Urdu?
>
> D. Yes, sir.
>
> T. And do you read Urdu?
>
> D. No, sir...I can read Arabic, very old, old, old Arabic.
>
> T. So you can read Koran then in Arabic?
>
> D. Yes, sir.
>
> T. And you can speak Urdu, but you don't read Urdu.
>
> D. No, sir.
>
> T. And what about Gujarati?
>
> D. The same, sir.
>
> T. You can speak it. And do your relatives speak that, do you speak Gujarati and Urdu to them?
>
> D. Yes, sir.
>
> T. Which was your main language, would you say?
>
> D. My main language, I think it used to be Urdu, but now I speak English with my Dad and Mum...but my Mum doesn't know English very well.
>
> T. She speaks Urdu, does she?

Neither David nor his English are 'problems' for his teacher. In many schools this would have meant that no one would ever know what is revealed about David's linguistic history by sensitive and interested questioning.

In the last three chapters I have tried to hear and to understand a little of what some adults and young people have to say about being bilingual. Apart from their bilingualism and the fact that they all live in a society which, despite its Celtic fringes, behaves as though it were monolingual, it could be said that their lives are more dissimilar than similar. The languages they speak, the context in which they acquired a second or subsequent language, the kind of support they received while doing so, their motives for learning and their memories of doing so, display a diversity and complexity, which make even a description of the state of affairs daunting. If we are to begin such a description, let alone to legislate for policies which might foster and capitalise on this curiously ignored collection of talents and experiences, we are not likely to plump for catch-all solutions.

Recent surveys suggest that between 14 and 15 per cent of London's school population are bilingual to some degree, and presumably, therefore, at least the same could be said of its adult population. If these particular bilinguals can, however minimally or partially, enlighten us about their difficulties as well as their achievements, schools and society generally would be indebted to them. I would expect the lessons we might learn from them to be in the territories of (a) language and learning as a continuous and developing relationship, (b) the ways in which the educational system might incorporate and maximise this kind of knowledge and understanding to benefit individuals, whatever their background, and (c) the texture of life lived by people in this country now, at a time when we are wrenching ourselves towards the recognition that we live in a multicultural society.

It is estimated that more than half of the world's population is bi- or multilingual; and in saying that I am clustering under one umbrella predicaments which can be quite different linguistically, socially and politically. It is important to retain the sense of individual experience and difference even as I move towards a narrowing of focus to some key themes. In the next chapters I shall start by attempting to locate the situation of bilingual speakers in this country within a broader picture of what bilingualism means and has meant internationally. Next, I shall consider some of the work which has been done by teachers, psychologists and linguists in the area of second-language learning. Since the early 1960s,[3] research into bilingualism has tended to emphasise the potential intellectual advantages of using two languages. Before that, and in certain places now, there was some consensus that bilingualism was probably a disadvantage. Research methodology, and its findings, can be modish, however, and it will be necessary to resist any sentimental embracing of the new optimism. None the less, there are impressive studies which suggest in some detail what advantages might accrue from using two languages; so that I shall move from a discussion of some of these to a final perspective: the educational implications for this country. And these will be set in the context of what is a large literature about possible educational responses to bilingualism in other parts of the world, particularly in Canada, America and Australia.

Before considering the question in these four ways, though, I want to return to what I take to be the most significantly recurring themes in the transcripts. The first I shall call the time dimension: a term capacious enough to include the ways in which language loyalty and competence change and fluctuate through time for any individual. What can seem like contradictions, ambivalences, dividedness and so on, must be unpicked, seen historically and developmentally and rematched with the conflations of a contemporary perception of them. All my bilinguals have been through a version of the immigrant experience, and asking them to account for their present attitudes to their languages has elicited something of the connection between language and individual development. Language choice and shift are culture-bound, dependent on 'atmosphere', place, interlocutor, context or topic; but they have also to do with a sequence in learning which marches with a sequence in experience. And, as I have suggested, this is a complex process, which mingles accretion with substitution, gain with loss, rigidity with flexibility, fossilisation with mobility.

Second, language and a sense of language are felt as aspects of relationships with other people: in childhood, with the family, with peers and a few specifically sited adults, and finally in an elaborate range of adult contexts. For bilingual children there can be an accentuated problem when, as young people, they feel drawn more sharply from their families by the blandishments of a mainstream culture. This can encourage an almost Oedipal guilt at being fitter and more competent than the parent. Seen within the time dimension this can produce distortions about the capacities of particular languages to express new experiences, distortions which blame one language while associating a new one with the more complex relationships inherent in growing into adolescence and adulthood. A Whorfian view of language as inescapably possessed of its particular cultural and intellectual determinations and ideologies may become more vulnerable when we consider development in this way and the attitudes of second-language learners to their target language.

A third theme is the learning of a second language. Most of us find it difficult to account for how we learned new knowledge and skills, and most of us tend to confuse teaching with learning. It is hardly astonishing, therefore, that most of my bilinguals attribute their learning of a second language to whatever process of instruction they went through. There remains the difficulty of accounting for all those other things they can do: tease, make jokes, use slang, understand clichés and so on. These accomplishments are vital to knowing a language and they suggest attentive and active learning rather than – though perhaps as well as – planned and structured teaching. Acting, role-play, mimicry, directed and undirected, begin to seem essential ingredients of second-language acquisition, as they are of first-language acquisition, and they are clearly involved in so-called monolingual skills like dialect shift and responsiveness to new registers, jargons and intralanguages.

If this natural part of language learning and use has its virtues for second-language learners it may also have attendant drawbacks. I have already suggested that it can, temporarily at least, tempt the learner into caricature or stereotypical expectations of linguistic (and other kinds of) behaviour, just as it can for those who resist the place of minority group cultures in our society. Simplification is seen by Selinker (1974) and Corder (1978) and others as an essential strategy in language and in learning and like other such strategies it is vulnerable to fossilisation. At its most spectacularly efficient, language learning comes out of and accompanies experience and action. Where that experience and action are missing abstraction and imagination have to serve instead. It is in this area, I believe, that the real challenge to education stands, on a spot which marks the meeting of individual development with the ways by which we understand each other and learn to live together.

5   The social perspectives of bilingualism

Bilingualism is a social phenomenon, and it is not possible to isolate it from its political context. By this I mean that its different manifestations are invariably shot through with the values accorded and attaching to them. Ervin-Tripp (1973) has put it like this:

> Bilingualism is an achievement that arrives by many routes. The bilingual-in-process might be a child growing up in a bilingual adult milieu, member of a bilingual family, or of a monolingual minority. He might be an adult who has moved to a different linguistic environment. The learning process might be casual or systematic pedagogy. The differences in what the learner hears, what he is expected to say, and how much formal correctness is demanded from the start make for radical differences in the process of acquisition according to age and milieu.

And then:

> Values play an important role in determining whether a given condition of social support will produce or sustain learning. At a gross level, beliefs about the ease or appropriateness of becoming bilingual may affect the probability of child or adult learning. In India it is assumed that children will readily become multilingual; in the United States bilingualism is taken as a matter of course only where the second language is English.

So, when, where, how and why are all questions which have to be asked about any individual or communal bilingual phenomenon. Motives for learning, rationales for pedagogy will vary, and these in turn will affect and be affected by attitudes to the languages involved. Such attitudes depend on who speaks which languages, to whom and for what purposes; and they will determine, in some cases, the extent to which a language may remain wholly or partly an oral resource.

110

I suggested in Chapter 1 that the phenomenon of bilingualism was almost invariably entangled with questions of class, and that this had helped to obscure the psychological and linguistic nature of the debate and to promote some anomalous educational responses to it. It would be true to say that for most of those societies where bilingualism or multilingualism is the norm, issues of status, access to education and literacy and international usefulness are likely to affect attitudes to the value attaching to one language rather than another. As Weinreich (1953) has shown, however, even in a country like Switzerland these are not simple matters. There is, for instance, the question of the proximity of one of the society's languages to a standard variant of that language used elsewhere in the world; and it is possible to come across contradictory views in a single speaker about the value of each of his languages. We heard a little of this when the group of six children were grappling with the distinction between a 'main' and an 'important' language. Similarly, an admired and high-status language may seem too formal, unresilient, humour-less a medium even for an expert and committed speaker of it. Many Indians feel like this about Hindi, for instance, and certainly many West Indians express that sort of view about the tensions between their own languages and the standard varieties of French and English which they may have willingly, if laboriously, mastered. Even amongst relatively high-status languages, there can be conflicts about a language which stands for a literature and a flourishing and shared culture, and another one which has developed technologically in ways which may make it a valuable economic asset. Two different versions of this might be the relation of French to English in Mauritius, and of Irish to English in Ireland.

Then, as both Weinreich and Haugen (1966) have shown, languages living cheek by jowl, so to speak, merge with one another in a variety of ways. Weinreich puts it like this:

First, language shifts should be analyzed in terms of the functions of the languages in the contact situation, since a mother-tongue group may switch to a new language in certain functions but not in others. For example, under a foreign occupation, or in migrating to a new country, the adult members of a mother-tongue group may come to use a new language in its

111

dealings with governmental authorities, while the children use it in school; at the same time, the old language may live on in the homes and at informal gatherings of the group. In such a case we might speak of a PARTIAL rather than a TOTAL shift. While language shifts among urban immigrants in America are usually rapid and total, the language shifts among rural immigrant communities are often rather of a partial type for two or three generations, at least.

Haugen describes a different kind of language shift in a community of Norwegian and Swedish speakers in America, where they have developed a version of Swedish which is regarded as comical in Scandinavia and whose mutant features cannot simply be attributed to the influence of English. Languages in contact with other languages are rarely static, nor are they, in any simple way, predictably exclusive or accommodating. Weinreich gives the example of Yiddish:

> A language which has, in the course of its history, experienced particularly multifarious and intimate contacts with others is Yiddish. The Yiddish language grew up on German dialect territory. One branch of it matured in Germany proper, a larger one in a Slavic environment; still others developed in contact with Rumanian, Hungarian, Lithuanian and Lettish. In Alsace and Lorraine, Yiddish evolved on the fringes of French-speaking territory. During the late nineteenth and early twentieth century, large segments of the Yiddish language community were withdrawn from the Slavic and other Old-World spheres of influence and brought into fresh contact with English, Spanish and Portuguese in the Americas. One finds, accordingly, in the history of Yiddish a certain basic structure now maintaining itself, now submitting to some outside interference, only to integrate the effects of this interference into a new, unique whole – depending on the specific historical circumstances. Such structural features in Yiddish as the opposition between some palatal and non-palatal consonants, for example, or that between perfective and non-perfective verbs, were at least partly acquired from, and supported by, contact with Slavic languages.

Clearly these differences in the effects of language contact, in their relative resistance to or absorption of one another, are subject to questions of status, group allegiance and particular social uses. It would be interesting to know what is happening to those Indian languages which have been brought here, often via parts of Africa.

E.G. Lewis (1976) reminds us that 'Polyglottism is a very early characteristic of human societies, and monolingualism a cultural limitation.' Nor does he suggest that the situation has radically changed over the centuries:

> In 1962 a survey of six nations revealed that a majority of Dutch and Belgian adults claimed a speaking competence in one or more languages other than their native tongues. Of the German and French who were questioned, 25% and 33% respectively made the same claim.... Russian is the second languae of 16 million non-Russians. The same urge to establish communication outside one's own group is characteristic of less modernized peoples also. In Central Africa, it has been claimed, the natives set out consciously to extend their identity beyond their native villages by deliberately choosing to incorporate in their conversations a vocabulary other than that of their native dialect.

If bilingualism then has been the norm its manifestations have always been variously prized. Lewis goes on:

> Because of bilingualism in medieval Europe, it is argued, 'people were forced into perpetual approximations in expressing their thoughts...forced as they were into an incessant movement to and fro between the two planes of languages' (Bloch, 1961). It is difficult to conceive how such an allegation can be validated or what criteria should be employed in any attempt to do so. Bilingualism has rarely been absent from important levels of the intellectual and cultural life of Europe, and nearly all European languages have had long, and in some instances, several successive periods of language contact. Bilingualism has been and is nearer to the normal situation than most people are willing to believe.

Yet if bilingualism can be seen to be a universal and continuing feature of nearly all societies, it has not only been differently valued but quite differently experienced. We might start by looking at two extremes on the continuum of ways in which it can be experienced. Leopold (1954) describes teaching his young

113

daughter to speak German as well as English in an American context where only he was available to her initially as a German speaker. His account of the fluctuations in her German, between obstinate dislike of using it to a sudden growth in her willingness and confidence in using German when she visited some of her paternal relatives in Germany, illustrates some of the problems of this kind of isolated fostering of bilingualism. More particularly, it shows how language use will be powerfully determined by the person it is used with and the purposes for which that relationship will make it seem appropriate. At another extreme might be communities in parts of India (or families like A.B.'s in Pakistan) where the possession of as many as three languages, and sometimes dialects of those languages too, and some elaborate knowledge about context and appropriateness, would be common to the majority of the population.

None of these forms of bilingualism is irrelevant in considering the individual and group experiences of people who have come to live in this country. Their past lives and the cultures they bring with them embody varieties of language contact and a whole range of attitudes to the languages they speak. That was apparent, I think, from the conversations I had with 'my' twelve bilinguals. Bilingualism means very different things for each of them. None the less, as I have already suggested, the one thing which those otherwise disparate bilinguals do share is their presence in a society which behaves institutionally as though it were monolingual. Such racial tolerance as exists here is founded on the premise that people who come to live here will want, and will find it easy, to assimilate to our culture and our language. It is as though the 'melting pot' image is the best we can do. Another anomaly is the one mentioned earlier: the discrepancy between the lip-service paid by our educational system to the learning of other languages and our refusal to admit that those advantages, if they are advantages, are already possessed by the large numbers of bilingual (and bidialectal) people who live here.

So that bilingualism, and I am for the moment excluding the Welsh and the Gaelic versions of it, is associated inevitably here with foreignness. A useful model for considering what this may mean for the 'foreigner', as for the host community, is provided by Schutz (1964), in his essay, 'The Stranger'. Here, Schutz contrasts what he calls 'a logic of everyday thinking', possessed and shared by members of a group, 'a knowledge of trustworthy *recipes* for interpreting the social world and for handling things and men in order to obtain the best results in every situation with a minimum of effort by avoiding undesirable consequences', with the strategies employed by a stranger to such a group, who 'does not share the...basic assumptions. He becomes essentially the man who has to place in question nearly everything that seems to be unquestionable to the members of the approached group.' 'To him,' Schutz continues,

> the cultural pattern of the approached group does not have the authority of a tested system of recipes, and this, if for no other reason, because he does not partake in the vivid historical tradition by which it has been formed. To be sure, from the stranger's point of view, too, the culture of the approached group has its peculiar history, and this history is even accessible to him. But it has never become an integral part of his biography, as did the history of his home group. Only the ways in which his fathers and grandfathers lived become for everyone elements of his own way of life. Graves and reminiscences can neither be transferred nor conquered. The stranger, therefore, approaches the other group as a newcomer in the true meaning of the term. At best he may be willing and able to share the present and the future with the approached group in vivid and immediate experiences; under all circumstances, however, he remains excluded from such experiences of its past. Seen from the point of view of the approached group, he is a man without a history.

Schutz includes language within this picture of reciprocal suspicion and likely misunderstanding, and in distinguishing between 'the passive understanding of a language and its active mastering as a means for realising one's own acts and thoughts' makes language an analogue for culture. In detailing the kinds of mental and emotional operation required of the stranger who wants to adapt to the host group, as well as the kinds of false expectation of what is involved in this which are likely to be entertained by the host group, Schutz illuminates some of the confusions which, at their worst, issue in racism and, even at their most benign, may cause waste and distress for large numbers of people. Learned with a first language, and by every child, is a rich and usually unexamined

115

tapestry of taken-for-granted knowledge about how the world works, how people behave and how, therefore, things can be expected to turn out in the future. Malinowski (1923) put it like this: 'language in its structure mirrors the real categories derived from the practical attitudes of the child'.

This way of looking at a child's mother tongue and at the particular cultural outlook which is learned through it – rather than as simply described by it – has two kinds of implication. The first involves the possibility that the unique quality of early development, in which language grows out of and accompanies experience, will mark that language in the mind of its user as different from other languages and as associated with particular kinds of learning. The second points to the possibilities for damaging misunderstandings, for confusion between personal and cultural forms of behaviour. In her remarkable novel, *The Woman Warrior*, Maxine Hong Kingston, a writer I shall want to return to, puts it like this:

> Chinese-Americans, when you try to understand what things in you are Chinese, how do you separate what is peculiar to childhood, to poverty, insanities, one family, your mother who marked your growing with stories, from what is Chinese? What is Chinese tradition and what is the movies?

Just as children are better at learning language and better at adapting to cultures than most adults are, so they become particularly vulnerable to the failure of adults to understand what kinds of adjustment are required of children at this stage. A telling example of this kind of misunderstanding is to be found in Brian Jackson's account (1979) of Beauregard starting school. He is the most neglected of the eleven children of a severely depressed Jamaican woman. Whereas he construes school in terms of what he has been told it is like, full of traps and punishments and detectors of his failings, his anxious and swift scuttling out of sight on his first day is seen at once as the wily and excitable behaviour of a spoilt West Indian boy who will need a lot of handling. His fear is construed as passivity or opposition, and in a matter of weeks there are plans to have him transferred to an ESN school. These are kinds of oversimplification and premature explanation of behaviour with which we are all familiar; scenarios which, so long as we treat them as provisional, may do no harm. They are

116

used by all of us as we begin to make ourselves familiar with the worlds we inhabit. Where they become potentially damaging, to both groups and individuals, is where the bedrock of expectations about the world, effortlessly garnered in childhood, is allowed to seem worthless as a provisional model for learning to understand a new world, and where mastering a new world is made to entail the abandoning or even desecration of the old one.

Before continuing with this question of how a child can best understand his new world I want to return to Schutz for a moment. His subtle image of the stranger is oversimplified in one respect for our purposes. For most bilingual children in inner-city schools there is no homogeneous world which they enter alone as strangers. Such homogeneity as there may seem to be is in fact an artefact, an illusion, which schools are often in the business of creating for purposes of control; so that the stranger is asked to believe that it is only he who lacks the knowledge which would make the new world intelligible to him. Children entering the majority of schools in inner London at the moment are in fact entering a society where that 'logic of everyday thinking' is not shared. It must be the business of schools to make that consolingly clear to all their pupils.

The arguments for making links between a child's own language and experience and the new language and culture of the school have too often concentrated on not much more than a generalised benevolence, however. Benevolence works with a deficit model of a child's linguistic and cultural 'gaps', ones to be filled with useful English tags or Christmas trees. Clearly much more than that is at issue here. What is needed is explicitness about the nature of the shifts in thought and behaviour people have to make when they approach other groups, the difficulties there are in doing so, the strategies they devise and the way they make use of connections, equivalences, differences in order to place themselves in acceptable relations with other people of all kinds. V.K. Edwards (1978) illustrates both the problems and the needs well, and it is clearly valuable to be reminded by her that the plight of bidialectal children resembles so closely that of bilingual children.

> The results of the attitude tests also suggest that the West Indians view themselves very negatively and these views reflect to a large extent the stereotype of West Indians which is

117

prevalent in Britain. It seems highly probable that a child's ability to learn is affected by his motivation and that his motivation is affected by the feedback he receives from society concerning his probable success. If this is the case, the plight of West Indian children in British schools is likely to continue to give rise to concern: not only is there evidence of extensive educational under-performance, but there are indications of far-reaching social malaise.

The importance of making available information which dispels the popular stereotype, therefore, cannot be overestimated. It is essential to show the linguistic validity of Creole – and, indeed, other non-standard varieties of speech – and to demonstrate that these varieties operate according to rules as regular, logical and systematic as those of the standard variety.[1] In the case of West Indian children, it would be informative to include discussion of verbal traditions in the West Indies in order to show the scope and flexibility of Creole and the importance attached to verbal skills. By the same token, priority should be given to sensitisation of teachers to the relationship between language attitudes and social stereotypes, and to the danger that these may be translated into reality.

From this it would follow that teachers need to understand more about language and more about learning in relation to cultural diversity.

Schutz, of course, specifically imagines his stranger as solitary and unencumbered. Only A.B. in my sample would fit such a portrait. What is likely to be much more common for bilingual children in this country is some variety of tug of war between the outside world and the family and home. Weinreich describes the kinds of effect on language use this situation can produce:

Whether the burden of bilingualism is borne by the group as a whole or to a greater degree by one part of it seems to depend both on the suddenness of the shift and the point to which it has progressed. In American immigrant families, for example, the children usually learn English most rapidly and in the early period it is they who switch back to the old-country tongue in communication with their elders. A generation later the grandchildren are often unilingual English and it is the parents and grandparents who must switch language in deference to their interlocutors.

An obsolescent language seems destined to acquire peculiar connotations and to be applied in special functions even after it has lost its main communicative role. Under a rapidly progressing language shift it acquires a certain esoteric value. On the other hand, the first generation to undergo the shift tends to learn enough of the obsolescent language to destroy this value; thus, many children of American immigrants 'know' just enough of the old folks' language to understand what the parents mean to conceal. Obsolescent languages also easily develop comic associations. Patois columns in French Swiss newspapers or Pennsylvania-German sections in certain Pennsylvania journals are mainly restricted to humorous material. Among children of American immigrants, the mere utterance of a word in their parents' language easily evokes laughter.

The stylistic specialization of an obsolescent language and the association of it with intimate childhood experiences is conducive to the borrowing of its lexical elements into the younger people's speech, especially in discourse that is informal and uninhibited by pretensions of high social status. Particularly apt to be transferred are colourful idiomatic expressions, difficult to translate, with strong affective overtones, whether endearing, pejorative, or mildly obscene.

Correspondingly, the 'new' language is likely to be viewed by members of the older age group as the epitome of fashion. This may lead, in turn, to heavy borrowing in the opposite direction; designed to make utterances sound more youthful, modern, or elegant. In Brazil, for example, highly mixed speech has been found to be a phase in the transition of Germans from their native language to Portuguese.

This is already beginning to be a recognisable pattern in this country; and though Weinreich is justified in seeing the conflict as a source of humour (one has only to think of New York Jewish novelists and some Irish writers to appreciate what he is saying) there may be real problems here for some children. The parental language or dialect may become associated only with 'babying' children or with an authority and surveillance which the children need to outgrow. In some cases there may be no appropriate common language to replace it.

119

Societies like ours have traditionally sanctified the family and relied on it as potentially consolidating and as a model for and reflection of social organisations of other kinds: government, work, school, church, all these institutions are allowed to depend on the image of the family to communicate ideas about how groups of people are most productively and harmoniously organised. New political attitudes to the role of women have begun to make inroads on an unconsidered faith in the family metaphor. Yet for many families who come to settle here the very forces which must seem to be undermining their own family structure are upheld by a hierarchy and beliefs which propose the family as a model for the existing power arrangements and the division of labour. There are many reasons for feeling that it is high time that this reliance on the family as an image of harmonious and hierarchical social organisation be relinquished. Be that as it may, the confusion in all this for youngsters growing up within families from other cultures can be seen at the very least to be unhelpful. Both Fatima and Mario are reacting to the authoritative paternalism of fathers who have been stripped of their authority outside the home.

Amrit Wilson (1978) has described the way in which some Asian parents 'regress' in cultural terms on their arrival here. Forced into an unfamiliar isolation, bereft of the status and the relationships with which they themselves grew up, some of them may feel the need to insist on aspects of their culture and on what these have to tell them particularly about controlling the younger generation which were perhaps, in their home countries, much more relaxed adjuncts to a whole way of life. Even where that is not true – and Amrit Wilson suggests that in many families, particularly ones from urban Hindu backgrounds, traditional views about marriage have not only been relaxed, but are often accompanied by high professional ambitions for their daughters – the accommodations are left for the families to make and not for the host institutions.

The problem is often exacerbated for these children by the kinds of ethnocentricism they may encounter in schools, attitudes which range from total ignorance of and/or scorn for their home culture to publicly articulated disapproval of their speech, eating customs, religious views, attitudes to clothes, and, particularly, views about sex and marriage. There is a sense in which these matters are both embedded in language and expressed by it. Amrit Wilson has this to say:

Only a minority of teachers I spoke to were interested in the way of life of their Asian pupils and an even smaller number knew anything about it. This lack of interest goes right through the educational system. In Ealing for example (an area where a high proportion of the population is Asian) not one school had facilities for teaching Asian languages. Of course an Asian child here must learn English, but must she or he forget their own language in order to learn English? A girl of ten told me that children in her school were punished if they spoke in their own language. An Indian teacher said that in his school Asian children's names were almost invariably mispronounced. But when in one class he had taken the register and pronounced their names correctly, there had been some laughter from non-Indian children (who were a minority in the class) but floods of embarrassed giggles from Asian children, who seemed to prefer their names to be mispronounced in school.

Culturally and linguistically these children operate an 'interlanguage', a more or less satisfactory series of overlapping approximations to a version of the target culture and language, which can sit with what they have learned within the family situation. Where there have been breakdowns for individuals or groups or whole communities, these have derived not simply from clashes between adult or adolescent immigrants and the host community or its authorities, but from conflict within families and within minority communities which might have provided support for children in difficulties, had they not themselves been undermined in their own way of life.

Some of this ambivalence about race and family and generation is caught on the wing, as it were, in the tape of a discussion I had with two twelve-year-old Jamaican girls, Ruth (whose poem adorns Chapter 1), Hilda and their St Lucian friend, Michelle (whom we met in Chapter 1 too). The three girls are not yet part of an adolescent culture. They are still echoing some of their parents' views, still deferentially inclined to give their white interviewer a comforting account of their own compliance with what they expect her to believe, still uncertain about those of their elders who are made angry by the position they are in. Our conversation illustrates, I believe, the kind of doubleness and ambivalence this situation can produce. At a later age the stress can be so great as to

121

drive young people into a wholesale rejection of all kinds of authority, whether it issues from the white community or the black.

I showed the girls an article and some pictures about The Black House, a hostel for black youngsters who have left home and have nowhere to live. Hilda read the article to the others, and they started to explain it to me. Ruth pointed out that these young people were 'Rastas', who are 'bad', a view indignantly denounced by Hilda, 'They're not bad.' None the less, Hilda explains, black children in their teens quarrel more irrevocably with their parents than white children do, and the Rastafarian cult, she believes, has something to do with it. Still explaining the situation to me, Ruth says, 'It's not that just that black people stay home with their parents after a period of time, after they've left school', revealing, I think, in the initial confusion of the sentence her own double and unresolved attitude to the subject. The only 'Rasta' boy in the school is lovingly described by Ruth and then laughed at as coming from the 'mad Mandingo tribe'. Parents are blamed for their children becoming Rastas, 'By the way some parents brought them up...they're Rastas. They go away from home because their parents don't like it.' I have the sense that my presence and my queries may be encouraging this doubleness. We start talking about primary school again, and I ask them about their earliest memories. In response to a question about whether Michelle remembers having any difficulties with English when she first went to school, since she spoke French patois at home, she imitates the teacher saying, 'You're talking bad language, bad English.' Asked what she thinks the teacher might have meant by 'bad', she replies, 'A different accent', and explains that she was taught English as a new language with drills and repetitions, mostly oral. She goes on, 'Parents don't want kids to speak Jamaican or patois. Don't know why.' She believes that a grammar school would insist that no one spoke patois, and would not like to go to one. 'You should be able to speak patois, Jamaican or English.'

When I ask Ruth about when, on what occasions, she speaks Jamaican, Ruth says, 'It just comes out.' Michelle talks about her parents, how they spoke 'just patois in the West Indies. My Mum can't speak it [English] properly, nor can my Dad', and she mimics him saying 'Starsky and Hutch' in an unforgivably foreign and comical way. 'If my Mum's quarrelling with someone she speaks patois,' Michelle goes on. The whole of this part of the conversation was conducted in their London speech and was couched in helpful, explanatory tones, intended for me.

Then, spontaneously it seemed, the girls returned to The Black House pictures and discussed them. They forgot about me, about the tape recorder and about their roles as instructors. For nearly ten minutes the conversation is in a different key, and all three girls (Michelle too) talk in London Jamaican. They are puzzled and excited suddenly:

Hilda	I couldn't live like dat. If he got leather jacket and shoes, where he got the money to buy it?
Ruth	Chure, maybe his parent gi, in it.
Mich-elle	Some of em tief it.
Ruth	True.
Hilda	Most people don't trust black people. Dey tink dem all de bad side.

Hilda goes on to tell the others a story about her sister beating up some insulting white girls. The three of them tell stories about 'bad blacks' and about 'bad black schools', at which they have friends who seem to them, oddly, to be happy there. I ask Ruth why she thinks that one of these schools is a 'bad' one, and she switches to her London speech to answer me and to explain why black schools are a bad thing.

These are twelve-year-olds, and perhaps their apparent ambivalence of attitude to blackness, their own languages, their parents and to particular manifestations of black culture is not surprising. When they talk about 'Rastas' the girls are giggly and excited and yet, ostensibly, disapproving. Hilda doesn't like them to be criticising Rastas in front of me. Yet she found it easier to describe the situation from the parents' point of view. As twelve-year-olds they are fascinated by but aloof from full-blown teenage culture. Their scorn for 'black' schools, and their admiration for their own, which they regard as a 'white' school, echoes their parents. Yet two of the girls refer wonderingly to friends at these despised schools who are happy at them. Hilda sees the racial situation from the white side, but quickly tells a story which shows that black children do not take insults from white children. Michelle laughs at her parents' English, but says that she likes speaking patois best.

123

She says, 'I don't know why' black parents discourage their children from speaking patois and follows this with, 'You should be able to speak patois, Jamaican or English.' Ruth's remark that Jamaican 'just comes out' is not the whole story, though it is demonstrated when the girls move into it as soon as they have eased me out of the conversation.

I have the impression that the culture of black youngsters in London is predominantly Jamaican. Michelle, from St Lucia, is as knowledgeable about Rastas and Jamaican music as the others, and, more importantly perhaps, spoke a form of London Jamaican with the other girls when they did. This suggests that apart from the versions of London English and Jamaican, which children of Jamaican origin can deal with so effortlessly, French-patois-speaking children may make themselves virtually tridialectal by taking on Jamaican speech as well as London English and their home language. There is growing evidence too of white London children switching to London Jamaican effortlessly when they choose to; and if their motives are occasionally hostile they are far more often friendly.

It is possible to see children like Michelle as having potentially richer language resources than other children. None the less, there are problems and confusions. Some of them may be purely linguistic and susceptible to linguistic approaches of the kind suggested by V.K. Edwards. Most of them, however, are cultural in a broader sense, and they are not helped by some parental expectations, nor by the school's ignoring the confusions, implicit in the girls' experience, between language and attitudes to language. The three girls are beginning to articulate a few of these muddles, but the muddles are not necessarily of a kind to melt away as soon as they are recognised. Their school's attitude to these girls' language is probably benign, but it is uninformed and unthinking, and the possibility is that before long the girls may react to that attitude with frustration, particularly if they are also confronted with any sort of school failure. If, for instance, their writing is thought inadequate by standards which have never been made explicit and whose underpinnings have not been explored openly and collaboratively, that is likely to confirm their sense that their own language is at fault.

I have already suggested that these kinds of confusion are characteristic of the move into adolescence and are not confined to bilingual and bidialectal children. It would be misleading too to suggest that confusions about language are of exactly the same kind for those moving between two languages as for those moving between two dialects. However, the business of sorting out such confusions can provide important intellectual and emotional lessons, and it would be quite untrue to say that more than a small minority of bilingual and bidialectal children grow up seriously impaired as learners and livers as a consequence of them. They are potentially damaging confusions, however, and by no means just for the members of minority groups. They are confusions about the nature of culture and the nature of language, which can block intellectual development if they remain unexamined and unarticulated. Allowing them to settle into prejudice is also potentially impoverishing to the school curriculum, which could make them a focus for a serious examination of the complexity and the relativeness of values in this area. As John Lyons (1968) says:

> entry is made into the semantic structure of another language in the area of cultural overlap; and once we have broken into the circle by means of the identification of items in this area...we can gradually develop and modify our own knowledge of the rest of the vocabulary from within by learning the reference of lexical items and the sense-relations that hold between them in the contexts in which they are used. True bilingualism implies the assimilation of two cultures.

This suggests to me the need for schools to make explicit the nature of the overlap as well as the differences, both general and particular, between cultures and between languages.

No one will want to argue with the need for all children to learn English well and to learn to enter and understand aspects of our by no means homogeneous culture and to make accommodations to it in their lives here. The issue finally is one which Schutz only partly touches on, and that is that these accommodations have to be made by both sides, and they are accommodations which involve an understanding of what is involved in learning a new language, indeed in learning language. M.A.K. Halliday (1973) reminds us that teachers have to do more than 'know about' language, they must learn what children believe language to be.

Perhaps it is characteristic, however, that the area in which host nations are apt to be at their most vigilantly concerned with new arrivals is in the teaching of their own language to speakers of other languages, though they have not always considered what is involved in doing this. In the next chapter I will be looking at the process of learning a second language and at what the nature of this process has been thought to be by teachers.

6 Learning first and second languages

It is clear that there are many ways of being or becoming bilingual, just as there is a variety of social conditions which determine how it happens. In this country, individual experiences are likely to share, at least, a relation to a mainstream culture which proposes, to some extent, to ignore or eliminate the using of languages other than English. There are societies where languages flourish alongside each other, though rarely in equality. If this is the terrain of sociology and anthropology, it is also where sociolinguistics has located itself: in a study of language variation in individuals, in groups and in language itself.

For Roger Bell (1976) code switching – the ability to adapt language to roles and situations – is an inevitable aspect of all language use, so that 'the notion of bilingualism is no more than a special case of such switching'. This raises not just the question of how we might usefully differentiate between language and dialect and code, but the broader one of discrepancies between linguists' models of language use generally and speakers' own accounts of their language behaviour. Those discrepancies may be illuminated by considering the issue on which Chomsky and Hymes have famously locked horns: the nature of 'competence' in language. On the one hand 'competence' is allowed to be an abstraction, drawn from a notion of an 'ideal' speaker of a language as the reposi-tory of data about that language. Against that is put a 'competence' which includes language 'performances', which are infinitely complex, variable and therefore beyond satisfactory definition.

That debate has important educational implications, and one of them is the relationship between speakers' (and therefore learners') perceptions of language (and their own using of it) and linguistic models. Another – and it will be central to this chapter – is the significance of what may remain implicit as theories of language and of learning which underlie all teaching approaches, whether they are amateur or professional.

127

I have already suggested that the apparent contradictions in the testimonies of my bilingual speakers came as no surprise; that such contradictions are expressed by speakers much nearer to a monolingual pattern too. There was the belief, on the one hand, that their languages were interchangeable and that, therefore, all languages are able to perform the same kinds of social and individual function. On the other hand, they were also ready to assert that one of their languages might be better for some purposes than others: joking or religion or talking about love or for particular educational aspirations. There were different views about whether or not it helped for the languages to be 'alike' or 'very far apart'; and about motives for successful second-language learning. These included sheer necessity, a sense of its usefulness and special educational or work purposes. There were those who believed that they 'just learned' it, because they were exposed to it. Clare Burstall (1978) has contrasted the relative success of learners whose motives she describes as 'integrative' with those whose reasons for learning the target language might be defined as 'instrumental'. This will be difficult to measure, since success itself will be realised so differently: making jokes, perhaps, on the one hand, reading scientific papers, on the other. The motives of the learner will be affected by his perception of the target language, its local and international status, its relation to educational and literate institutions, its proximity to a 'standard' version, the people who speak it and the purposes to which it may be put in the learner's immediate as well as future life.

Successful bilinguals offer different accounts of how their second or subsequent language was acquired, and they will often attribute to a form of teaching a success which might appear to transcend the consequences of the kind of instruction they underwent. Many will look back to a formal drilling in 'grammar', to exercises and a concentration on written forms. Others will remember just listening, to people talking, or to the radio and television. 'Having to speak' will be regarded by some as the breakthrough for them. Role-playing figures in some testimonies, feeling your way into 'being' a speaker of the new language; and if role-playing is also seen as an aspect of code-switching in all language use, then role-playing may be what my bilinguals mean when they attribute their ease with switching to an almost automatic response to changes in 'atmosphere', place, people, topic.

128

Before considering what this might indicate for schools I want to look at what linguists have had to say about bilingualism and about becoming bilingual. In doing so I shall focus on the complicated interplay between theories of language development generally, ways in which bilingual repertoires have been described, debates about the involvement of linguistic with social competence and implications which have been drawn for second-language teaching and learning.

Learning English as a second language is often, in practice, the first point of contact between the new arrival in this country and the host community. It can be for both learner and teacher (and by teacher I mean the first English speakers with whom the learner tries to communicate) the terrain where cultures and languages meet and where incompatibilities are first encountered. Underlying this relationship will be unspoken attitudes about how second languages are learned and how a second language sits with a first language in the mental processes of bilingual speakers. There will be people in that 'teacher' role who believe that no language but their own is a real one, others who may 'believe' in the other's first language but who are convinced that it must be expunged before a second is learned, still others who are familiar with bilingual speakers and expect the learner to use his first language, if only in order to help him learn a second. Anyone, whether professionally or casually involved, works to a theory of what learning and language *are*. It is necessary only to hear very young children 'teaching' their language to someone else to realise that they will have clear ideas about what is useful, easy or appropriate, what is rule-governed and what is random. To some degree all such teachers will be responding to Lyons's reminder that 'entry is made into the semantic structure of another language in the area of cultural overlap'.

The relation between linguistic theory and language teaching is difficult to chart. Developments in both have derived from different sources, and each has used the other for its own purposes. Successful practice will generate its own rationale, and this will sometimes involve a raiding of the insights of linguists who are not primarily concerned with language teaching. Some of the most recent and interesting work, for instance, in the area of second-language learning, takes as its starting point the active strategies of the learner, rather than assuming an easy correlation between the method of teaching and the quality and extent of mastery. Analyses of the learner's current language performance have concentrated on different aspects of it. A 'contrastive analysis' concentrated on 'errors' which were believed to result from 'interference' from the first language. 'Error analysis' considers the learner's deviations from the target language in much broader terms, as windows on the strategies the learner is bringing to the process. This approach introduced the notion of 'interlanguage' as a description of the language the learner was actually producing. So that 'interlanguage' is analysed as language which is changing, provisional, but none the less rule-governed; the product of much more than the influences of the first language on a partially understood version of the second.

An analysis of interlanguage has, more recently, moved beyond its 'errors' to an attempt to describe the learner's whole perform- ance in real-life discourse. The concentration on what the learner of a second language *does*, rather than on what he ought to do or does not do, was fathered by Selinker (1974) and clearly inspired by Chomskian ideas about the essentially creative, active and rule-governed nature of first-language acquisition. This has had two principal consequences: it has suggested that in important ways learning a second language is more like first-language acquisition than had been thought hitherto. It has also brought second-language learning within the same general theories of learning which have changed approaches to the teaching of reading.

Frank Smith (1975) and the Goodmans (1977), as psycho- linguists, ask us to focus on the strategies used by someone who already has language when he intends to make sense of an unfamiliar version of the language he knows: its written form. An implicit knowledge of language and the experience of the world that language accounts for will support the learner's predictions as to the meaning of unfamiliar forms. The message for teachers from this altered focus is that they may have to relinquish what have often been magical and retrospective rationalisations about what teaching and learning *ought* to have gone on for us to have become literate or fluent second-language speakers. Instead, they are asked to consider what purposes and expectations the beginning reader or second-language speaker is likely to have working for him. Whether the learner is in the process of learning to read or learning a second language such information can be gleaned in part from a scrutiny of 'errors' or 'miscues'. This scrutiny will be useful not for what it reveals of the learner's ignorance but for what it yields about the learner's current range of methods for approaching unfamiliar language. In the case of the beginning reader, for instance, the teacher may discover that when the learner meets an unfamiliar word he plumps for its first letter and ignores contextual, semantic and syntactic clues. Another reader will guess a word which makes sense in the context, will read *ship* for *boat*, perhaps. In order to read well the learner will need to develop alternative and additional strategies and to make maximum use of redundancy in the language.

This view of language learning rests on a model of language use as continuous, variable and dependent upon thought. It is the learner's intention to make sense of unfamiliar language on the basis of his own experience of language which will propel him into new learning. The earlier 'contrastive' view of how second and subsequent languages were acquired was premised on a different notion of the relation between thought and language, and this in turn proposed a model of translation as a kind of traffic between languages, which might even be separately located in the brain. A recent example of that tradition might be George Steiner, who, while proclaiming that one of his

> principal contentions[1] [has been] that translation is 'an exact art' whose 'theory', in fact, amounts to a large corpus of intuitive, metaphoric and local suggestion, that there can be no genuine 'theory' of translation so long as there is no satisfactory 'theory' of how the human mind produces meaningful speech, let alone interlingual transfers of such speech,

can also believe that if there were to be such a theory,

> it would put forward a topological model of the 'location' of different languages in the same human mind and of the possible matrices of contact and exchange between such locations.

There are at least two reasons why it is difficult to accept versions of bilingualism which insist on duality and contrast, rather than on a continuity which includes a variety of ways of thinking and of language use. One derives from the likelihood that thought precedes language in individual development, and the other is that if all language use is characterised by an ability to switch codes in response to social situation then bilingualism is different only in degree not in kind.

For a long time people have invoked Weinreich's categories of compound, coordinate and subordinate bilinguals. I shall quote John Macnamara's account (1972) of these categories (though it is not a friendly one) because I find it the clearest of the many exegetical glosses on them.

> In that book[2] he tentatively suggests that on semantic grounds bilinguals seem to fall into three types, which I shall call by the names which have subsequently become standard. 'Coordinate' bilinguals are those for whom the corresponding pair of terms in two languages signify two distinct semantemes. 'Compound' bilinguals are those for whom corresponding terms signify a single semanteme. 'Subordinate' bilinguals are those for whom a term in L2 signifies first a term in L1 and signifies a semanteme only indirectly...
>
> In Ervin and Osgood [1954] the subordinate type is subsumed into the compound one and criteria are given for judging to which of the two remaining types a bilingual belongs. Compounds are those who either learned one language through the medium of the other, as in old-fashioned language classes, or learned both languages in the same context, the home for instance. The coordinates or 'true' bilinguals are those who learned the two languages in different contexts, such as L1 at home and L2 at school (presumably by the direct method) and at work.

These slippery categories are further complicated by the quite different use Lambert (1969) has made of the compound/coordinate distinction, which amounts roughly to using the first to indicate *early* bilingualism and the second to indicate *later* bilingualism. Macnamara's objections to both the Whorfian view of language as cognitively and culturally determining and to these extrapolations from such a view issue from his sense that they work with an inadequate theory of semantics:

> If Whorf's hypothesis were true, if it were the case that differences among languages caused substantial differences in

cognitive functioning, the bilingual person would be in a curious predicament. In his cognitive functioning, the bilingual would have to conform to one of three patterns, and each of the three would involve serious inconveniences. He might when using L1 or L2 always function cognitively in the manner appropriate to L1 say; he would then have great difficulty in understanding speakers of L2 or in being understood by them. Alternatively, he might always function cognitively in a manner appropriate to neither language and run the risk of understanding or being understood by nobody. Or he might have two cognitive systems, one for each language. He could then communicate with speakers of either language but he would have great difficulty in 'communicating' with himself. Whenever he switched languages he would have difficulty in explaining in L2 what he had heard or said in L1.

In extension of this argument Macnamara gives an example:

French uses the word *couper* in connection with the cutting of hair with a scissors and also the cutting up of a joint of meat with a knife; standard English divides the function of *couper* between *cut* and *carve* respectively. It follows that a coordinate French-English bilingual could well have different mediating processes associated with *couper* and *cut*.

It is important to consider what the implications of Macnamara's strictures might be. In proposing the need for a semantic theory to explain the operations of bilinguals he is, first of all, suggesting that linguistic functioning is to a great extent dependent on non-linguistic functioning of many sorts. He is returning to Piaget and to Vygotsky, to different but similar reminders that the origin of thought is distinct from the origin of language, 'and that insofar as the two are related in the early stages, language is the dependent partner'. It is not difficult to recognise the source of Macnamara's belief that the equivalences between languages, their essential translatability, is dependent on fundamental and therefore universal features of human intelligence, a belief which requires him, inevitably, to assert that there could, therefore, be no possibility of bilingualism affecting, adversely or otherwise, basic intelligence. He makes an important proviso, however: 'of course a second language usually means access to a whole new

133

world of people, literature, and ideas, and so bilingualism can be an enormous advantage'.

In the next chapter I will be taking up the claims and counter-claims that bilingualism may affect intelligence as well as school performance. For the moment, though, I wish to return to the implications of Macnamara's rebukes. Broadly, they are telling us that thought stands to the acquisition of the second language as it stands to the acquisition of the first, and that, if we accept his invitation to return to Vygotsky (1962), this could be seen to involve a 'saccadic' (as Vygotsky puts it) and spiralling interaction between thought and language. Macnamara is clearing the decks for considering second-language learning as language learning, pure and simple.

What is often called the Sapir-Whorf hypothesis, the idea that a person's language *forms* their perception of reality, has been fiercely disputed on several grounds. In its strongest, most absolute version it is hard to hold to. Cromer's weaker version (1975), however, may at the very least be important for its echoing of what bilinguals and bilingual translators testify to as the impossibility of finding a match at all times between languages. Macnamara, as a linguist who works from the tenet that thought precedes language, so that languages must grow from universal mental structures, is, therefore, unwilling to allow that there can be bilinguals of quite different types. But if this seems to suggest an inflexible model of bilingual thinking and language use it may be helpful to return to Bell's suggestion. If variation and variability are essential ingredients of all language use it seems likely that bilinguals will not always operate in one way, whether as 'compound' or 'coordinate' bilinguals. They will sometimes translate between their two languages, sometimes effortlessly switch, sometimes use both and sometimes be driven by their meanings and experiences into one language rather than the other.

To see bilingualism as the interplay of systems is to leave language as an abstraction rather than to focus on the way in which people enter into using it. It is when we look at the second-language *learner* that we may find Macnamara's emphatic simplicity unrealistic. Certainly some sense of meanings adhering in a special way to the language which first expressed them is clung to by teachers and learners alike. It may be that we must suspend any total rejection of Whorf's determinism while considering what learners do before they move into the new language as 'a means for realizing one's own acts and thoughts' as Schutz puts it; before, that is, they become 'true' bilinguals.

Norman Segalowitz (1977) suggests that the learner of a second language is likely to pass through stages at which his languages are in different relations to each other and to thought and that this will be dependent on what may be optimal ages or conditions for becoming bilingual. He offers

the prediction that it would be easier to learn a second language together with the first than to learn it at a later date. The reason is that it would be difficult to differentiate an already developed cognitive network into two relatively distinct ones since new labels and syntactic processes would have to be built into the network where perfectly satisfactory ones already exist.

This picture of the differences there might be between a child learning two languages simultaneously and the mature adult moving towards a second language depends on a model of language which has been called the weak version of the Sapir-Whorf hypothesis. It suggests that we are likely to find that there are different stages of psychological development and experience (many of them connected with age) which could account for learners approaching a new language with particular expectations and intentions and strategies and difficulties. This would produce fluctuations in the strength and fluency of one language in relation to the other. Ervin-Tripp (1973) points to different learning strategies and problems for different learners, though she is anxious to insist that it would be a mistake to suppose that it is always adults who come off worse:

There is strong evidence that for children under eleven language is sound, for adults, sense. Children generalize more between words alike in sound, give more clang associations, confuse the meanings of similar-sounding words. . . . In adults, similar behaviour appears in feeble-mindedness and under drugs. One might say that for adults language is transparent, since adults rapidly penetrate the surface of an utterance to its meanings, to a network of connected thoughts. ... Children attend more to the surface, just as they also connect speech more to the immediate situation in which it occurs.

Later she will go on to explain that adults in certain situations learn second languages as easily as young children do, but that such adults tend to be people for whom language learning has not, as it often does, atrophied or ceased as a conscious process. This may be a crucial insight and one which may partly explain why people who are already bilingual often find it easier to learn yet another language than monolinguals do. Claydon, Knight and Rado (1977) speculate interestingly about another potential difficulty for the adult learner, whom, by the way, they are at pains to defend from assumptions about any inferiority to the young child as a second-language learner:

> In contrast [with the L1 learner], the L2 learner has no comparable natural selection device in his cognitive development, which is usually more advanced than that of the L1 learner. Even a moderate difference in cognitive maturity might affect rule application procedures. It seems that simultaneous rule application is a feature of L2 acquisition by the older learner. This suggests that the attention of the L2 learner will be directed to the total corpus available and he will try to observe a large array of linguistic facts. By using his previous linguistic knowledge and by attempting to match the new language with his intellectual capacities, he will overload his language processing system, eventually making it more difficult to separate the incorrectly observed forms from the correct ones.

What may significantly be conferred by bilingualism is a language-learning capacity, which is consciously used. It may turn out that this is the most vital of the advantages possessed by bilinguals, and the one we should consider in relation to educational possibilities for all children. Such a capacity would come out of the experience of having learned and used a language and out of a sense of the intentions and purposes which might be realised by learning a second.

Selinker and the group of linguists and teachers who have worked in his wake have been asking us, in effect, to abandon ways of language teaching which are founded on either a contrastive account of the similarities and differences between particular languages, or on systems which have been developed inductively by native speakers as sequences or vertically isolated structures and functions. They are directing us through 'error analysis' to an understanding of the rules and dynamics of 'interlanguage'. This shifting corpus of strategies includes language, and ideas about language, deriving from the mother tongue. Just as importantly it will include perceptions, constantly modified, of the target language.

Selinker proposed five visible manifestations of the interlanguage process, each of which is vulnerable to 'fossilisation', either temporary or permanent. The first of these he called *language transfer*, by which he meant any kind of appropriation of forms or features from the first language. The second he called *transfer of training*, a category of 'error' deriving from the particular mode of instruction received by the learner. *Strategies of second-language learning*, the third, might be seen as individual or more generally used short-cuts, simplifications or provisional usages, which come out of the learner's sense of the target language and of his successes and failures in mastering the language to date. *Strategies of second-language communication*, Selinker's fourth category, are 'errors' or non-native items of usage, which continue to be used by the learner because they have worked, been communicatively effective, despite their being contrary to other rules of the language which the learner knows. The fifth category, *the overgeneralisation of target-language linguistic material*, includes 'errors' involving the overgeneralisation of learned rules about inflection or pronunciation or usage. All five categories can, of course, include 'errors' in idiom, vocabulary, pronunciation or grammar.

These categories have yielded a great deal in terms of research, hypotheses and pedagogy; and though it is not part of my intention to consider more than a fraction of the refinements to and expansion of these categories, I shall want to look at some of their implications. Jack Richards[3] in particular, who has written and edited some of the most useful work in the area, enriches the notion of 'interlanguage' by reminding us that it is both a cultural phenomenon and characteristic of communities as well as of individuals; so that pidgins and Creoles might helpfully be described as 'interlanguage', with pidgins created out of immediate communicative need on the part of groups of people with different languages, and Creoles establishing themselves as a more stabilised or even 'fossilised' form of such languages. As Richards points out (1974), 'Features attributable to interlanguage processes can thus achieve stabilization through identification with ethnic roles.' Bell (1976) invests this model with an essential dynamism and variability:

> It seems realistic to explain the varying abilities of the bilingual in whom change and development of the interlanguage are still going on, as moving from co-ordinate to compound but, and this is the point, not at an equal rate in all linguistic or social skills. In order to communicate efficiently, the speaker needs to control, not only the linguistic code but the choices of channel through which the code is actualized, the situational variables which modify such choices and the sociolinguistic rules which permit cohesive discourse and sustain or create social relations. The achievement or mastery over such a range of diverse skills can hardly be expected to occur instantaneously and so, in some spheres, a bilingual will have a compound-like control, in others co-ordinate, in yet others even subordinate.

The notion of 'interlanguage' is necessary to any model of language use which is neither monolithic nor static. It encourages a view of language users as potentially learning as well as switching between codes or dialects or even languages in response to social as well as linguistic demands. The central notion of a dialect continuum, which allows that most speakers will operate a language repertoire, from, crudely, the more formal kind of language to the more intimate, and that this will involve a sensitivity to variety of dialect form and to appropriateness of style, must be set against the likelihood that individual and group repertoires may overlap but can be very different. It seems possible to guess, for instance, that General de Gaulle at his most intimate may well have used language more formal and public than the language of a trades union leader speaking at a large public meeting. More than that, it is possible to hypothesise that though every speaker will develop a repertoire he will not be equally effective in all aspects of it. He may, for instance, be a master of abuse in the dialect form he uses with contemporaries of his own sex and be inexperienced at writing in that dialect. Similarly, if we are to see bilingualism as a version, or part, of that repertoire, as a form of code switching, we will have to accept that though he may 'know' two languages, there will be topics and social situations in which one of those languages will seem to him inadequate, if only because he has not used it for those particular purposes. This may affect a learner's attitude to particular languages and to their speakers, encouraging a sense that that language is in itself inadequate to certain tasks; and this will, in turn, affect areas of a speaker's language learning and even his achieved repertoire. This is significant in terms of recent developments in second-language teaching and is illuminated, I think, by Tucker's vital reminder (1978) that 'a student can more effectively acquire a language when its learning becomes incidental to the task of communicating with someone about an inherently interesting topic'.

It is S.P. Corder[4] who makes the most interesting connections between the practice of 'error analysis' and its possible fruits for pedagogy, by suggesting what it is that learner strategies can tell us about the effects of formal as against informal language learning, and therefore teaching. He begins by proposing 'interlanguage' as a dynamic process, neither the mother tongue, nor the target language, nor something discrete between them, but a kind of universal pidgin, and, therefore, 'the product of the innate cognitive and perceptual processes of the human mind'.The interlanguage user behaves, therefore, much as the first-language learner does, so that 'the learner's possession of his native language is facilitative and...errors are not to be regarded as signs of inhibition, but simply as evidence of his strategies of learning'. I referred to some of these strategies while considering my bilinguals and their testimony: operations based on a perceived 'distance' between the languages, for instance, so that, as Corder puts it, 'It is one of the strategies of learning to find out just how far down the scale it is going to be necessary to go before starting to build up again.'

Another strategy Corder points to is the conscious step-by-step progress made by the learner from the simpler to the more complex, a scale which is not always matched by the teacher's version of such a programme and which Corder sees as parallel to what the young child does as he learns his first language. It is interesting to compare what Leopold was writing about this in 1949, when he was still at an early stage in his study:

> The child's interest, in a much wider sense, determines the choice, and the limelight does not always fall on the phonetically easier words. We get much farther when we add the simple,

non-technical psychological insight that the fine differentiation of the adult's phonetic system does not correspond to the child's capacity in early stages; that he simplifies the delicate phonemic mechanism into a much simpler, coarser pattern of contrasts, which becomes very gradually more and more refined as the rough outlines of the child's early picture of the world acquire more and more detail; that the child, often quite able to hear and even to imitate certain complicated sounds and combinations of sounds, rejects their regular use because a simpler system of sounds is as yet more congenial to his state of mind.

Brown and Bellugi (1964) have studied the ways in which young children develop certain grammatical structures out of their simplest and earliest, single-word utterances, and this gives substance to Leopold's account of his daughter's phonetic development.

Most importantly, perhaps, Corder sees second-language learning as on a permanent and dynamic continuum of language use and language learning. 'We do not kick the ladder down of our own linguistic development, but keep it available for climbing up and down, all our lives.' Language learning, like all learning, involves taking risks, making mistakes, entering into the possibilities of developing an instrument for our own purposes. The achievements of 'my' bilinguals are ones which provide a model and encouragement for other sorts of learning, and for this to be made explicit, and therefore useful, we need to look for a moment at what recent workers in the field have to say about the relative efficacy of formal second-language teaching as compared with informal learning.

Let me return for a moment to Selinker's point:

the second language learner who actually achieves
native-speaker competence, cannot possibly have been taught
this competence, since linguists are daily – in almost every
generative study – discovering new and fundamental facts about
particular languages. Successful learners, in order to achieve
this native-speaker competence, must have acquired these facts
(and most probably important principles of language
organization) *without* having explicitly been taught them.

There have been teachers who have taken Selinker's point to propose language-teaching programmes based – and this is oversimplifying their position – on the teaching of functions rather than of structures. Daphne Brown (1979) makes a good case for being wary of leaving children to the sort of 'natural learning' which may, but doesn't necessarily, take place when they are left amongst their native-speaking peers in the classroom or the playground. She may, however, be confusing the gains from concentrated individual attention from an adult with those aspects of language which she believes can only be taught formally. It appears that ideal second-language learning involves a wish to speak to target-language speakers about things which are interesting, and that this is sometimes inhibited, even impeded, in the classroom. Ervin-Tripp has a salutary reminder for us:

> But we know that in formal instruction there is frequently emphasis on structure devoid of semantic context, practised in instances where meaning is either unclear or trivial – e.g. in transformation drills. So it cannot surprise us when after an hour of practising turning statements into questions a student intent on getting a question answered, after class, produces a question that is a word-for-word translation of his mother tongue and shows no impact whatever of the drill. *What means this word, Mrs Tripp?*

Corder takes this to its possible conclusion:

> The wise course would be to relax even further our control over the linguistic forms he is exposed to, indeed perhaps to abandon all control of a structural sort.

In fact, in a later piece (1978b), when he is discussing the, as he sees it, tenuous relation between 'well-formed utterances' and 'error-free performance' he goes so far as to suggest that a second-language teaching programme might do well to incorporate the learner's early simplifications and 'errors' as acceptable, provisional features of his target language.

This has been a somewhat perfunctory exploration of some views of what is involved in learning a second language. It was undertaken, and is offered here, partly as an attempt to fill out some of the more opaque and mysterious pronouncements in the

141

testimonies of the bilinguals discussed in previous chapters. It seems that second-language learners share with their teachers a sense that an ordering and structuring of teaching items is bound to correspond to the way by which a learner most naturally comes to 'know' his second language. I am sceptical of this; and my scepticism is due in part to the relative failure of that sort of approach when applied to foreign-language teaching. It should also be said that unaided immersion in a new language is likely to end in a drowning.

Clearly, questions of learner motive, attitudes to mother tongue and to target languages, what are seen as cultural constraints or invitations, social context and the perceived status of particular languages – all these can be seen powerfully to influence on the second-language learner's success or failure. Perhaps as crucially, however, some of this recent work points to the ways in which second-language learning repeats, extends, reflects and is parasitic upon first-language learning. It is language learning, simply, and therefore most satisfactorily undertaken by children and by adults who are actively, consciously and exuberantly engaged in the business of language learning. Teachers will certainly not be put out of a job by recognising this. On the contrary, it may (indeed I shall want to show later, already has done) make their work more interesting as well as more successful.

In the next chapter I shall be looking at some claims for the possible cognitive advantages of being bilingual. I will need to return to the implications of this chapter: to Macnamara's doubts about language being at all likely to influence intelligence and to his readiness to concede that 'of course a second language usually means access to a whole new world of people, literature and ideas, and so bilingualism can be an enormous advantage'. It will also be necessary to hold in mind the possibility that this kind of active, risk-taking and rewarded learning can provide a model and encouragement for other kinds of learning, and that it may demonstrate how an insistence on a monocultural and monolingual curriculum is not just dangerous socially and, perhaps, emotionally, but is capable of narrowing intellectual options, of failing to take up the slack of human potential. If this is true, it will be true for all children, not just for children from minority groups.

7   Do bilinguals think better?

I have already begun to suggest that there might be cultural and linguistic advantages for bilingual speakers. There has, in recent years, been a considerable amount of research into the possibilities of these kinds of advantage and, particularly, into the question of there being cognitive benefits for children who grow up speaking two languages. These are significant claims and worth considering both for what they may contribute to the debate about the relation of thought to language and because they may have something to say about the educational achievement of particular children from minority groups.

As Verity Khan (1978) has pointed out, there is an obligation on us to show in what ways bilingualism can be advantageous if we are to encourage the maintaining (learning or relearning) of the first (or parental) language alongside the provision for second-language English learning. There is even more of an obligation on us to do so if we are to work towards any forms of bilingual education and changes in the curriculum which accord with new social needs and a different population. My examples of successful bilingualism and my ignoring of what is sometimes called 'semi-lingualism' (a disabling inadequacy in two languages) may be thought to have left the question of such advantages as more attractive than proven. The sense that such advantages must be seen and understood to be measurable ones is a difficult aspect of the whole subject, as it is in most areas of educational research. It may seem disingenuous to meet such appeals for quantitative proof with the assertion that at the very least there has been no satisfactory proof of the opposite. That said, there has been a good deal of careful and intriguing research in the territory, which is particularly well summarised by James Cummins in his paper of 1973, in which he dates the first serious entry into this territory from Peal and Lambert's 1962 paper. In this they reported on some possible advantages possessed by both their anglophone and

143

francophone bilingual groups in Canada, in relation to mono-lingual groups. As I mentioned in the first chapter, studies of a comparable kind had been conducted before that date, and most of them were characterised by findings which showed that bilinguals were likely to suffer as far as their school performance was concerned. Perhaps Peal and Lambert's most important contribution was to remind us that sample groups for research of this sort needed to balance for social class, extent of experience in each language and language and cultural bias in the tests themselves. It was they who first drew attention to the distinction between tests which revealed something about surface language ability and tests which revealed non-verbal as well as verbal capacities.

Cummins has entered into public debate with Macnamara and he is certainly not prepared to accept Macnamara's adamant insistence that, according to any Vygotskian or even Piagetian account of the relation of thought to language, bilingualism could not be expected to have an influence on cognitive development. Indeed, Cummins quotes from Vygotsky's paper, 'Multilingualism in Children' (1975), in which Vygotsky expressed doubts as to there being any advantages for the 'spontaneous bilingual child' and then counters such doubts with the speculation that where the position is made explicit the child might be oriented towards more abstract thought processes and away from what Vygotsky else-where (1962) called 'the prison of concrete language forms and phenomena'.

Cummins, then, is cautiously optimistic about some of the work that has been done which shows particular superiorities in the mental operations of bilingual children; though he is anxious to remind us that in accepting such conclusions we must confine ourselves to talking about a certain threshold of functional bilingualism, for, as he says,'failure to resolve difficulties in coping with two languages over a prolonged period of time can negatively influence an individual's rate of cognitive development', though, he goes on, 'the threshold hypothesis assumes that when a certain level of competence in two languages has been attained there are aspects either of a bilingual's present access to two languages or of his bilingual learning experiences which can positively influence his cognitive functioning' (1974, with Gulutsan).

So what kinds of claim have been made? In 1972 both Ben-Zeev and Ianco-Worrall published the results of studies which they believed showed a superiority for bilinguals in what they called 'cognitive flexibility'. This work was extended by Cummins and Gulutsan in 1974 in a return to the form of Peal and Lambert's earlier experiment; and they were able to report 'a significantly higher level both on measures of verbal and non-verbal ability and on one measure of divergent thinking, i.e. verbal originality'. Also in 1974, Bain conducted two studies which showed that 'children who had become bilingual before coming to school showed higher levels of concept formation'. I shall want to consider Ben-Zeev's 1972 and 1977 studies in more detail; but before doing so I shall return to Ianco-Worrall's work and to her findings.

Briefly, she claimed that bilingual children showed a more flexible manipulation of the linguistic code and were more advanced in concrete operational thinking. Her findings support Leopold's hypothesis that simultaneous acquisition of two languages in early childhood accelerates the separation of sound and meaning, or name and object. Of her four-to-six-year-old bilinguals she found that fifty-four per cent consistently chose to interpret similarity between words in terms of a semantic rather than an acoustic dimension. 'Bilinguals,' she says, 'brought up in a one-person, one language environment, reach a stage in semantic development...some 2–3 years earlier than their unilingual peers. A high percentage of these bilingual youngsters perceived relationships between words in terms of their symbolic rather than their acoustic properties.'

Ben-Zeev conducted her studies with a group of Hebrew/English-speaking children in 1972 and repeated and extended her experiments in 1977 with a group of Spanish/English-speaking children. I want to look at her account of what she takes to be the particular intellectual superiorities of her samples of bilinguals.

First she points to the bilinguals having a superior capacity to do what she calls *analyse language*; and she attributes this to the positive effects of interference working as a 'stimulus to the individual acts of thought'. She also reiterates Ianco-Worrall's claims that this analysis involves an ability to separate meaning from sound and to state the principle of naming.

A second category of superior mental operation in bilinguals she describes as *sensitivity to feedback cues*. This may involve an ability to switch and to respond to language register in other speakers. It might also include a tendency towards elaboration in, for instance, constructing a narrative from a series of pictures. Torrance *et al.* described this in 1970 as a better-developed capacity for picking out the necessary details for linking picture episodes. It is clear that the capacity to do such an exercise could subsume a variety of essential operations, and it would be interesting to know whether such tests could discriminate expert from inexpert comic-strip readers. Ben-Zeev also included in her category of sensitivity to feedback clues a more general responsiveness to social uses of language, since 'anxiety over confusion and ridicule may be a strong motivation for development of sensitivity to perceptual feedback cues pertaining to language'.

A third category of superior operation described by Ben-Zeev is one she calls *maximisation of structural differences between languages*. This is a complex hypothesis, which she accounts for by saying 'that bilinguals become aware of their languages as internally consistent systems more than do other children', a possibility she is prepared to qualify: 'The bilingual might grasp general rules and extend them more quickly, but by the same token they may be slower in attending to the increasingly detailed modifications of rules within the language as they conflict with other rules of the language.' I take this to propose the possibility that a bilingual child will be attentive to the differences between his languages, and, therefore, to certain constants and variables in language generally, but may, relatively to a monolingual child, be insensitive to some of the complexities within each of his languages.

Her fourth category, *neutralisation of structure*, she describes in these words:

in many cases structural simplification, including relative
absence of marking, is the result of a positive strategy which has
as its purpose the prevention of interference between languages
by means of temporarily neutralizing the structure of one of the
languages at a point of conflict.

What is indicated here, I think, is that where benefits are seen to accrue to the bilingual child they are in the area of his awareness of the separateness of his languages. If the languages were really to merge for him such advantages would cease to exist.

In her 1977 study Ben-Zeev refined these categories, elaborated

146

on her tests and gave much more detailed information about the particular difficulties which some of the bilingual children had with what she characterises as generally surface language features, particularly in the extent of their vocabulary in each language. Her conclusion to this study seems to me worth quoting in full, particularly since it is more careful and temperate than her earlier one:

> We may conclude that the effort to become bilingual results in greater ability to process systemic structures, even for bilinguals in relatively disadvantaged circumstances, in which there are fewer opportunities to encounter outstanding speech models and fewer special rewards for complex verbalization. The Spanish-English bilinguals of this study also differ from the Hebrew-English bilinguals of the previous study in that their two languages are much more similar to each other in structure and in vocabulary (there are very few Hebrew-English cognates). In a way, the language similarity promotes interlingual transfer and thus greater interference, but, on the other hand, changing from one language context to the other or translating from one to the other is less of a challenge to reorganizational ability.
>
> Although translation ability was not found to be related to performance in either study, different approaches to translation between the two bilingual groups may be related to the differences between them in the intensities of the strategies they manifest. Among the Hebrew-English bilinguals a child who was balanced in that he could translate as well in one direction as the other also tended to have fewer total translation errors. For the Spanish-English bilinguals, on the other hand, a high balance score could be achieved through few errors, but it could also be the result of performance containing many errors which went in both directions equally. Yet the balance score did have validity, since it was highly related to ability to tell a story in one language without inadvertently slipping into the other language.
>
> Perhaps some of the Spanish-English bilinguals were concentrating not on learning how to switch from one language to the other, which involves interlingual analysis, but rather on learning how to stay within the confines of one language at a time without slipping into the other and causing themselves

embarrassment. This would require attention to details of structure and to social aspects of the environment more than to reorganization. Other bilinguals in this group seem more like those in the previous study.

Whatever advantages were seen for the bilinguals in structural processing were usually more marked among the younger bilinguals. The same was true in the earlier study. It is not clear why this should be, but possibly it concerns the fact that the younger bilinguals are closer in time to the initial confrontation between the two languages. The advantages seemed to be maintained better in the earlier study, where motivational conditions were more favorable to maintaining bilingualism, so it may be that long-term maintenance of the effects of bilingualism on cognitive processing depends upon the circumstances of the confrontation between the two languages, in addition to sheer exposure.

Broadly then, Ben-Zeev clusters her bilingual advantages under two headings: *attention to structure* and *readiness to reorganise*, notions I shall want to open up to possibly wider connotations by calling them *language awareness* and *language-learning readiness* – a reformulation of Ervin-Tripp's account of the optimal conditions or states of mind for second-language learning.

In 1974 Cummins and Gulutsan investigated whether bilingualism affected memory, reasoning and creative thinking ability and whether it influenced the way in which a child represented his world. Their conclusions were that

> having two words for the same referent not only directs the child's attention to the conceptual attributes of objects in the external world...but also focuses his attention on his linguistic operations themselves...this can lead the child to contrast and compare his two languages and can account for his superior performance on measures of verbal intelligence.

They came down for the proposition that 'bilingualism confers some type of "verbal enrichment", i.e. a greater facility at representing the world through linguistic mediation as opposed to imagistic'.

Kolers (1968), having investigated the information processing of bilinguals, has this to say:

148

Suppose one wanted to give a student two lessons in geography. If the student knew two languages, he would retain as much geography from one lesson in each language as from two lessons in one of them. Moreover, he would be able to talk about geography readily in both languages. On the other hand, teaching him geography in one language and also teaching him a second language would not necessarily enable him to express his knowledge of geography in the second language without some kind of additional instruction. The information one has and the mechanisms or rules used to acquire it are clearly separate aspects of memory.

There seem to me to be suggestions here which might be taken up in terms of 'language across the curriculum', an aspect of the educational implications of bilingualism which I will consider in the next chapter.

This is far from being a comprehensive account of research into the cognitive effects of bilingualism. Saville-Troike (1973), Evans,[1] Jones (1959), Fishman (1965) and many others have considered similar kinds of possible advantage and disadvantage in being bilingual.

There are difficulties in settling as simply as one might wish to for findings from research projects of this sort. Partly they are to do with the dilemma of controlling for essential social, intellectual and educational factors. There are difficulties in taking on trust tests of the kind which are used and in accepting the hypotheses developed out of children's success or failure at them. We are also likely to have serious reservations about accepting a simple cause/effect relationship between bilingualism and kinds of verbal and cognitive performance.

One reason for offering even such a brief survey as this of some of the findings in the area is to draw attention to the kind of hunch many of these researchers have started from. I have shared those hunches and seen some signs in bilingual as well as bidialectal children that there may be something to them. I want to suggest, however, that my enlargement of those Ben-Zeev categories, to *language awareness* and *language-learning readiness*, may serve to account for the majority of these hunches. The first would include an implicit understanding that language is both rule-governed and arbitrary, that it is variable and yet constant in so far as all human

149

beings share the using of it. From this follows the second category: that language is never learned once and for all, but accompanies and adapts itself to new experience, so that it cannot be complete, nor can there be a complete description of it.

In the next chapter I shall be considering the educational implications of bilingualism in terms of this country now. Before doing that, however, I want to return to some of the ideas of Margaret Donaldson (1978) which I invoked at the beginning of the book and which I would want to make at least partly responsible for the direction my argument has taken and, indeed, for the character of the curriculum innovations I shall want to propose. I shall quote at some length from her chapter 'What the School Can Do', in which she discusses the kinds of preparation and awareness of language which she believes must precede and accompany learning to read:

> So the preparation for reading should include, as a most
> important component, attempts to make children more aware of
> the spoken tongue. It is not just a matter of helping them to use
> speech more effectively, it is a matter of helping them to notice
> what they are doing. For instance, many of them will never
> before have realized that the flow of speech, which they have
> been producing and interpreting unreflectingly for years, is
> composed of *words*. Yet this realization is indispensable if they
> are to deal sensibly with the grouped and spaced marks on paper
> which, as they must now come to see, correspond to the spoken
> language. Awareness of this correspondence – even of its
> existence, much less of its nature – should never be taken for
> granted. It is essential to make certain that the child understands
> that the marks on paper are a written version of speech. And it is
> important thereafter to help him to recognize the special
> functions and usefulness of this written version – as an aid to
> memory, as a means of communicating at a distance and so on.
> If these preliminaries are well taken care of then he will see the
> sense and purpose of what he is about to do and will be rescued
> from the bewilderment of struggling to master an activity the
> nature of which he does not comprehend.

Lest this be thought remote from the question of the possible advantages of having two languages for use, let me follow this passage with another taken from a little further on in her book. I think it makes my point for me:

> The hope, then, is that reading can be taught in such a way as greatly to enhance the child's reflective awareness, not only of language as a symbolic system but of the processes of his own mind. Important as reading is, however, there is no reason to suppose it is the only way. As Vygotsky put it: 'All the higher functions have in common awareness, abstraction and control.' And he believed that all of the school subjects could be made to contribute to the growth of 'consciousness and deliberate mastery', which he called 'the principal contributions of the school years'.... For instance, if the child is taught to operate with the decimal system without coming to understand that it is one system among other possible ones then, to quote Vygotsky once more, 'he has not mastered the system but is, on the contrary, bound by it'.

Leopold felt confident in asserting on the basis of his day-by-day case study of his daughter that 'Bilingualism may well be a gain because it induces concentration on the subject matter instead of the words.' This might be taken to be a somewhat less sophisticated version of what Vygotsky (1962) saw as an intrinsic stage in the development towards higher-order mental operations:

> In the beginning, only the nominative function exists; and semantically, only the objective reference; signification independent of naming, and meaning independent of reference, appear later and develop along the paths we have attempted to trace and describe.
>
> Only when this development is completed does the child become fully able to formulate his own thought and to understand the speech of others. Until then, his usage of words coincides with that of adults in its objective reference but not in its meaning.

At the centre of what Donaldson takes and develops from Vygotsky is the need for a stance towards language on the learner's part which allows him to reflect on its nature and on its use. This, it is suggested, is essential if he is to move towards literacy and towards what Vygotsky sees as the genuine manipulation of concepts. He will learn to use his language for creative

151

thinking rather than depending on the categories proposed by the language of his everyday experience.

It may be that it is to analysis and insight of this sort that we should be looking for confirmation or support of hunches that where bilingualism is not allowed to be a disadvantage it can provide very real advantages. We should welcome the empirical work which gives encouragement to the kind of theory put forward by Vygotsky and others, while remaining wary when it is based on tests which seek to isolate cognitive attributes from affective ones and from the social context in which both operate and grow together. Any solutions to these issues in educational terms will have to take on the whole individual and his relation to the world he inhabits. So that, necessarily, any possibilities for curriculum innovation, new and better educational provision, are likely, and rightly so, to be concerned with the whole school-age population and not just with those who may have an inestimable advantage in being or becoming bilingual.

8 The educational implications of bilingualism

In considering the educational implications of bilingualism for this country I shall want to allude to the background of experience and research in bilingual education programmes which operate in other parts of the world. I shall also want to suggest the need for a sensitivity to local differences and a responsiveness to what might be useful to the whole school population.

It is clear that there can be advantages to possessing two functioning languages. They are advantages of a practical, intellectual and cultural kind and they are not much attended to in this country. It should also be said that bilingualism has been allowed to seem a disadvantage (sometimes by default) here and elsewhere, and that educational provision has often, if covertly, worked to extirpate these supposed disadvantages. Many of the programmes in America, Canada and Australia are founded on and financed out of a notion of compensation. The EEC Directive of 25 July 1977[1] 'on the education of the children of migrant workers' to which the British government is in principle committed, could be said to intend not much more than the safeguarding of a government's right to employ foreign labour while discouraging permanent immigration.

Another difficulty in looking outside this country to responses made, to bilingualism elsewhere is that they tend to come out of relatively clear-cut bilingual situations rather than multilingual ones: either in the English/French parts of Canada, or communities in America, where schools can safely assume that their population will be made up either of Spanish/English children or children speaking an Indian language and English. The Australian experiences described in *Curriculum and Culture* by Claydon, Knight and Rado have more to offer us in that they involve several languages and come out of inner-city schools.

We have, none the less, a good deal to learn from the experiences of other countries, and it might be well to start from

Fishman's reminder (1976) that 'Bilingual education need not be entirely compensatory or minority-group-oriented. It can also be a type of "alternative" education for mainstream children.' This is a necessary antidote to the current tendency to make educational provision a matter of showing that you have noticed a problem. Whether it has been a matter of offering facilities for mother-tongue maintenance or learning, second-language teaching in English or a variety of bilingual education, there has usually lurked in it a response to evidence that children from particular minority groups were performing less well than they should. Some of that response issues from a refusal to confront the relation between social class and educational attainment. Of course, language is involved in that. It may be, however, that a more positive consideration of what is involved in successful bilingualism will take us further than any consideration of the place of language in learning which concentrates exclusively on what children cannot do.

In their *Languages and Dialects of London Schoolchildren* Rosen and Burgess describe the survey they carried out to discover the extent and nature of language diversity in London schools. The survey covered 4,600 pupils in their first year at twenty-eight secondary schools. The authors do not claim to provide a representative picture of the whole country, but their survey is able to suggest the complexity of the situation in many large cities, where the populations of schools which are geographically close can vary enormously. One of their interesting findings was that of the sixteen most commonly spoken languages only four were ones which are taught in those schools as foreign languages, and they were Italian, Spanish, French and German (Table 1). This has meant that the first languages of the majority of bilingual children in London are likely to be ones which few of us know much about and may be predisposed to look down on. This has often affected the speakers of these languages, and has encouraged them to reduce or abandon their use. I showed earlier how both Najat and Mario had been ready to give up their mother tongues and had later discovered important needs for them as they were reaching adulthood.

The issues of mother-tongue maintenance are not easy ones, and no neat legislation is likely to deal with them in ways which are practicable and acceptable to the people involved. For instance, a

154

Table 1   Distribution of languages other than English,
where spoken by more than 14 pupils

	Number of pupils	*Percentage of all 749 bilingual pupils in the sample* %
Greek	165	22
Turkish	97	13
Italian	46	6
Gujarati	41	5
Spanish	35	5
Cantonese	33	4
French Creoles	33	4
German	30	4
Portuguese	28	4
Bengali	20	3
Punjabi	18	2
French	17	2
Yoruba	17	2
Arabic	16	2
Hindi	15	2
Urdu	15	2

melting-pot approach to the question, which proposes the swift
and efficient acquisition of English rather than the maintaining of
two languages, is one to which many members of minority
language groups themselves subscribe. This is not the whole story,
however; for such apparent willingness to abandon a mother
tongue has to be seen within a context where maintaining it can
involve long hours of after-school study and the possibility that
children will be damagingly marked out for this sign of separateness from their school peers. More importantly still, many parents
are vulnerable to the suggestion, which is likely to be made by
schools and by society generally, that holding on to the mother
tongue may interfere with the development of their English.

We are still ignorant about a number of things: about the extent
and character of languages other than English which are spoken
here, and of their speakers' allegiances to these languages. And we

need to consider what kind of within-school provision or support for their own initiatives these communities want. Verity Khan[2] is currently at work in answering the first question, having already (in 1978) pointed to some of the needs as well as the experiences of and provision for mother-tongue teaching which already exist. Harold Rosen (1979b) has made a useful survey of current provision for language teaching in England and Wales. John Wright (1978) – and I shall be returning to him – has studied the international experience and suggested some guidelines for possibilities here. D. Sharp (1973), A.D. Edwards (1976), V.K. Edwards (1979), J. Derrick (1977) and Arturo Tosi (1979) have discussed the problems and implications of adapting schooling to the presence of bilingual or potentially bilingual children here and have described some efforts already made.

Joshua Fishman has had an important influence on the development of forms of bilingual education and the evaluation of actual programmes. His four models (1976) are often invoked in relation to local and national proposals as being more or less relevant to what he saw as four 'differing kinds of community and school objective'. It may be useful to consider these:

1 *Transitional bilingualism*, which implies the use of the mother tongue in early schooling 'to the extent necessary to allow pupils to "adjust to school", and/or to "master subject matter" '.
2 *Monoliterate bilingualism*, which allows for oral development in both languages but literacy only in English.
3 *Partial bilingualism*, which 'seeks fluency and literacy in both languages, but literacy in the mother tongue is restricted to certain subject matter, most generally related to the ethnic group and its cultural heritage'.
4 *Full bilingualism*, where 'students are to develop all skills in both languages in all domains'.

It is easy to feel daunted by even the first of these models, let alone the fourth, when we are considering schools where ten or more languages may be spoken by anything from a single pupil to a group of ten or more in a single class. It is not surprising, therefore, that most mother-tongue teaching is locally initiated, by churches or embassies or consulates or by groups of teachers or parents. It may be characteristic of the British reliance on the *ad hoc* and the voluntary that despite exhortation from central and local government (in, for example, the Bullock Report or the 1977 ILEA document, *Multi-Ethnic Education*) and quite apart from EEC directives, things have largely been allowed to rest there. I have already suggested why this is unsatisfactory.

In 1978, John Wright produced an important and useful paper on the possibilities of adapting Fishman's third model, 'partial bilingualism', for use in English schools. Having associated the ILEA Bilingual Education project, with which he had been involved, with Fishman's transitional model, he began by declaring his opposition to Macnamara's assertion (1974) that 'Only a decadent society relies on schools to maintain languages, morals, ethnic identity, religion. The fate of these is determined outside the schools, and the most that we can expect of schools is that they support society in its stated or unstated ambitions, or at any rate the nobler ones among them.' Wright replies to this with the speculation that 'it could be that bilingual education programmes function as the catalyst to organised community action for so long as their adoption by the state system remains a campaigning goal. In this sense such programmes foster solidarity and group identification.' His proposals, which I shall consider, are important for coming out of this joint perspective: the ways in which bilingual advantages might be generalised across the school population and the political role of the schools in promoting and protecting the interests of minority groups. There is an inevitable significance attaching to what is institutionalised within the curriculum and what is left out of it; and that significance is educational as well as politically symbolic.

John Wright offers six criteria for the form of Fishman's 'partial bilingualism' which he is advocating and starts from the principle that such a model must offer 'the option of bilingualism to *all* students', which would entail the possibility of learning a 'community' language as well as or instead of a traditional 'modern' language. It is worth considering his criteria in some detail. His first, 'The motive for introducing minority languages into the learning situation must be utilitarian, not tokenist', is glossed with the following examples:

So, the languages, when used, should be used as the medium through which information of various kinds is made available and accessible: taped folk tales from different cultures in the

listening corner of the infant classroom; books on countries of
origin in languages of those countries in the junior school
library; works of reference on subjects such as chemistry,
biology, psychology etc. in the departments in secondary
schools, and in the libraries, a selection of literature in the
languages of minority group students.

While agreeing entirely with John Wright's insistence on utility
and not tokenism, it is easy to feel that his distinction raises
problems. Bilingual experience is real experience, planted in real
lives and needs, and its virtues, like its drawbacks, are not to be
transmitted simply in the classroom. This is not to undermine
Wright's first criterion, but to suggest that the situation may not be
best dealt with by all-or-nothing solutions. We need to avoid the
pitfalls of 'tokenism', while acknowledging too that schools and
teachers begin where they can. We need also to be wary of an
enthusiasm which is in danger of relying on more language
teaching, of more languages, as the solution to educational and
social problems. His examples of work which could go on in a
multicultural classroom do show, however, the dimensions of what
could be achieved and they also point to an area where national
and local provision and support are needed: books and resources
and people from the community, who are involved in the school's
work, not just as fleeting visitors, but as serious contributors to the
education of their own and other people's children.

Wright's second criterion has other important implications:
'Integrate the work stimulated by minority language books/tapes/
workcards etc. with the mainstream of class activity.' Most
provision for the needs of children speaking languages other than
English has involved taking them out of ordinary classrooms for
some, if not all, of the time. There will be those who argue that
this is sometimes essential, despite the difficulties for the children
involved, who will be missing large parts of the curriculum as well
as delaying their entry into the life of the school. Some teachers of
English as a second language feel that this kind of withdrawal will
not be in the best interests of their pupils. Language lessons will
become just that, the practising of language for its own sake,
rather than for the purposes the learner has in his immediate life:
whether in the subjects he is studying in school or in the outside
world.

In recent years some non-ESL specialists have worked in classrooms alongside trained language teachers. The collaboration has been enormously useful for both kinds of teacher. Mainstream teachers have been obliged to focus on the language demands they and their subjects make on children and on the talking and writing tasks they foster in the classroom. ESL teachers have seen their role as the supporting of active learning, done by their pupils in collaboration with native English-speaking youngsters of the same age. Such work inevitably reminds both kinds of teacher that they are dealing with potentially bilingual pupils, and that this will involve encouraging children to use their first language as they learn a second and to use both in order to learn across the curriculum. There are now some excellent examples of this kind of collaborative work between teachers from different traditions. Examples like the SLIPP project and work done within the Schools Council Language for Learning Project[3] point to the possibilities of working in ordinary classrooms with children who are learning English and doing so in ways which promote language learning through cooperation between children and through, for instance, the Maths or Geography work which is part of the curriculum. (See, for instance, J. Levine, 1981.)

Wright's third criterion points to the ways in which bilingual children's knowledge and expertise might be usefully generalised for monolingual children: 'Provide within the classroom the opportunity of developing and refining the skills of bilingualism – translation and interpretation – not only of language but of cultural experience.' Children who grow up in schools where the population is culturally and linguistically diverse may, even before teachers encourage them to, have learned a good deal about other languages and cultures: perhaps quite simple things, like knowing that people who don't speak English do speak other languages, that other children's parents will look and dress differently from their own. In schools where the population is predominantly of one race and culture, if not entirely so, that learning will not go so smoothly, and pain and misunderstanding can produce prejudice and exclusion. Wright's suggestion here is that translating and interpreting should be consciously worked at, both as useful activities in themselves and as ways of mediating for children the social conflicts which, in the classroom, can be disruptive and damaging. Clearly, there are chances here for developing more

159

advanced language and cultural studies, of a kind which is rooted in the diversity of a community's own experience, but which moves towards more sophisticated knowledge and analysis.

Wright's fourth criterion, 'Provide language learning opportunities, and the opportunity of becoming bilingual, to *all* students – even though a very small minority of English-speaking students would take up the option', is more difficult to put into practice. One London school has introduced Arabic into its curriculum; and though it is far too early to say whether this has been a success or not, its introduction was debated with some passion. First, there was the question of which minority-group language should be taught and what criteria would govern the choice. There is also the question of the form of the language which should be taught. While Classical Arabic could be said to be the language of millions of people it is actually spoken by relatively few, particularly in London, where children are more likely to speak a variant or dialect of it.

Arturo Tosi (1979) has described the anomalies of teaching Italian to the children of families from Southern Italy, who came to live in Bedford more than twenty-five years ago. The children were born here, may have forgotten or never spoken Italian and are now required to learn a version of it which neither their parents nor their relatives in Southern Italy understand. There are schools where the number of languages spoken either fluently or at all by their pupils is so large that the school could only offer those languages in the most 'tokenist' way as a part of the curriculum. So there are difficulties. There are also possibilities. Some schools have begun to offer Greek, Turkish, Hindi, Gujarati; and English-speaking children and some teachers as well have started to learn these languages, though it seems unlikely that this will have happened in ways which meet Wright's fifth criterion: 'Never segregate the minority group for mother-tongue learning...without explicitly inviting *all* pupils/students to join the group.'

His sixth criterion too may be more controversial than it seems: 'Preserve and defend the minority group students' right to choose for her/himself the balance of minority and majority group language and culture which best meets the desired identity of the individual.' I think I have already suggested some of the reasons for the difficulties inherent in this proposal. The children of minority groups frequently feel under pressure to drop their home languages and dialects. The pressure is a general social one, and it is often supported by schools and by families. Very often young people in their teens will want to regain that language, use it with peers and assert it as an intrinsic part of their identity. This makes it difficult to legislate in a simple way for school support for mother tongues. If teachers and schools are to respond positively to Wright's suggestion they will need to work first to build up in all their pupils a respect for and understanding of language diversity and then find ways of making it possible for young people to take up the option to learn or relearn their parents' language when they need to.

Since it is never possible to discuss curriculum priorities in this country without reference to public examinations I shall give some attention to the particular problems they present for children who are either fully bilingual or are becoming so.

Children whose first language is not English may need more, not fewer, certificates than other children when they compete for jobs or places in further and higher education. Indeed, their families may have come here for the education particularly. In considering how courses and examinations might be made more appropriate for children like these there can be no question of proposing easier options or asking for handicap conditions. They will need certificates which are genuinely informative about them and which rate as testimony to their achievements and abilities. In most cases they will want to participate straightforwardly in British society and would reject any notion that they are in need of benevolent special pleading.

This will mean an enlarging and elaborating of the curriculum not a withering of it. The languages they speak, the cultures they are part of, cannot be ignored by schools or left unvalued by certification. Knowledge of Ibo language, of Islamic thought, of Indian film, for instance, are assets in national as well as individual terms. So too, and it should not need saying, is a flexible and confident use of the English language. Need one preclude the other? On the one hand the extent of diversity to be found in Britain today, of culture and of language, suggests a need for a broader curriculum, susceptible to evaluation on several levels. On the other it demands a radical rejigging of priorities, to allow for talents which are unrecognised to be recognised and for talents which are currently insisted on to be scrutinised for ethnocentricity and irrelevance.

A child arriving in the fourth or fifth year of secondary school may have interrupted an education differing noticeably from what is on offer here. He will be expected to learn English while dealing, in English, with a curriculum directed towards fifth-year examinations. He will need more time, and possibly financial help, in order to fulfil his potential within the English school system. There are some subjects which he might be able to study, and be examined in, in his own language, either by continuing courses he had already begun at home, or by following adapted versions of courses taught here.

It is possible to take many of the languages spoken by minority groups at O level. Most of these examinations are modelled on the foreign language papers taken in French, say, by native English pupils. These have two disadvantages. They require, in general, a ludicrously low level of knowledge of the language concerned (ludicrous, that is, for speakers of the language), and they depend on a fairly sophisticated knowledge of English. Children's experience of their home country, culture and language is unlikely to be adequately mirrored in exercises requiring translations, some exercises in structure and two or three hundred words of continuous prose. It is absurd to suppose that a child who speaks and understands Chinese and can read and write in it only deserves a certificate to say he can do those things if he can also prove that he can translate what he knows into English. Eventually, of course, he will be able to do that too.

Some children may never have learned their parents' mother tongue, others may forget it and wish to relearn it. For them examinations in these languages on the model of our foreign languages examinations may be more suitable. A society like ours needs teachers (and other people) who speak more than one language. One way of ensuring that we get such people is to capitalise on the language resources the country already possesses by validating at several levels the languages with which children are acquainted when they come to school. The same principle can be applied to the evaluation of knowledge and skills in other parts of the curriculum. There are schools which have introduced Asian Studies into their CEE work, and others which have negotiated Mode. 3s with particular boards to allow for the studying of

162

Caribbean or African literature. It is possible to imagine syllabuses for History, Geography, Social Studies, Religious Knowledge, Domestic Science, Music and Art from CSE to A level standard which might include sizeable options on, as it were, Turkish history, industrialisation and the Third World, a comparison of domestic customs in different societies. This is not a prescription for cultivating only your own back garden, small-scale chauvinism, but a suggestion for building a programme of diversity and relativism into the curriculum for all children. The other side of the coin would be the encouragement of determined efforts to eradicate damaging cultural bias and the sorts of ethnocentricity, or Euro-centricity, which is disabling for children and for us all.

The question of how best to assess the progress or achievement of a pupil who is learning English as a second language is a different but no less crucial one. There are by now several syllabuses, and proposals for more, for examining English as a second language. These have different emphases. Most are modelled to some extent on a view of the way second languages are most often taught (rather than learned): as a series of structures to be learned in isolation, vertically, as it were, rather than horizontally, with no relation to any other language or languages, and ordered in a somewhat arbitrary way from easier to more difficult items. Some proposals see a kind of hierarchy of language functions, which begins with something in the nature of 'survival' language and moves upwards to something else called 'the language of education'. With some exceptions the stress is on written forms and on accuracy, rather than on spoken language to use and make sense of. And as C.J. Brumfit (1981) has put it, fluency is more likely to be a useful way to get to accuracy than the other way round. Most of the syllabuses regard the language pupils need and use to think, recall, imagine and speculate as secondary to the language needed to write, say, a letter of application or pass an examination. Only one syllabus I know of proposes that the learning of English as a second language happens, necessarily, within a bilingual context. Few see the learning of first and second languages within the context of multiculturalism, so that literature, film, television, sport and school activities of all kinds both contribute to and motivate language learning. 'Usefulness' is certainly not to be sneered at, but it is a difficult idea to wield with conviction, and the drawback to most of the proposals for assessing attainment in English as a second language is that the acquisition of such a 'useful' language is divorced from the sort of process in first-language learning which allows us to become the best judges finally of what is 'useful' to us for particular purposes.

At its starkest, the need for certification to mark the stages reached in learning English is attested to by teachers in sixth forms and FE colleges. It is for an O level certificate (or its equivalent) for students pursuing studies in other subjects, who need such a qualification for a job or for further training. Both CEE and CSE provide some scope for manoeuvre in terms of the kind of literature and culture which might be studied and for a variety of spoken and written tasks.

The other area of need may be a more transitional one, where certification is needed to guarantee for employers a high level of *progress* in learning English, which provides grounds for expecting that a young person is likely to become proficient with time, experience and encouragement. Again, this proposes a level of attainment and of validation, which is realistic in terms of the student's engagement with the language at that moment.

One of the most imaginative draft proposals for a syllabus for this group of young people concentrates on the collection by children on tape of examples of language in a variety of situations; examples which might be used as models and for study of function and register. This proposal has a scope which would make it viable as a language programme for all sixteen-year-olds, whatever their first language.[4]

Many children have skills, bilingual or bidialectal ones, which vastly transcend those of their teachers, their examiners, or their monolingual classmates. They may be able to shift, to adopt a metalinguistic approach to the differences and similarities between languages and dialects, to develop a whole extra range of interpretative and performing abilities, which are in no way rewarded by the examinations as they stand. What is needed, then, is not a range of easier options, but a flexible scheme for assessing a far broader spectrum of skills and knowledge than is currently thought worthy of being honoured by certification.

An impatience with the present system of examining school students is shared by people who have vastly different reasons for wanting things changed. It would, however, be a tragedy if these changes were allowed to happen without reference to what is probably the most important complex of events to affect this country in the twentieth century. We need a different examination system because we are a different kind of society, and we need one as well because we have endured for far too long a system which relies on techniques for detecting inadequacy and which insists on failure. There are things we need to find out. Any serious investigation into what is actually involved in acquiring language competence of the sort employers and educators say they want and don't get must be accompanied by just as serious an investigation into the array of language abilities which children in fact possess. There is currently a proliferation of examinations, of a usually vocational kind, which offer certification for English as a foreign or second language. Such proliferaton needs to be scrutinised in the context of language learning and assessment generally and in relation to the central role language plays in social, cultural and educational experience. To pay attention to the advantages and the disadvantages enjoyed by children who are bidialectal or bilingual is to do no more than accept that the examination industry, like many other aspects of education in this country, has inclined towards too simplistic and monolithic an account of social priorities and their possible solution.

I want to concentrate for the rest of this chapter on one particular curriculum development and its implications. The Survey of Language Diversity described by Rosen and Burgess (1980) started in classrooms where teachers and pupils and researchers collaborated to collect information. The experience was enlightening, and several teachers were determined to build on their new insights. The result of their work was a collection of material, which the ILEA English Centre has published, tried out in classes and revised. What is now called *The Languages Book* (Raleigh and Miller, 1981) is the outcome. The work began with the collecting and describing, by the children themselves, of the languages and dialects spoken in their particular class. From this, the notion of 'diversity' developed into something multidimensional: varieties of English and their history, group languages, slangs and jargons and styles, written forms, the language of thinking, private languages, 'anti' languages and languages associated with sex or age or class or occupation.

Central to this work on language variety are attitudes to

language: ideas about effectiveness, appropriateness, correctness, the understanding of judgments made about language being 'good' or 'bad'. An essential aim of the work is to increase awareness of the ways in which language can exert power or confirm weakness.

It would be easy to see this work as simply an updated language course, immaculately delivered out of sociolinguistics just as an older style of language work was born from a dependence on a prescriptive view of grammar or the traditions of rhetoric or even the study of belles-lettres. There are, it seems to me, two kinds of significant difference. The first is that the study of language as variable and changing starts from the pupils' own experience of its being that, and from the conflicts and confusions that poses for them. The second is that the intention here is to bridge what has been a gap between study and use, to make this a course about using language, doing things with language in ways which generate questions about language. Questions like, How are we able to understand new speakers, unfamiliar dialects, written language? What is a mother tongue? Which of a speaker's languages or dialects or registers is more appropriate with some people or in some situations? On what do people base their judgments of the value of particular kinds of language, spoken or written? How is writing different from talking? Why did writing develop and where is it more or less useful than talking? And so on.

Many teachers have found this work particularly useful in helping their pupils to understand the relation of their own dialects to versions of Standard English and to writing. V.K. Edwards, amongst others, has suggested that there may be greater problems for a dialect speaker moving towards standard than for speakers of other languages altogether. This might be because the dialect speaker is confronted with the contrasts between two languages, which overlap far more than they diverge, while the learner of English as a second language is braced for differences. It seems likely, at any rate, that some dialect speakers have difficulties with some written conventions because the shift they need to make is often a subtle one and is not understood by the teacher or not, at any rate, made explicit. I have already suggested that the relative success in mastering written conventions by dialect speakers in those parts of the country where the dialect features are shared by a majority of children (perhaps by the teacher too) may be attributable to an explicit concentration on problem areas thrown up by that particular dialect. Language work which enables children to examine the exact nature of the relation between their speech and the conventions of writing in a context where their dialect is valued, and where its relation to other forms of English is openly discussed, are likely to find the process of operating bidialectically easier, from an emotional, social and linguistic point of view.

David Halligan (1980) spent some time in classrooms where this kind of work was going on. His account reminds us that such learning has vital social implications in the classroom as well as educational ones. It is likely to alter the role of the teacher, the relations between pupils and, vitally, the sense of what counts as knowledge:

Three incidents. A group is waiting for their teacher to give out materials; Jimmy says, 'How many words for football do we know?' I start them off with the Italian, Carlos follows with the Spanish, Amir with the Arabic and Jimmy calls across the room to Kolyo for the Bulgarian. Later Mohammed comes to me with the opening of the Koran; he's pleased and excited to see it, but criticises the translation we had used which is not the one he's used to; later he explains the Islamic prayer obligations and says that he thinks 'Koran' should really have been written 'Quran'. Another group has three West Indian boys in it and turns its attention to the meaning of dialect: 'It's like different languages in English, like Jamaican', says one of them and the conversation turns, as we work on a questionnaire about the linguistic diversity in the classroom, to whether the boys can read and write in West Indian dialects. 'You don't write it', argues one of the boys, so I show him a poem written in Jamaican. 'But my mum and sister write to one another in English', he argues....

The expertise belongs – as I believe it should – with the children, and not with us, the teachers. If they wanted to know about the languages spoken by the children in the class it was to one another that they had to turn, not to us. Secondly the cultural focus of the classroom became a necessarily pluralist one because language use cannot be severed from the culture in which it is embedded. So for Mohammed, to find classical Arabic in the booklet led at once to his wishing to talk about the

167

circumstances in which he encounters it – the Mosque. Finally, both children and teachers were forced to confront their own attitudes to language – the issue which arose when the last group I mentioned discussed whether or not it was appropriate to write in a dialect other than the standard one.

There is a dimension here which is not denied by John Wright but which could be thought dangerously close to his caricature of the 'tokenist' approach. I would want to dispute that and to suggest that it may be that in this sort of work we will find a way of remaking curricula which assorts with the experiences of children in schools today, while helping teachers to see their role differently.

In attempting to provide a rationale for work of this sort I shall want to return to the last chapter, in which I extrapolated from the work of Ben-Zeev two broad notions of what bilingual children seemed better at than monolingual ones. These I called *language awareness* and *language-learning readiness*. I made a link between those possibilities and Margaret Donaldson's hypothesis about what children need to know about language systems if they are to detach themselves from them sufficiently to develop the reflexiveness needed to deal with abstract thinking, and her suggestion that teachers might start by 'helping them to notice what they are doing'.

In recent years there have been several innovations in what is sometimes called Language Study. They have been spawned in some cases by the separate but parallel growth of linguistics and its proliferating branches of study. These new approaches have often been welcomed by teachers, sometimes as a way of replacing more formal language work, but also as productive of much more than exercises in or a rationale for 'correctness' in writing. The best-known example of this work is probably *Language in Use* (Doughty *et al.*, 1971), which encouraged teachers to explore the 'relationship between pupils and their language. This relationship has two major aspects: what pupils should know about the nature and function of language and how they can extend their command of their own language in both speaking and writing.' The materials and the underlying ideas of this work have had considerable appeal, though by no means all teachers have recognised its invitations and possibilities. There were difficulties too; similar ones to those found in new courses which set out to teach or improve 'language skills' in isolation both from the languages pupils know and use and from the range of language performances which they encounter as listeners and readers.

M.A.K. Halliday has always been associated with *Language in Use*, and yet it is possible to feel that this programme evades one of Halliday's most insistent premises: that 'Language study is not a subject, but a process' and that 'the child knows what language is, because he knows what language does', so that 'the child's internal "model" of language is a highly complex one; and most adult notions of language fail to match up to it' (1973). This shifts the emphasis, I believe, from teacher to pupil, from passive consumer of language to active manipulator of it, from a need to use language appropriately to a need to use it creatively and for understood purposes. Halliday continues,

> We shall ask, in effect, about the child's image of language: what is the 'model' of language that he internalizes as a result of his own experience? This will help us to decide what is relevant to the teacher, since the teacher's own view of language must at the very least encompass all that the child knows language to be.

This may be a different kind of 'knowing' from the much more problematically unconscious 'knowing' upon which Chomsky's theory of language acquisition depends,[5] in that it may be unformulated, but is not, in principle, unformulatable, since it comes out of learning and using language. If teachers were to make themselves sensitive to what children do with language it might be easier for them to consider what it is that children 'should know' which they don't know, and how they might best learn it.

John Dixon (1979) picks out three strands in language study as it has developed in sixth forms and further education colleges:

> A specialist interest in language and its analysis may currently take several different forms; unfortunately these are not too well integrated in practice, though there is some overlap between them. The oldest is the study of language of earlier English texts, an analysis of changes in grammar and vocabulary that owed a good deal to classical studies. The second is the more systematic treatment of spoken and written language that developed in 'general linguistics'. The third arose from the study

169

of individual language development and has come to include the social context for its use.

Two other emphases are worth noting at this point: the first is also John Dixon's and is embodied in the A level Communication Studies syllabus[6] he was instrumental in creating. In this he proposes that it is in performance, in the making of language constructs, and the using of traditional and technological media for doing so, that students begin to understand language and extend their powers as language users. A more depressing development has been in the isolating of what are seen as discrete language skills, which may range from spelling and handwriting to public speaking or talking on the telephone, and 'teaching' them in ways which may encourage students to expect formulae to answer their needs.

More recently, F.C. Stork (1980), a linguist, offered his services, as it were, on the grounds that 'the study of language will probably teach more about how the human mind works than any other subject'. Such a claim may be acceptable, but it issues from a view of what linguistics has to offer which has something of the programmatic, the necessary body of knowledge about it; and he is openly hostile to those who have felt that, as he puts it, 'the only justification for learning *about* language is any effect it might have on performance skills'. That is, I suspect, something of a caricature of what Halliday and others would wish to suggest as a connection between study and use, and it evades the dilemma. Tony Burgess (1980), in an article which seeks to reconcile Dr Stork with some of his critics,[7] puts it like this:

> The task for the pupil must always be to articulate the connections between the language he knows and what he knows of language. The difficult question in this debate is not what understandings from linguistics to select and make available, but, rather, what sort of practice might be indicated which allowed connections between use and study to be made and preserved.

Later in the same article he writes, 'use *is* study and study use.... We have to avoid a curriculum model, however contemporary in content, which yields knowledge of the human mind only at the end of a long haul, meanwhile denying pupils knowledge of their own minds and experience as human.' We might return at this point to Ervin-Tripp's reminder of the optimal age or stage for language learning, most characteristically present in early childhood, but repeated where adults or older children know that they are learning and behave towards language as learners.

If bilingualism is to be put to work in our schools it should be, I believe, with this kind of view of learning and language, as a differently known and *current* experience, to be shared, extended and connected with the current experiences of other children, who may be monolingual or bidialectal. Certainly, it should also be possible for all children to learn languages spoken by members of the community in which they live. Their knowing these languages becomes, in any case, an educational as well as a social resource. If we are not careful, though, bilingual education may begin to take its place alongside other curriculum debates: integrated studies, how many separate sciences and for how long, social studies versus sociology, and I believe that this would be to reduce its significance. It is not that these issues are unworthy of our attention, but that they shift our focus from pedagogy to content, from learning to teaching. David Halligan (1980) finishes his appraisal of the *Languages* (Raleigh and Miller, 1979) work he watched in this way:

> A notion of progress emerges which is based on children looking more reflexively at their own language use, but we should beware of asking for abstract formulations of linguistic principles at too early a stage, or straight answers to hard questions at any stage. We are all too close to the powerful influences that shape our language use for such answers ever to come easily.

If we return to Ben-Zeev's findings and to my extrapolations from them: to the possibility that bilinguals develop greater language awareness than monolinguals and that part of that awareness consists of a sense of themselves as currently learning language, we may begin to see, in Tony Burgess's terms, the outlines of 'what sort of practice might be indicated which allowed connections between use and study to be made and preserved'. Such practice would not concentrate on surface features of language or on conventions and appropriateness, but on language as it is learned within a culture and as it develops for groups and

171

for individuals within social and cultural constraints. It is some-where in the experience of using language that the real knowledge is to be found, and it is unlikely to be knowledge of a low-level or ungeneralisable kind.

It is easy to feel daunted by the task of remaking education for a multicultural society. It is less daunting when we realise that we have some of the understandings, incipient though they may be. The possibilities for making use of the advantages of bilingualism seem to me to march with the insights of Britton (1972) and Dixon (1975) about language and learning, about children taking responsibility for their own learning and for learning proceeding from what is known through processes of reorganisation to new knowledge. Certainly, there is also a need for funding, for radical changes in the examination system and for research on several fronts. There is also a need for a thorough-going scrutiny of material used in school which makes damaging or obtuse assumptions about languages and cultures. There is a beginning to be made, though, which makes use of what most classrooms already contain, a diversity of experience in the using of language, and there are insights which children have had about that which owe nothing to linguistics.

By no means all of those people who have grown up as bilinguals or have operated bilingually for a part of their lives remember the process as easy. There will have been tensions, frustrations and conflicts. In suggesting that such experiences can also be produc-tive ones I am not minimising the difficulties, which may, nevertheless, be versions of difficulties which many people encounter as they grow up into the complexity of cultural divisions and the problem they pose for individuals in relation to them. An understanding of the nature of such conflicts must anyway be part of what education provides. In my final chapter I shall be looking at some bilingual writers who have put such experiences at the centre of their work. Isolation, division, misunderstanding have characterised their own lives and have often done so in the context of some of the most important events and conditions of modern times: colonialism, exile, immigration, for instance, and the conse-quence of prejudice against people on grounds of race and class and sex and religion. if some of them have written out of the deepest pessimism about the world they have also made something of their predicament which may offer possibilities for a new optimism.

9   Writing in a second language

Some of the most powerful writing of this century has come from writers who have been bilingual. Conrad, Kafka, Borges, Beckett, Nabokov and Bashevis Singer are some of them. For these writers, as for some others I shall be considering, bilingualism has meant very different things. Many nineteenth-century Russian writers were bilingual, returning as writers to a language which had stood for them as the language of childhood, of a world remote from literature, as, indeed, a language associated with illiteracy and the oral tradition of the majority of the population. Most African writers and writers from the Indian sub-continent speak more than one language, and frequently one of them has been English. Other writers, like Hugh MacDiarmid or V.S. Naipaul or Irish writers like James Joyce or Seamus Heaney, have consciously worked within the tensions produced for them by the colonising thrust of Standard English and the language of English literature, to raid or resist, accommodate or remake.

If we were simply to consider the ways in which English has been revitalised in this century by writers who are speakers of North American or Irish English and by writers moving into English from the traditions of dialect speech or from other languages altogether, it is possible to see reflected in their work some of the most significant twentieth-century dilemmas. Roughly, these might be seen as a variety of exasperations with a world which seemed to be moving towards homogeneity, unity and a kind of levelling, but which simultaneously encouraged national distinctiveness, the separation of identities and a reclustering of affinities and cultural allegiances. Universality has been pitted against cultural particularity, classlessness against an awareness of class, and versions of colonialism against its breaking up. Language has always been central to such conflicts.

Out of these tensions has come the search for new forms and new language, and that search has often been accompanied by a sense of loss. The growth in literacy and mass communications both threatens and encourages diversity, and in either case the result can be the unsettling of what were settled cultures and cultural identities. The fear has been that in spreading a dominant culture, whether to groups of people who had been excluded from it or to parts of the world where it was foreign and unfamiliar, there would be a thinning and impoverishing, an encouraging of false unities and conformities. Such tensions are susceptible to quite different explanations.

Eliot's 'Waste Land', for example, can be read as a dirge for Western culture under the threat of barbarisms within it, at a time when the vitality of its myths and religious expression, its languages and its classical inheritance, are nearly exhausted, barely more than stumps and relics in the imaginations of his readers. How, the poem seems to ask, can a literary tradition so careless of its origins survive? There is another version of that lament. Leavis and, in a different way, the writers of 'The Movement' in the 1950s and 1960s have been accused of parochialism and xenophobia because of their insistence on the centrality of a particularly English tradition at the expense of a conversance with non-English cultures or with cultures within England, working-class ones, for instance, which had been subverted by education and its fostering of some exclusive notion of what culture really is.

That kind of debate can seem old-fashioned now, if only because both sides to it shared an assumption that there was somehow a central, shared and probably English culture, to which all writers in English must adhere, though they diverged when it came to the question of what kind of knowledge of other cultures a writer or reader might usefully bring to it.

The debate is differently located now, and that is largely due to the sound of voices formed by quite different experiences. While those voices sometimes speak English, it may be an English learned and used as a second language or an English which still embodies its dialect origins. These voices remind us that language and culture disseminated from a central point change *en route*. Culture remakes itself on its travels. Artists like Chinua Achebe, R.K. Narayan and Satyajit Ray have not merely received English from us. Having read our literature and seen our films they have remade what they have received and given back something entirely of their own. Bilingual writers do not simply move from one language to another. The journey involves, for them and for us, the discovery of new territories and categories of experience.

Kafka spoke Czech and German, but he wrote only in German. His father, on the other hand, grew up as a Czech speaker, and moved, with prosperity, towards German, though he never mastered its written forms. Kafka often described his commitment to writing – 'I *am* literature' – as his identity, as a besieged refuge from the anomalies of being a German-speaking Jew in Prague, a condition which he seems to have associated resentfully with his father and with betrayal. Erich Heller remarks that

> Certainly, the sense of being an outsider, of having no existence except a literary one, was no prerogative of the 'Prague School': the complaint was not unknown in Dublin and Lübeck or Paris. Yet in Prague it had a poignancy all its own: for the homelessness of the artist was superimposed upon the estrangement felt by the Jews among gentiles, of German-speaking Jews among Czechs.

In 1921, in a letter to his friend Max Brod, Kafka wrote about the way writers like himself might invade the German literary language and imagination, which he regarded as moribund as the expression of specifically German traditions. Such writers would be 'boisterously or secretively or even masochistically appropriating foreign capital that they had not earned but, having hurriedly seized it, stolen'.

This complex image, of appropriation, of remaking another's language, of raiding a culture from outside and remaking it for new purposes which the operation and the language can reveal, illuminates, I believe, the work of many of the writers I shall be considering. Out of a sense of loss, of exclusion, foreignness, of having no demarcated culture of your own, can come this sort of assertiveness, even aggression, a conviction that there is something of spectacular importance in the outsider's stance *vis-à-vis* a society's taken-for-granted assumptions. It is possible to see many of these writers revitalising the culture which they submit to a sometimes baffled as well as angry scrutiny. In many ways this is a reversal as well as a confirmation of Schutz's model of the stranger entering an established group.

Henry Roth, in his novel *Call it Sleep*, made of the sufferings of

175

the outsider, the obscured and twilight world of displaced languages and of the misunderstandings produced by that displacement, a harrowing critique of the optimistic melting-pot of American myth. For his young David, growing up in a network of wary ghettoes in New York during the earlier years of this century, the world is full of dangerous secrecies, expressed as versions of English which separate people from each other and make them all variously incomprehensible to a child. His predicament is not eased by the invoking of American English as a guiding star, from which will come clarity, a meeting ground, since that too will deny, or fail to make sense of, the mysteries in his own life and the mutterings of adults in Polish and Yiddish and Russian and Hebrew as they move towards kinds of broken and groping English. The novel is a *tour de force* in many respects, and not the least of these is Roth's extraordinary ability to represent this Babel in English and to suggest the mutilations of feeling and language which the melting-pot aspiration could encourage.

For many writers a second or third language has opened up another world and produced a need to express their fascination with it. Such new experiences are not always inviting ones. They have involved exclusions, mystifications, the helplessness of the individual at the mercy of the powerful, who already possess the language towards which they themselves are moving. Kafka, perhaps more than any other writer, has given us this double sense of what an acquired language meant to him. German, the language of power, could be entered 'boisterously or secretively or even masochistically', and using it with genius was also a kind of usurpation directed against a father who had opted for the language of power out of mere expedience. The son's fictions might thus be seen both as an attempt to enter the fatherly and excluding citadels and as a lament for the father's as well as the son's failure and betrayal.

For Pushkin, Gogol, Tolstoy and Turgenev, forging Russian as a literary language was a cultural and political act of reclamation. It was a way of identifying Russianness as something distinct from Europe and distinct from a European view of Russia as exotically medieval and barbaric. The productiveness and confidence of Russian novelists, poets and critics during the middle years of the nineteenth century came out of a shared political energy which embraced both a sense of national consciousness and an aware-

176

ness, among those for whom French was the language of 'culture', of Russian and Russianness as an expression of the submerged, invisible majority of the population. Gogol at one time planned to write an 'Explanatory Dictionary of the Russian Language', and in his introduction to it he wrote:

> The need for such a dictionary seemed all the more necessary to me because, within the foreign life of our society, which accords so little with the spirit of the land and the people, the direct and genuine meaning of indigenous Russian words is distorted: and some of them ascribed different meanings, while others are entirely consigned to oblivion.

Something like that is happening in parts of Africa, where writers are reclaiming a vernacular, often regarded with contempt as a literary language, and are doing so within a similar political atmosphere. Clearly this reclaiming of a language for literature, rather than Kafka's 'appropriation' of a language already used confidently by writers, must feel very different. Yet both kinds of operation have in common exactly the sense of remaking language which only a handful of writers in their own language have managed to achieve and which has been felt as an impossibility by writers of all kinds. Dorothy Richardson, for instance, makes this sense of language as impermeable and constraining a central theme of her novel: '*All* that has been said and known in the world is in *language*, in words' and, later, 'Language is the only way of expressing anything and it dims everything.' The dilemma is partly resolved for her heroine by her discovery of the strengths inherent in the shared nature of language and of other aspects of culture.

Amongst many bilingual writers, however, there has been an approach to the culturally dominant language which is more ironic than aggressive. Many, that is, emerging from a colonial past, have deliberately and expectantly moved towards the colonial language, French or English or Portuguese or Spanish. For writers like Chinua Achebe, or Buchi Emecheta, or R.K. Narayan, English has been the language of colonialism, of education and of literature; and the route by which they have come to English has made it for them the language which can contain and express recent history and the contradictions of their place within it. English is both the language in which they can communicate with people like themselves and also the language in which, while addressing their oppressors, they assert what is special in their experience. It seems no coincidence that all three writers are superb ironists, that using English is part of that irony and that the irony is at their own expense and yet subtly destructive of an outsider's mockery. Raju, Narayan's pickpocket in the story 'Trail of the Green Blazer', 'got his chance when the other passed through a narrow stile, where people were passing four-thick in order to see a wax model of Mahatma Gandhi reading a newspaper'.

This is an irony imbued with ambivalence and pain, and its being in English is part of that. Narayan is speaking in English *about* people who don't know English and *to* people who do. It can seem as though Narayan is both inviting us to laugh at people he understands better than we do, and is fond of, and warning us as he does so that we mock them at our peril. Another version of this irony is sharply caught in the predicament of Adah, a young Nigerian woman who is bringing up her five children in Kentish Town. She is the heroine of Emecheta's first novel, *In the Ditch*.

> Trouble with Adah was that she could never speak good London English, or cockney. Her accent and words always betrayed the fact that she had learned her English via *English for Foreign Students*.

It is an English which Emecheta has herself developed into a language for her novels, and they deal not only with the immigrant experience in England, but with the displacements and dividedness of African life as well. Her novels are about blackness and about class and about being a woman, so that English stands here for the complexities of a society which will not ease her passage, but which, instead, expects her to be reduced by language.

> There was much to explain, so Adah put on her studied African look, shut her lips, and would say nothing. That was very easy to achieve because she had a tight scarf over her head knotted determinedly under her chin. Her face was shiny and unmade-up, her lips hanging down. She reserved such looks for places where she knew society expected her to look poor.
> 'Don't you understand English?' the girl clerk demanded, exasperated.
> 'No, no, no want that 'ouse. No want,' Adah replied, shaking her head like a toothless baby.

It is also characteristic of bilingual writers that they should be moving into a language which can seem bookish, which they have encountered through education and through reading. It will often remain oddly impregnated by its having been both a target and a product of education, divorced from, and even inimical to, the culture of childhood. The American writer Richard Rodriguez gives a moving account of his growing up as a 'socially disadvantaged' Mexican child, who wanted more than anything else to speak a 'public language', which meant English for him, and English as it could be learned from books. He took with great literalness his school's exhortations to 'Read to Learn', to 'Open your mind with books.' 'I could say something', he writes, 'about Greek tragedy and Marx and sentimental novels. But I was not a good reader. I lacked a point of view when I read. Rather *I read in order to acquire a point of view*.' Rodriguez is scathing about 'bilingual education', scathing too about any welcoming of his own culture, which he saw as already truncated, taken over, impaired and corroded and overwhelmed by the mainstream culture. What, he felt, did his Spanish-speaking parents, reduced by their poor English and their poverty, have to offer him, let alone the world? Yet, in recording his special vulnerability to the bookish blandishments of education he also suggests that it derives from the undermining of his home language and culture. Of course, bookishness, a particular faith in and need for literature, even something approaching Kafka's 'I *am* literature', could be said to characterise many young people who become writers. It acquires, I believe, a special quality when that turning to literature comes out of a sense of rootlessness, ambivalence, duality and isolation.

For some writers turning to a second or third language has been a consequence of living in a different country, but it may also have involved conscious and even perverse decisions and choices. Conrad, Beckett and Nabokov are striking examples of how such shifts can enter into a writer's work centrally and creatively. For each of these writers the shift to another language coincided with a release into the possibilities of new and welcome identities, new subject matter and new attitudes to that subject matter.

Marlow, in Conrad's *Heart of Darkness*, is considering other examples of people like Kurtz, people who have chosen, or been driven, to live far from their own civilisations and to construct provisional social arrangements for themselves. 'He has to live in

179

the midst of the incomprehensible,' he concludes. Conrad's novels are full of characters like this: uprooted, travelling men, usually multilingual and living amongst people from all kinds of background and nationality. Darkness, mystery, secrecy and incomprehensibility are themes and images in all his work. As Leavis (1948) has pointed out, 'Conrad, of course, was a *déraciné*, which no doubt counts for a good deal in the intensity with which he renders his favourite theme of isolation.' It is always, though, isolation within a bustling, noisy world of talk and variety, vividly remembered and presented by the Marlow of *Youth* in passages like this one:

> And then, before I could open my lips, the East spoke to me, but it was in a Western voice. A torrent of words was poured into the enigmatical, the fateful silence; outlandish, angry words, mixed with words and even whole sentences of good English, less strange but even more surprising. The voice swore and cursed violently; it riddled the solemn peace of the bay by a volley of abuse. It began by calling me Pig, and from that went crescendo into unmentionable adjectives – in English. The man up there raged aloud in two languages, and with a sincerity in his fury that almost convinced me I had, in some way, sinned against the harmony of the universe.

Scenes like this one came out of real experience and out of literature and they are the other side of Conrad's own isolation and exile. As Norman Sherry (1966) points out:

> Conrad's own sense of isolation must have been strong – most of his life was spent as a kind of outcast from society. As a boy he was exiled with his father, and as a young man speaking a strange tongue he was an exile in the sense that any sailor is.... Even in England Conrad lived exiled from the social world.

This may partly have been temperament. It was felt as language. Ford Madox Ford writes that

> Conrad spoke with extraordinary speed, fluency and incomprehensibility, a meridional French with as strong a Southern accent as that of garlic in *aioli*.... Speaking English he had so strong a French accent that few who did not know him well could understand him at first.

In accounting for Conrad's place in his 'Great Tradition' Leavis has to cope with the reality of Conrad's 'foreignness':

> that he was a Pole, whose first other language was French. I remember remarking to André Chevrillon how surprising a choice it was on Conrad's part to write in English, especially seeing he was so clearly a student of the French masters. And I remember the reply, to the effect that it wasn't at all surprising, since Conrad's work couldn't have been written in French. M. Chevrillon, with the authority of a perfect bilingual, went on to explain in terms of the characteristics of the two languages why it had to be English. Conrad's themes and interests demanded the concreteness and action – the dramatic energy – of English. We might go further and say that Conrad chose to write his novels in English for the reasons that led him to become a British Master Mariner.... Here, then, we have a master of the English language, who chose it for its distinctive qualities and because of the moral tradition associated with it.

Leavis's account of the appeal of English for Conrad raises some interesting questions. It suggests, first of all, deliberate choice, and choice based on the writer's sense of a particular language embodying particular traditions of thought and culture, uniquely expressed by that language. It also suggests that a writer might be drawn to a language solely through its literature, even to the exclusion of the possibilities of that language serving real-life purposes. Many writers have posed their multilingualism different-ly. Nabokov and Gerhardie (particularly in his *Memoirs of a Polyglot*), for instance, and other writers brought up in multiling-ual families, have started from a view that their languages were interchangeable for them, transparently equivalent ways of ex-pressing the same things. Where they have played, for instance, with macaronic language[1] in their writing it has been to suggest aspects of their own experience and to associate with particular languages styles or atmospheres, rather than meanings which could be expressed in no other langage.

George Steiner, in *After Babel*, is a particularly interesting case of this. 'I have no recollection whatever of a first language', he writes:

> So far as I am aware, I possess equal currency in English, French, and German. What I can speak, write, or read of other languages

has come later and retains a 'feel' of conscious acquisition. But I experience my first three tongues as perfectly equivalent centres of myself. I speak and I write them with indistinguishable ease.

What is odd about this conviction of the equivalence of his three languages for him is that it comes within an argument about language and translation that proposes something a good deal more Whorfian and determinist than any universalist view of languages as 'interchangeable'. Yet some such theory would certainly be needed to account for what Steiner claims about his own trilingualism. He is also able to say:

> There is room, I submit, for an approach whose bias of interest focuses on languages rather than Language; whose evidence will derive from semantics (with all the implicit stress on meaning) rather than from 'pure syntax'; and which will begin with words, difficult as these are to define, rather than with imaginary strings or 'pro-verbs' of which there can never be any direct presentation. I question whether any context-free system, however 'deep' its location, however formal its *modus operandi*, will contribute much to our understanding of natural speech and hearing. Investigation has shown that even the most formal rules of grammar must take into account these aspects of semantics and performance which Chomsky would exclude.

This discrepancy accords strikingly with the way other bilinguals see their situation. Many multilingual speakers insist on the character of particular languages as something inherent in those languages and independent of their particular use of them, while also insisting that there is no possibility of difficulty in transferring from one to another. Polanyi, in *Personal Knowledge*, takes a similar view:

> The most pregnant carriers of meaning are of course the words of a language, and it is interesting to recall that when we use words in speech or writing we are aware of them only in a subsidiary manner. This fact, which is usually described as the *transparency* of language, may be illustrated by a homely episode from my own experience. My correspondence arrives at my breakfast table in various languages, but my son understands only English. Having just finished reading a letter I may wish to pass it on to him, but must check myself and look again to see in

what language it was written. I am vividly aware of the meaning conveyed by the letter, yet knowing nothing whatever of its words. I have attended to them closely but only for what they mean and not for what they are as objects. If my understanding of the text were halting or its expressions or its spelling were faulty, its words would arrest my attention. They would become slightly opaque and prevent my thought from passing through them unhindered to the things they signify.

It is not an easy terrain. Most of us do view language as a system existing outside ourselves as well as one which we, personally, generate. Language *is* both of those things. Perhaps there is no reason why multilingual people should make more sense of this than the rest of us. Consciously acquired languages, in Steiner's terms, can seem to offer alternative ways of expressing the same thing. Yet translation from one language to another is bound to remind us that language variety is more than difference of form. It always involves us in working between sharp differences in social meaning. At the end of *After Babel* Steiner quotes a speech by Hamm in Beckett's *Endgame*, claiming (wrongly) that Beckett wrote this in English and then translated it into French. The point is that Steiner, while admitting to the flawlessness of the transfer, is reduced to insisting on the effect of the differences between the two versions in terms of cadence, tone and association. Clearly there are such differences, and they may be ones which matter to readers and to writers. Does that, though, make it possible to say that these qualities in a particular language inevitably determine, for a writer in that language, what it is possible to feel and think and say and write?

Richard Coe, in his *Samuel Beckett*, juxtaposes his view of why Beckett first flourished as a writer in French with the author's own characteristically laconic explanations. There are significant differences. Coe writes:

Beckett's reasons for turning to French are by now fairly clear. The peculiar characteristics of English as a language are, firstly, its comparative freedom from grammatical rigidity, and secondly, the extraordinary powers of sensory evocation possessed even by the most insignificant of words. In English, the words do half the poet's work for him, and the temptation is to let them do more and more, to let them take over directly from a subconscious which gives the impulse but which does not direct, and for the writer merely to follow withersoever the whim of language wanders...and so long as the subject-matter remains on the whole deliberately commonplace, earthy and 'real'...the independent creative powers of language are a valuable asset. But gradually Beckett's purpose changes. His subject-matter begins to drift further and further away from the realms of common 'reality' towards that Nothingness which is ultimate reality. And the Nothing is that which, by definition, *cannot* be expressed directly in terms of language. All language, therefore, is specious, and the independent language of poetry, the most dangerous and misleading of all. Beckett, in the final analysis, is trying to say what cannot be said; he must be constantly on his guard, therefore, never to yield to the temptation of saying what the *words* would make him say. Only when language is, as it were, defeated, bound hand and foot; only when it is so rigorously disciplined that each word describes exactly and quasi-scientifically the precise concept to which it is related and no other, only then, by the progressive elimination of that which precisely *is*, is there a remote chance for the human mind to divine the ultimate reality which *is not*. And this relentless, almost masochistic discipline, which reaches its culmination in *Comment c'est*, Beckett achieves by writing in a language which is not his own – in French.

In some ways this is persuasive, though it begs the question most seriously where Coe is insisting on the 'extraordinary powers of sensory evocation' in English, without considering the extent to which such powers depend on the writer's and the reader's active participation in them from their own experience as speakers and hearers of a language. Here, though, is Beckett himself, quoted by Coe:

> To Herbert Blau, Beckett confided that French 'had the right weakening effect'; to Niklaus Gessner, that 'in French it is easier to write without style'; to myself, that he was afraid of English 'because you couldn't help writing poetry in it.'

What is interesting about these remarks and Coe's quoting of them is that where Beckett concentrates on his own relation to his two languages, Coe extrapolates from Beckett's remarks descriptions of those two languages as systems which may have attracted or repelled Beckett, who had, as it were, something to say outside either language, which only needed the right language for its expression. For Beckett, the move into French must also have allowed for an escape from the language of his childhood, of his mother, of Ireland and of Joyce. English for him was bound to be a language with 'extraordinary powers of sensory evocation' because of such associations. He sought difficulty and a language which allowed him to write 'without style' because it was his second language. And out of this language, stripped of the possibilities for poetry and style, and 'weakening' to him, he found what it was he wanted to say, not just a way of saying it.

For Nabokov the journey among possible languages was different from Beckett's; so was the outcome. More of an émigré than an exile or *déraciné*, he carried his foreignness with him like some superior passport. Andrew Field (1977) describes how Nabokov at Cambridge 'became a Russian poet in earnest...was more Russian there than at any time before or after in his life'. Nabokov apparently also believes that he 'might have been a great French writer'. Before deciding to settle in America he spent some years in Germany, writing in Russian, and proudly isolated within a Russian émigré world which scorned the learning of German. Field remarks that Nabokov 'has written that he looks back upon this period of his as if he were a multiplicity of strangers' and quotes the Soviet writer Dimitri Eisner as describing him as 'an artist with no theme'.

There is no doubt that Nabokov relinquished Russian reluctantly and painfully, and he had been in America for some time before he reemerged as an English writer. During this time he wrote in a letter to his wife:

On my walk I was pleasantly pierced by a lightning bolt of inspiration. I had a passionate desire to write, and write in Russian, and I must not. I don't think that anyone who has not experienced this feeling can really understand its tortuousness, its tragic aspect. The English language in this light is illusion and ersatz. I am in my usual state of affairs, i.e., occupied with butterflies and translations or academic writing, and so I am not fully caught up in the sadness and bitterness of my situation.

Nabokov's stance as a writer is the stranger's. His theme came out of his sense of English as 'illusion and ersatz', a superb description both of the English he evolved as a writer and of the world of America which novels like *Lolita* and *Pale Fire* differently account for. Humbert Humbert is a superior European figure, in love with the America of motels and highways, but scornful of its newness and of its poor sense of history. Nostalgia characterises his Russian work, which is often in danger, as Gerhardie's is, particularly in his overrated first novel, *Futility*, of recreating, with a modicum of irony, the world of a pampered St Petersburg childhood as it might have been described by an aristocratic master of the nineteenth century. Snobbery, a need to display his credentials, operates in these early works to put in aspic a life which has been obliterated. English allowed the same snobbery to emerge differently. America is loved for its naivety, its crassness and barbarism. It is also sneered at; but Nabokov's English, donnish, precious, occasionally ferocious and always civilised, provided him with a focus and a subject matter he would not otherwise have found.

Conrad, Beckett and Nabokov are writers who found their distinctive voices first in a language which was not their mother tongue, and whether they might not have done so eventually in their first language is a useless speculation. What can be said is that becoming writers in a second language involved particular challenges and head-on confrontations with the problems of language and point of view; that in such confrontations their 'themes' were revealed to them and, finally, that the languages and the literatures to which their talents were released were greatly enriched by the process.

All the writers discussed so far have testified to the stresses of multiculturalism. For most of them writing is a form of assault on a mainstream culture, an assault demanding inclusion in and extension of that culture. For others, it has involved a reclamation of a language and a culture which have become attenuated by a culture more powerful and pervasive. For all of them, however, there has been newly discovered territory which demands redefinitions of language and culture. That territory has often been located within the confusions inherent in the merging of cultures. Cultures and languages have always been unequal in their will and capacity to impose an identity or a way of life, particularly on the young. The ideal of cultural equality can obscure the sheer strength of mainstream English culture in the minds of majority and minority groups.

186

In two remarkable novels, *The Woman Warrior* and *China Men*, Maxine Hong Kingston begins from the quality of dislocation which characterises those whose culture is preserved in defiance of, and in resistance to, the majority. She herself was born and grew up in California as the daughter of parents who had left China in their youth. In different ways both books invent her parents' childhood, their China and their early days in America out of her mother's stories and the myths and fragmented history of the Chinese community in America. The invention is an answer to the silence, the 'invisibility' of this group in American eyes. It develops out of her own dividedness and becomes an imaginative explanation for it. They are extraordinary novels in several ways: written in an excited, new-made English, which is able to represent both her own educated Americanness and the strangeness to her of her mother's 'talk-stories'; and they account both for a unique and personal experience and for a more recognisably common confusion:

> Whenever she had to warn us about life, my mother told stories that ran like this one, a story to grow up on. She tested our strength to establish realities. Those in the emigrant generations who could not reassert brute survival died young and far from home. Those of us in the first American generations have had to figure out how the invisible world the emigrants built around our childhoods fits in solid America.
>
> The emigrants confused the gods by diverting their curses, misleading them with crooked streets and false names. They must try to confuse their offspring as well, who, I suppose, threaten them in similar ways – always trying to get things straight, always trying to name the unspeakable. The Chinese I know hide their names; sojourners take new names when their lives change and guard their real names with silence.
>
> Chinese-Americans, when do you try to understand what things in you are Chinese, how do you separate what is peculiar to childhood, to poverty, insanities, one family, your mother who marked your growing up with stories, from what is Chinese? What is Chinese tradition and what is the movies?

V.S. Naipaul has concentrated in his novels on the plight of the permanently exiled, as people who may be especially susceptible to the distorting accounts cultures give of themselves. It is the other face of the colonial predicament. As Naipaul wrote in *The Middle Passage*:

> to be a colonial is, in a way, to know a total kind of security. It is to have all decisions about major issues taken out of one's hands. It is to feel that one's political status has been settled so finally that there is very little one can do in the world.

One of the things such a person *could* do is escape, even perhaps into writing. In *A Bend in the River* his hero, Salim, an Indian who has grown up in East Africa and has already been forced to move to Central Africa, is once again on the move. His arrival in London is a terrible 'home-coming', his destination a city constituted, it seems to him, by and for the excluded and the immigrant, whose tragic expectations have rested on a vista of English culture which is, ultimately, a hopeless illusion.

> The Europe the aeroplane brought me to was not the Europe I had known all my life. When I was a child Europe ruled my world. It had defeated the Arabs in Africa and controlled the interior of the continent. It ruled the coast and all the countries of the Indian Ocean with which we traded; it supplied our goods. We knew who we were and where we had come from. But it was Europe that gave us the descriptive postage stamps that gave us our ideas of what was picturesque about ourselves. It also gave us a new language.
>
> Europe no longer ruled. But it still fed us in a hundred ways with its language and sent us its increasingly wonderful goods, things which, in the bush of Africa, added year by year to our idea of who we were, gave us that idea of our modernity and development, and made us aware of another Europe – the Europe of great cities, great stores, great buildings, great universities. To that Europe only the privileged or the gifted among us journeyed. That was the Europe Indar had gone to when he had left for his famous university. That was the Europe that someone like Shoba had in mind when she spoke of travelling.
>
> But the Europe I had come to – and knew from the outset I was coming to – was neither the old Europe nor the new. It was something shrunken and mean and forbidding. It was the Europe where Indar, after his time at the famous university, had

suffered and tried to come to some resolution about his place in
the world; where Nazruddin and his family had taken refuge;
where hundreds of thousands of people like myself, from parts of
the world like mine, had forced themselves in, to work and live.

Of this Europe I could form no mental picture. But it was
there in London; it couldn't be missed; and there was no
mystery. The effect of those little stalls, booths, kiosks and
choked grocery shops – run by people like myself – was indeed
of people who had squashed themselves in. They traded in the
middle of London as they had traded in the middle of Africa.
The goods travelled a shorter distance, but the relationship of
the trader to his goods remained the same. In the streets of
London I saw these people, who were like myself, as from a
distance. I saw the young girls selling packets of cigarettes at
midnight, seemingly imprisoned in their kiosks, like puppets in a
puppet theatre. They were cut off from the life of the great city
where they had come to live, and I wondered about the
pointlessness of their own hard life, the pointlessness of their
difficult journey.

What illusions Africa gave to people who came from outside!
In Africa I had thought of our instinct and capacity for work,
even in extreme conditions, as heroic and creative. I had
contrasted it with the indifference and withdrawal of village
Africa. But now in London, against a background of busyness, I
saw this instinct purely as instinct, pointless, serving only itself.
And a feeling of rebellion possessed me, stronger than any I had
known in my childhood. To this was added a new sympathy for
the rebellion Indar had spoken of to me, the rebellion he had
discovered when he had walked beside the river of London and
had decided to reject the ideas of home and ancestral piety, the
unthinking worship of his great men, the self-suppression that
went with that worship and those ideas, and to throw himself
consciously into the bigger, harder world. It was the only way I
could live here, if I had to live here.

Yet I had had my life of rebellion, in Africa. I had taken it as
far as I could take it. And I had come to London for relief and
rescue, clinging to what remained of our organised life.

Naipaul has sometimes been criticised for his pessimism and for
his exasperation with the political solutions envisaged and hoped

for by people who have escaped from imperialism. His humour is often sad, and he can be contemptuous of the aspirations of those who are powerless and cut off from their own cultural strengths. We need, none the less, to listen to accounts like his of societies where multiculturalism is already a fact of life, if often a contentious and painful one, because it will not be easy to change if we are not able to understand the nature of cultural and linguistic dislocation. Those who most confidently participate in a mainstream culture will have to give ground, and they are likely to discover, even as they do so, that voices as powerful as Naipaul's or Maxine Hong Kingston's have already invaded and occupied the territory which they were so anxious to protect from change. It is not, of course, just a matter of giving ground. Something more difficult and delicate is required. We have to recognise that people who grow up here, though they or their parents may have come from other places and ways of life, will not simply move between two cultures, comparing and contrasting, as it were, and making judicious selections from each. They will want to raid ours and reject a good deal of it, and they will be transforming the one they come from in the process. This will not be sad if it is understood, if what is lost and what is gained are properly valued. It will be the job of education to mediate this process for all young people, whatever their languages and cultures, and there are not likely to be simple ways of going about it.

I have wanted to scrutinise the experience of being bilingual; and in looking to the work of some bilingual writers I have hoped to deepen this scrutiny and to point to ways in which their possession of two languages has been central to their development as writers. It has seemed to me that bilingual people have, potentially, special strengths, and that these may be of a cognitive as well as a cultural kind, which might endow them with particular confidence as learners. In bilingual writers it is possible to see the same kind of strength, writ large perhaps, because of the writer's avowed and explicit dependence on language. In many cases bilingualism can seem to provide specific challenges as well as an ability to stand outside facile assumptions about language and culture in a critical way. It also seems possible to suggest that the constraints and difficulties involved in writing in a second language may release creativity in the using of language, may even be responsible for the originality and power of some of the work of these writers. Such writers have revitalised the languages and the literatures into which they have moved, and they have often done so by asserting as central their outsider's focus on the world.

What, then, might be the implications of all this for education? First, it encourages us to consider what have often been hidden strengths in pupils who have been allowed to seem wanting in language abilities. It opens up as fruitful areas for research the relation of second- to first-language acquisition, and the relation of second-order language skills (particularly reading and writing) to first-order ones. It also encourages us to extrapolate from a sense of what bilinguals can do to what dialect and monolingual speakers can do, and to consider what it is that bilinguals know about language and their own use of language which might be useful for all children.

Second, bilingualism provides us with a window on thousands of young people poised not only between home and school, but between two languages and between two cultures. They are poised not stranded, and their position is mobile and is powerfully battered as well as buttressed from both sides. It is possible that young people positioned like this may be especially well placed to stand back from and deal positively with potential cultural conflict, by seeing their situation in terms not of one culture versus another, but in terms of the arbitrariness of each. Out of such perceptions could grow the possibilities of new, critical attitudes which squarely face the causes of division and exclusion and attempt to bridge them.

Third, we are faced with the need for a radical overhaul of the curriculum, for changes which centre on the notion of diversity. This is not just a question of developing tolerance, but of analysing the consequences of certain beliefs and social arrangements as against others, of making explicit the differences and the connections. Assimilation does not work, and its opposite, the coexistence of separate, intact cultures, appears to be unrealistic. Young people, individuals and groups must be given time and support to make their own accommodations to living here, and such accommodations are not made within politically neutral or ahistorical perceptions of how societies maintain themselves and cope with intrusions.

Finally, I want to return to Kafka's remarks about how writers like him might enter another's language 'boisterously or secretively or even masochistically appropriating foreign capital that they had not earned but, having hurriedly seized it, stolen'. In so far as the English language exists as a system somewhere outside the ways in which it is individually and collectively used by its speakers, it is a system which has been able to withstand invasions and recuperate. It will continue to do so. We need to encourage in pupils for whom English is a second language something of Kafka's aggression and disrespect for the pieties, traditions and rules of another language. This does not mean that we should not help them to learn English, but that we return to Corder's reminder that 'interlanguage', though provisional, is language in action and therefore potentially something more important to its speakers than simply a primitive variety of some ghostly target. Young people who never become confident writers have often been bamboozled by rules and conventions and bound by a sense of those being the ultimate definitions of successful language use. Having something to say makes light work of rules and it also language a valuable possession rather than a grudging loan.

Wai Keung is a fifteen-year-old London schoolboy, who is learning how to use English to say what is important to him. Here he is writing about his arrival from Hong Kong:

> I put my hands into my two little pockets. I found a photograph. I took it out, it was my grandfather. I lived with him since I was born, but now 11 years, I have to go away from him and my country. My tears came out. I clean that off quickly with my hands, tried to not let people saw me. I didn't know why I would do that, perhaps because I was new from here.
>
> I kissed the photograph and then put it back inside my pocket carefully because that was the only thing my grandfather had left for me. But perhaps I couldn't say that it was the only thing. I still have my memory.
>
> I saw my parents and my uncle. They took my luggage into the taxis. My father told the taxi driver our address. I felt interesting that my father could talk another kind of language. I thought how could I learn English. It would be hard for me, I thought again. I cried again, but not from my eyes, but from my heart.

We need to make sure that the curriculum allows all young people to develop and reflect on their language by using it purposefully

192

and confidently, to learn about themselves in relation to cultural diversity.

There are no simple solutions. Varieties of bilingual education, support for mother-tongue maintenance and learning, a concentration on helping children to make the passage towards spoken and written English and a consideration of ways in which the curriculum and the examination system could better reflect and encourage the languages and cultures of children in school: all these are important, though on their own, and for different reasons, they can be crude or unworkable, or both. We need first to develop an understanding of what is involved in operating more than one language or more than one dialect, and it may be that the confident bilingualism of the minority and of writers can help teachers to make fruitful connections for their pupils between the language they use and the languages they need to learn how to use.

Notes

1 The dimensions of bilingualism in London schools

1 This poem is quoted by Cazden, C.B., in an article called 'How Knowledge About Language Helps the Classroom Teacher – Or Does It: A Personal Account'.

2 This figure is taken from Rosen, H. and Burgess, T., *Languages and Dialects of London Schoolchildren: An Investigation*. A more recent survey by the ILEA puts the figure nearer fifteen per cent.

3 See, for example, Jones, W.R., *Bilingualism and Intelligence*.

4 Peal, E. and Lambert, W.E., 'The Relation of Bilingualism to Intelligence', 1962. This paper, as I explain in Chapter 7, marked a turning point in research of this kind.

5 For a recent and comprehensive view of the state of bilingualism in Wales see Sharp, D., *Language in Bilingual Communities*.

6 It is only necessary to consider the extent to which parents are prepared to sacrifice themselves financially to pay for their children to attend *lycées* and other 'international' schools all over the world, and see that their children acquire French through 'exchanges' and visits abroad, to perceive the anomalies in this.

7 In Cazden, C.B., 'The Situation: A Neglected Source of Social Class Differences in Language Use' there is an interesting discussion of a point made by Chomsky, N. and Halle, M., in their book, *The Sound Patterns of English*. I shall quote the argument in its entirety:

One new question about social class differences in word knowledge also derives from Chomsky's work. It is the relation between a person's understanding of the sound system of English and his knowledge of a particular part of the English lexicon, i.e., learn-ed or Latinate words. Briefly, if our knowledge of the sound system of English were limited to the sounds present in words as spoken, we would not understand morphemic relations such as: histor -y, histor -ical, histor -ian; anxi -ous, anxi -ety; courage, courage -ous; tele -graph, tele -graph -ic, tele -graph -y. The only way to account for this system of sound relationships is to postulate the underlying structure which consists of a single and highly abstract 'lexical representation' of each morpheme (a unit of meaning, whether free like *courage* or bound like *-ous*). This underlying representation is related to the surface representation of the morpheme – its sound as spoken – by a complex set of phonological rules which somehow become part of the implicit linguistic knowledge of the native

194

speaker.... According to Chomsky and Halle the underlying system of lexical representations conforms extremely well to standard English spelling, contrary to popular notions of chaotic irregularities. But only someone who had acquired this full system, by familiarity with Latinate words, could take full advantage of that regularity in learning to read. This is one very specific but one very important aspect of language where lower-class speakers may be at a disadvantage.

Cazden is right to make this point, and yet it is possible to see this as another area in which schools could use what pupils already 'know' to enlarge their understanding of how languages make use of accretion and borrowing.

8 Indeed, this has often been how people have encountered language system for the first time. In my final chapter on bilingual writers I shall want to suggest that writing in a second language opened up for them the quality of particular languages and of their own power to manipulate and exploit them.

9 This example is based on work done at Vauxhall Manor School, which is written up in *Becoming Our Own Experts*, written and published by the Talk Workshop Group, 1982.

10 A useful evaluation of a project undertaken in the USA and based on the belief that pre-school literacy in the mother tongue is an advantage to the second-language learner when he goes to school is given in Christian, C.C., 'Social and Psychological Implications of Bilingual Literacy'.

11 A discussion of the question of whether it is in fact easier to learn a second language as a young child, and if so, why that should be, must wait until Chapter 6.

12 It is now accepted by linguists and psychologists that there is much more than a need to communicate involved in a child's learning to speak. For a particularly intriguing illustration of this, see Luria, A.R. and Yudovich, F. Ia., *Speech and the Development of Mental Processes in the Child*.

13 This is an issue I discuss in greater detail in Chapter 5, where I draw on some of the insights provided by Weinreich's *Languages in Contact*.

14 There are drawbacks to using the word *language* for the dialect of a language. I do use it here (though I shall differentiate between them in other parts of the book), not because Michelle's dialect is so aberrant as to seem quite different from English, but because it works as a complete and coherent system for her, which cannot simply be judged in terms of its divergences from Standard English. A blurring of the distinction between 'language' and 'dialect' is also appropriate here, in my view, because the problems they pose for the child in school have so much in common.

15 This capacity to shift between two or more dialects of English is at last being recognised; and some superb documentation is coming out of London schools at the moment. For examples of this, see Richmond,

J. (1982), and a story written by Sandra Herridge and included in an unpublished paper by McLeod, A., 'Writing, Dialect and Linguistic Awareness'.

16 In *The Study of Non-Standard English*, William Labov studies the way in which a particular group of dialect speakers clearly understand most Standard forms, though they do not always reproduce them.

In repetition tests with fourteen-year-old Negro boys, members of the peer group we have known for several years, we find that many unhesitatingly repeat *ask Albert if he knows how to play baseball* as *axe Albert do he know how to play baseball*. On the other hand, if the test sentence was *ask Albert whether he knows how to play baseball*, most of the subjects had far more trouble.

Cazden (1970) makes the comment,

Correct translation of a Standard English sentence into the speaker's NNE, the particular dialect, presupposes correct understanding of the original. While NNE speakers ask questions in the *do he know* form, they understand the Standard English use of *if* but not *whether*.

17 This is harsh, for there are now several inner-city schools where other languages and dialects are welcomed, as Mr Orme welcomes them. It is just that there are not nearly enough of them, nor of outside support for local initiatives.

18 I am thinking, for instance, of the Bullock Report, *A Language for Life* (1975), the two DES Educational Surveys, *The Education of Immigrants* (1971) and *The Continuing Needs of Immigrants* (1972), the Council of Europe's Directive of 25 July 1977 (77/486/EEC) and the ILEA document, *Multi-Ethnic Education* (1977).

19 For useful accounts of some local schemes of this sort, see Khan, V.S., *Bilingualism and Linguistic Minorities in Britain: Development and Perspectives*, a briefing paper. Also Rosen, H., *Comparative Study 1: Language and Literacy: Education for Multicultural Societies. England and Wales*.

20 Two useful accounts of rather differently undertaken projects are Wright, J., 'Bilingualism and Schooling in Multilingual Britain', and Tosi, A., 'Semilingualism, Disglossia and Bilingualism: Some Observations on the Sociolinguistic Features of a Community of Southern Italians in Britain'.

21 For an amusing and self-critical account of this phenomenon see Cazden, C.B., 'How Knowledge About Language Helps the Classroom Teacher – Or Does It: A Personal Account'.

2 *'So I think I'll stay halfway'*

1 This was written by an Apache child in Arizona and is also quoted in Cazden, C.B. (1976).
2 This was published by the ILEA English Centre in 1978.
3 Both stories appeared in the anthology *Our Lives*, Raleigh and Symons (eds) (1980).

3 'Urdu has very deep manners'

1 For an account of Whorf's position here, see 'The Relation of
Habitual Thought and Behaviour to Language' in Whorf, B.L.,
Language, Thought and Reality. This view of language will be
discussed in detail in later chapters.

4 'It's a positioning of the self within the language'

1 There is a return to these definitions in Chapter 6.
2 For a useful discussion of the notion of aspects of language being
intrinsically easy or difficult for the second-language learner, see
Richards, J.C. (1974).
3 Perhaps an arbitrary date, but in 1962 'The Relation of Bilingualism to
Intelligence', by Peal, E. and Lambert, W.E., appeared and has since
generated many of the studies looked at in Chapter 7.

5 The social perspectives of bilingualism

1 This is patently true and worth getting children to understand. It may
be important to say too that the equivalence of languages and dialects
lies as much in what can be done with them as in their system and
logic.

6 Learning first and second languages

1 Steiner is referring (1979) here to his book, *After Babel: Aspects of
Language and Translation*.
2 Weinreich's *Languages in Contact*.
3 Richards, J.C., has edited and contributed to both *Error Analysis* and
Understanding Second and Foreign Language Learning.
4 These ideas are developed in two essays: 'Idiosyncratic Dialects and
Error Analysis' in *Error Analysis*, and 'Language Learner Language'
in *Understanding Second and Foreign Language Learning*.

7 Do bilinguals think better?

1 S.J. Evans. Writing of Welsh children in 1953, Evans is referred to by
T.M. Ilams as having 'Welcomed bilingualism because learning two
languages simultaneously "frees the mind from the tyranny of words".
Any individual who can dissociate thought from words has an
advantage, he believed, over people whose thinking is restricted by
language' (in Simoēs, 1976).

8 The educational implications of bilingualism

1 The obligations embodied in this directive: the teaching of the official
language, adequate training of teachers to implement this, the

197

teaching of the mother tongue of the country of origin, and the fulfilment of these principles within four years, would be difficult, if not impossible, for this country to put into practice were it not for the loophole provided by Article 3, that member states should take appropriate measures 'in accordance with their national circumstances'. Our national circumstances include the fact that we are not, for the most part, talking about the children of migrant workers, and that these children are British citizens, who are likely to go on living here.

2 Dr Verity Khan is the Senior Research Officer of the Linguistic Minorities Project, which is based at the University of London Institute of Education.

3 For details of these research and development projects see Bibliography.

4 This is Jean Ure's 'English Language and the Community: an approach to the teaching of English through bilingual and bidialectal skills'.

5 Michael Dummett has written about this dilemma in Chomsky's work in a review of *Rules and Representations* by Noam Chomsky in *London Review of Books*, vol. 3, no. 16, September 1981.

6 'A' Level Communication Studies, AEB.

7 See articles by W.H. Mittins and M. Torbe in *English in Education*, spring 1980.

9 Writing in a second language

1 I am referring particularly here to Nabokov's novel *Ada*, of which Andrew Field writes: 'The catherine's wheel of languages in *Ada* is the way the Nabokovs, not just Vladimir, really do speak – in the households of Nabokov's father and grandfather it was French at the table, English in the nursery, and Russian elsewhere, with complete freedom to use macaronic combinations as the mood or need was felt – and so in this respect, too, *Ada* is an historically accurate voice of a family.'

Bibliography

ADLAM, D. and SALFIELD, A. (1980),'The Diversion of Language. A Critical Assessment of the Concept "Linguistic Diversity" ', *Screen Education*, spring.

ALATIS, J.E. (1979), *International Dimensions of Bilingual Education*, Georgetown University Round Table on Languages and Linguistics.

ANDERSSON, T. (1977), 'Philosophical Perspectives on Bilingual Education' in Spolsky, B. and Cooper, R. (eds), *Frontiers of Bilingual Education*, Newbury House.

ARMSTRONG, M. (1980), *Closely Observed Children*, Writers and Readers.

BAIN, B. (1974),'Bilingualism and Cognition: Toward a General Theory' in Carey, S.T. (ed.), *Bilingualism, Biculturalism and Education*, proceedings from the conference at Collège Universitaire Saint Jean, University of Alberta.

BALLARD, R. and BALLARD, C. (1977), 'The Sikhs' in Watson, J.L. (ed.), *Between Two Cultures*, Blackwell.

BARAN, H. (ed.) (1976), *Semiotics and Structuralism*, International Arts and Sciences Press.

BARATZ, J. and SHUY, R. (1969), *Teaching Black Children to Read*, Washington Center for Applied Linguistics.

BELL, R.T. (1976), *Sociolinguistics*, Batsford.

BENJAMIN, W. (1977), 'The Task of the Translator' in *Illuminations*, Fontana.

BEN-ZEEV, S. (1972), 'The Influence of Bilingualism on Cognitive Development and Cognitive Strategy', unpublished PhD dissertation, University of Chicago.

BEN-ZEEV, S. (1977a), 'Mechanisms by which Childhood Bilingualism affects Understanding of Language and Cognitive Structures' in Hornby, P.A. (ed.), *Bilingualism: Psychological, Social and Educational Implications*, Academic Press.

BEN-ZEEV, S. (1977b), 'The Effect of Bilingualism in Children from Spanish-English Low Economic Neighbourhoods on Cognitive Development and Cognitive Strategy' in *Working Papers on Bilingualism*, no. 14.

BERGER, P. and LUCKMAN, T. (1971), *The Social Construction of Reality*, Penguin.

BERNSTEIN, B. (1971), *Class, Codes and Control*, 3 vols, Paladin.

BICKERTON, D. (1975), *The Dynamics of a Creole System*, Cambridge University Press.

BLOCH, M. (1961), *Feudal Society*, Routledge & Kegan Paul.

199

BOLINGER, D. (1975), *Aspects of Language*, Harcourt, Brace, Jovanovich.

BORGES, J.L. (1972), *Selected Poems 1923–1967*, ed. N.T. di Giovanni, Allen Lane.

BOURHIS, R.Y. and GILES, H. (1977), 'The Language of Intergroup Distinctiveness', in Giles, H. (ed.), *Language, Ethnicity and Intergroup Relations*, Academic Press.

BOWEN, J.D. (1977), 'Linguistic Perspectives on Bilingual Education' in Spolsky, B. and Cooper, R. (eds), *Frontiers of Bilingual Education*, Newbury House.

BRIGHT, W. (ed.) (1966), *Sociolinguistics*, Mouton.

BRITTON, J. (1972), *Language and Learning*, Penguin.

BROWN, D. (1979), *Mother Tongue to English: The Young Child in the Multicultural School*, Cambridge University Press.

BROWN, R. and BELLUGI, U. (1964), 'Three Processes in the Child's Acquisition of Syntax', *Harvard Educational Review*, vol. 34, no. 2.

BRUMFIT, C.J. and JOHNSON, K. (eds) (1979), *The Communicative Approach to Language Teaching*, Oxford University Press.

BRUMFIT, C.J. (1980–81), In ESOL Department of University of London Institute of Education *Newsletter*, no. 3.

BULLOCK, A. (Chairman) (1975), *A Language for Life*, HMSO.

BURGESS, T. (1980), 'Language Study in Secondary Education: A Further Comment', *English in Education*, summer.

BURROWS, G. (1978), 'Bilingualism and Mother Tongue Teaching: A Select Bibliography', Bedfordshire Education Service, Resources Unit, September.

BURSTALL, C. (1978), 'Factors Affecting Foreign-Language Learning: A Consideration of Some Recent Research Findings' in Centre for Information on Language Teaching and Research, *Language Teaching and Linguistics: Surveys*, Cambridge University Press.

CAMPBELL-PLATT, K. (1976), 'Distribution of Linguistic Minorities in Britain' in *Bilingualism and British Education*, CILT.

CAMPBELL-PLATT, K. (1978), *Linguistic Minorities in Britain*, The Runnymede Trust.

CANDLIN, C. and DERRICK, J. (1973), *Language*, Commission for Racial Equality, 2nd edn.

CAREY, S.T. (ed.) (1974), *Bilingualism, Biculturalism and Education*, proceedings from the conference at Collège Universitaire Saint Jean, University of Alberta.

CARRINGER, D.C. (1974), 'Creative Thinking Abilities of Mexican Youth: The Relationship of Bilingualism', *Journal of Cross-Cultural Psychology*, no. 5.

CAZDEN, C.B. (1970), 'The Situation: A Neglected Source of Social Class Differences in Language Use', *Journal of Social Issues*, vol. 26, no. 2.

CAZDEN, C.B. (1972), *Child Language and Education*, Holt, Rinehart & Winston.

CAZDEN, C.B. (1976), 'How Knowledge About Language Helps the Classroom Teacher – Or Does It: A Personal Account', *Urban Review*.

CHOMSKY, N. and HALLE, M. (1968), *The Sound Patterns of English*, Harper & Row.

CHRISTIAN, C.C. (1976), 'Social and Psychological Implications of Bilingual Literacy' in Simoẽs, A., *The Bilingual Child*, Academic Press.

CILT REPORTS AND PAPERS 14 (1976), *Bilingualism and British Education: The Dimensions of Diversity*, May.

CILT (1978), *Language Teaching and Linguistics: Surveys*, Cambridge University Press.

CLAYDON, L., KNIGHT, T. and RADO, M. (1977), *Curriculum and Culture: Schooling in a Pluralist Society*, Allen & Unwin, Australia.

COE, R.N. (1970), *Samuel Beckett*, Grove Press.

CONRAD, J. (1924), *Notes on Life and Letters*, Dent.

CORDASCO, F. and BERNSTEIN, G. (eds) (1979), *Bilingual Education in American Schools. A Guide to Information Sources* (vol. 3 in the Education Information Guide series), Gale Research Company.

CORDER, S.P. (1974), 'The Significance of Learners' Errors' in Richards, J.C. (ed.), *Error Analysis*, Longmans.

CORDER, S.P. (1978a), 'Language-Learner Language' in Richards, J.C. (ed.), *Understanding Second and Foreign Language Learning: Issues and Approaches*, Newbury House.

CORDER, S.P. (1978b), 'Error Analysis, Interlanguage and Second Language Acquisition' in CILT, *Language Teaching and Linguistics: Surveys*, Cambridge University Press.

COUNCIL OF EUROPE (1977), Directive 77/486/EEC, 25 July.

CROMER, R.F. (1975), 'The Development of Language and Cognition: The Cognition Hypothesis' in Foss, B. (ed.), *New Perspectives in Child Development*, Penguin.

CROSS, C. (1978), *Ethnic Minorities in the Inner City*, Commission for Racial Equality.

CROSS, D.C. (1978), 'Exploiting Urdu in the Classroom', *Modern Languages*, December.

CUMMINS, J. (1973), 'Abstract: The Influence of Bilingualism on Cognitive Growth: A Synthesis of Research Findings and Explanatory Hypotheses' in *Working Papers on Bilingualism*, no. 9, April.

CUMMINS, J. and GULUTSAN, M. (1974), 'Some Effects of Bilingualism on Cognitive Functioning' in Carey, S.T. (ed.), *Bilingualism, Biculturalism and Education*, proceedings from the conference at Collège Universitaire Saint Jean, University of Alberta.

DAVIES, A.-M. (1980), 'How do you spell bomb?', *The English Magazine 3*, ILEA English Centre, spring.

DERRICK, J. (1966), *Teaching English to Immigrants*, Longmans.

DERRICK, J. (1977), *Language Needs of Minority Group Children*, National Foundation for Educational Research.

DES DOCUMENT (1963), *English for Immigrants*, Education Pamphlet 43, HMSO.

DES DOCUMENT (1971), *The Education of Immigrants*, Education Survey, HMSO.

DES DOCUMENT (1972), *The Continuing Needs of Immigrants*, Education Survey, 14, HMSO.

DIEBOLD, A.R. (1968), 'The Consequences of Early Bilingualism in Cognitive Development and Personality Formation' in Norbeck, E., Price-Williams, D. and McCord, W.M. (eds), *The Study of Personality*, Holt, Rinehart & Winston.

DIXON, J. (1975), *Growth Through English*, Oxford University Press.

DIXON, J. (1979), *Education 16–19: The Role of English and Communication*, Macmillan.

DONALDSON, M. (1978), *Children's Minds*, Fontana.

DOUGHTY, P., PEARCE, J. and THORNTON, G. (1971), *Language in Use*, Schools Council Publications.

DOUGHTY, P., PEARCE, J. and THORNTON, G. (1972), *Exploring Language*, Edward Arnold.

ECKMAN, R. (ed.) (1977), *Current Themes in Linguistics*, Hemisphere Publishing Corporation.

EDWARDS, A.D. (1976), *Language in Culture and Class*, Heinemann Educational.

EDWARDS, V.K. (1976), 'Effects of Dialect on the Comprehension of West Indian Children', *Educational Research*, 18.

EDWARDS, V.K. and SUTCLIFFE, D. (1978), 'Broadly Speaking', *The Times Educational Supplement*, 13 October.

EDWARDS, V.K. (1978), 'Language Attitudes and Under-performance in West Indian Children', *Educational Review*, vol. 30, no. 1.

EDWARDS, V.K. (1979), *The West Indian Language Issue in British Schools*, Routledge & Kegan Paul.

ELBAJA, M. (1978), *My Life*, ILEA English Centre.

EMECHETA, B. (1979), *In the Ditch*, Allison & Busby.

EPSTEIN, N. (1977), *Language, Ethnicity and the Schools*, George Washington University.

ERVIN, S. and OSGOOD, C.E. (1954), 'Second Language Learning and Bilingualism', *Journal of Abnormal and Social Psychology* (Supplement), no. 49.

ERVIN-TRIPP, S.M. (1973), *Language Acquisition and Communicative Choice*, Stanford University Press.

EVANS, S.J. (1953), Address of the Conference of Headmasters of Grammar Schools, Wales, in Central Advisory Council for Education, *The Place of Welsh and English in the Schools of Wales*, HMSO.

EYERS, S. and RICHMOND, J. (1977), *Jennifer and Brixton Blues*, Vauxhall Manor Local Centre for English.

FERGUSON, C.A., HOUGHTON, C. and WELLS, M.H. (1977), 'Bilingual Education – An International Perspective' in Spolsky, B. and Cooper, R. (eds), *Frontiers of Bilingual Education*, Newbury House.

FIELD, A. (1977), *Nabokov: His Life in Part*, Hamish Hamilton.

FISHMAN, J.A. (1965), 'The Status and Prospects of Bilingualism in the United States', *Modern Language Journal*, vol. 49.

FISHMAN, J.A. (1966), *Language Loyalty in the United States*, Mouton.

FISHMAN, J.A. (ed.) (1968), *Readings in the Sociology of Language*, Mouton.

FISHMAN, J.A. (1971), 'National Languages and Languages of Wider Communication' in Whiteley, W.H., *Language Use and Social Change*, Oxford University Press.

FISHMAN, J.A. (1976), *Bilingual Education: An International Sociological Perspective*, Newbury House.

FISHMAN, J.A., COOPER, R.L. and ROSENBAUM, Y. (1977), 'English the World Over: A Factor in the Creation of Bilingualism Today' in Hornby, P.A. (ed.), *Bilingualism: Psychological, Social and Educational Implications*, Academic Press.

FISHMAN, J.A. (1977a), 'The Sociology of Bilingual Education' in Spolsky, B. and Cooper, R. (eds), *Frontiers of Bilingual Education*, Newbury House.

FISHMAN, J.A. (1977b), 'Language and Ethnicity' in Giles, H. (ed.), *Language, Ethnicity and Intergroup Relations*, Academic Press.

GENESEE, F. (1977), 'Summary and Discussion' in Hornby, P.A. (ed.), *Bilingualism: Psychological, Social and Educational Implications*, Academic Press.

GERHARDIE, W. (1971), *Futility*, Penguin.

GERHARDIE, W. (1973), *Memoirs of a Polyglot*, Longmans.

GIGLIOLI, P.P. (ed.) (1972), *Language and Social Context*, Penguin.

GILES, H. (ed.) (1977), *Language, Ethnicity and Intergroup Relations*, Academic Press.

GILES, H., BOURHIS, R.Y. and TAYLOR, D.M. (1977), 'Towards a Theory of Language in Ethnic Group Relations' in Giles, H. (ed.), *Language, Ethnicity and Intergroup Relations*, Academic Press.

GOLDENBERG, S. *et al.* (1978), *Language: The English Programme, Thames Television*, Hutchinson.

GOODMAN, K.S. and BUCK, C. (1973), 'Dialect Barriers to Reading Comprehension Revisited', *The Reading Teacher*, vol. 27, no.1.

GOODMAN, K.S. (1977), 'Acquiring Literacy is Natural: Who Skilled Cock Robin?', *Theory into Practice*, Ohio State University, vol. XVI, no. 5, December.

GOODMAN, K.S. and GOODMAN, Y.M. (1977), 'Learning about Psycholinguistic Processes by Analysing Oral Reading', *Harvard Educational Review*, vol. 47, no. 3.

GUMPERZ, J. and HYMES, D. (eds) (1972), *Directions in Sociolinguistics*, Holt, Rinehart & Winston.

GUNDARA, J.S. (1980), 'From a Marginal Man to a Plural Person' in Salmon, P. (ed.), *Coming to Know*, Routledge & Kegan Paul.

GUNN, THOM (1977), Essay in Hayman, R. (ed.), *My Cambridge*, Robson.

HAKUTA, K. and CANCINO, H. (1977), 'Trends in Second-Language Acquisition Research', *Harvard Educational Review*, vol. 47, no. 3.

HALLIDAY, M.A.K. (1973), *Explorations in the Functions of Language*, Edward Arnold.

HALLIDAY, M.A.K., MCINTOSH, A. and STREVENS, P. (1973), *The Linguistic Sciences and Language Teaching*, Longmans.

203

HALLIGAN, D. (1980), 'Working Together on Language', *The English Magazine 3*, ILEA English Centre, spring.

HARRISON, D. and TRABASSO, T. (eds) (1975), *Seminar on Black English*, Hillsdale, New Jersey, Erlbaum.

HAUGEN, E. (1966), 'Dialect, Language, Nation', reprinted from *American Anthropologist*, vol. 68, in Pride, J.B. and Holmes, J. (eds), *Sociolinguistics*, Penguin (1971).

HAUGEN, E. (1973), 'The Curse of Babel', *Daedalus*, vol. 102, no. 3.

HAUGEN, E. (1977), 'Norm and Deviation in Bilingual Communities' in Hornby, P.A. (ed.), *Bilingualism: Psychological, Social and Educational Implications*, Academic Press.

HAWKES, T. (1977), *Structuralism and Semiotics*, Methuen.

HAYDON, C. (1980), 'Mother Tongue Teaching: The Outsider', *The Times Educational Supplement*, 22 February.

HAYMAN, R. (ed.) (1977), *My Cambridge*, Robson.

HELLER, E. (1974), *Kafka*, Fontana.

HESTER, H. *et al.* (1977), *English as a Second Language in Multiracial Schools*, NBL.

HESTER, H. (Director), *Second Language Learners in Primary Schools Project* (SLIPP), ILEA Centre for Urban Educational Studies (CUES).

HIGONNET, P. (1978), 'Reading, Writing and Revolution', a review of Furet, F. and Ozouf, J. (eds), *Lire et Écrire*, Eds de Minuit, and of Cherval, A., *Et il fallut apprendre à écrire à tous les petits français*, Payot, *The Times Literary Supplement*, 13 October.

HORNBY, P.A. (ed.) (1977), *Bilingualism: Psychological, Social and Educational Implications*, Academic Press.

HUXLEY, R. and INGRAM, E. (eds) (1971), *Language Acquisition: Models and Methods*, Academic Press.

HYMES, D. (1971a), 'On Communicative Competence' in Pride, J.B. and Holmes, J. (eds), *Sociolinguistics*, Penguin.

HYMES, D. (1971b), 'Competence and Performance in Linguistic Theory' in Huxley, R. and Ingram, E. (eds), *Language Acquisition: Models and Methods*, Academic Press.

IANCO-WORRALL, A. (1972), 'Bilingualism and Cognitive Development', *Child Development*, 43.

ILEA (1977), *Multi-Ethnic Education*, joint report of the Schools Sub-Committee and the Further and Higher Education Sub-Committee presented to the Education Committee on 8 November.

JACKSON, B. (1979), *Starting School*, Croom Helm.

JANOUCH, G. (1971), *Conversations with Kafka*, trans. Goronwy Rees, André Deutsch.

JEFFCOATE, R. (1979), *Positive Image: Towards a Multi-racial Curriculum*, Chameleon.

JOHN, V.P. and SOUBERMAN, E. (1977), 'Educational Perspectives on Bilingual Education' in Spolsky, B. and Cooper, R., *Frontiers of Bilingual Education*, Newbury House.

JONES, W.R. (1959), *Bilingualism and Intelligence*, University of Wales Press.

KHAN, V.S. (1976), 'Provision by Minorities for Language Maintenance' in *Bilingualism and British Education*, CILT.

KHAN, V.S. (1978), *Bilingualism and Linguistic Minorities in Britain: Development, Perspectives*, briefing paper, The Runnymede Trust.

KHAN, V.S. (ed.) (1979), *Minority Families in Britain*, Macmillan.

KINGSTON, M.H. (1980), '"How Are You?" "I Am Fine, Thank You. And You?"' in Michaels, L. and Ricks, C. (eds), *The State of the Language*, University of California Press.

KINGSTON, M.H. (1981), *The Woman Warrior*, Picador.

KINGSTON, M.H. (1981), *China Men*, Picador.

KOLERS, P.A. (1968), 'Bilingualism and Information Processing', *Scientific American*, 218, 3.

KRASHEN, S. (1981), *First Language Acquisition and Second Language Learning*, Pergamon.

LABOV, W. (1969a), *The Study of Non-Standard English*, Clearinghouse for Linguistics, Center for Applied Linguistics, quoted in Cazden, C.B., 1970.

LABOV, W. (1969b), 'The Logic of Non-Standard English' in Alatis, J. (ed.), *Linguistics and the Teaching of Standard English to Speakers of Other Languages or Dialects*, Georgetown University monograph series on Language and Linguistics, No. 22, Georgetown University Press.

LABOV, W. (1970), 'Finding Out About Children's Language', paper delivered to the Hawaii Council of Teachers of English, July.

LAMBERT, W.E. (1967), 'A Social Psychology of Bilingualism', in Pride, J.B. and Holmes, J. (eds), *Sociolinguistics*, Penguin (1971).

LAMBERT, W.E. (1969), 'Psychological Studies of the Interdependencies of the Bilingual's Two Languages' in Puhvez, J. (ed.), *Substance and Structure in Language*, University of California Press.

LAMBERT, W.E. (1972), 'A Pilot Study of Aphasia among Bilinguals', in Lambert, W.E., *Language, Psychology and Culture*, Stanford University Press.

LAMBERT, W.E. (1972), *Language, Psychology and Culture*, selected and introduced by Anwar S. Dil, Stanford University Press.

LAMBERT, W.E. and TUCKER, G.R. (1972), *Bilingual Education of Children: The St Lambert Experiment*, Newbury House.

LAMBERT, W.E. (1977), 'The Effects of Bilingualism on the Individual: Cognitive and Sociocultural Consequences' in Hornby, P.A. (ed.), *Bilingualism: Psychological, Social and Educational Implications*, Academic Press.

LEAVIS, F.R. (1948), *The Great Tradition*, Chatto & Windus.

LEOPOLD, W.F. (1954), *Speech Development of a Bilingual Child: A Linguist's Record*, 4 vols, Northwestern University Press.

LE PAGE, R.B. and TABOURET-KELLER, A. (1982), 'Models and Stereotypes of Ethnicity and of Language', paper delivered to the *Language and Ethnicity* seminar organised by the Linguistic Minorities Project and the British Association of Applied Linguistics, January.

LEVINE, J. (1981), 'Developing Pedagogies for Multilingual Classes', *English in Education*, vol. 15, no. 3, autumn.

LEWIS, E.G. (1970), 'Immigrants: Their Languages and Development', *Trends in Education*, no. 19.

LEWIS, E.G. (1972), *Multilingualism in the Soviet Union*, Mouton.

LEWIS, E.G. (1976), 'Bilingualism and Bilingual Education: The Ancient World to the Renaissance' in Fishman, J.A. (ed.), *Bilingual Education: An International Sociological Perspective*, Newbury House.

LIEDKE, W.W. and NELSON, L.D. (1968), 'Concept Formation and Bilingualism', *Alberta Journal of Educational Research*, no. 14.

LURIA, A.R. and YUDOVICH, F.IA. (1973), *Speech and the Development of Mental Processes in the Child*, Penguin.

LYONS, J. (1968), *Introduction to Theoretical Linguistics*, Cambridge University Press.

MACKEY, W.F. (1970), 'A Typology of Bilingual Education', *Foreign Language Annals*, no. 3.

MACKEY, W.F. (1971), *Bilingual Education in a Binational School*, Newbury House.

MACNAMARA, J. (1966), *Bilingualism and Primary Education*, Edinburgh University Press.

MACNAMARA, J. (1967), 'The Effects of Instruction in a Weaker Language', *Journal of Social Issues*, no. 23.

MACNAMARA, J. (1972), 'Bilingualism and Thought' in Spolsky, B. (ed.), *The Language Education of Minority Children*, Newbury House.

MACNAMARA, J. (1974), 'What can we expect of a Bilingual Programme?' in *Working Papers in Bilingualism*, no. 4, October.

MALINOWSKI, B. (1923), 'The Problem of Meaning in Primitive Languages', Supplement 1 to Ogden, C.K. and Richards, I.A., *The Meaning of Meaning*, Routledge & Kegan Paul.

MCCORMACK, P.D. (1977), 'Bilingual Linguistic Memory: The Independence-Interdependence Issue Revisited' in Hornby, P.A. (ed.), *Bilingualism: Psychological, Social and Educational Implications*, Academic Press.

MCDONOUGH, J.E. and MCDONOUGH, S.H. (1978), 'Teaching English as a Foreign Language and Mother Tongue Teaching: Some Parallels', *Educational Review*, vol. 30, no. 3.

MCLEOD, A. (1979), 'Writing, Dialect and Linguistic Awareness', privately circulated, includes 'Mauta Massy', story by Sandra Herridge.

MEDWAY, P. (1980), *Finding a Language*, Writers and Readers, with Chameleon.

MELETINSKI, E.M. (1976), 'Primitive Sources of Verbal Art' in Baran, H. (ed.), *Semiotics and Structuralism*, International Arts and Sciences Press.

MICHAELS, L. and RICKS, C. (eds) (1980), *The State of the Language*, University of California Press.

MILLER, J., Conference papers for Language and the Inner City (research based in the English Department of the University of London Institute of Education):

MILLER, J. (1977), 'A Description of a First-Year Class', unpublished paper for conference on Language and the Inner City.

MILLER, J. (1978), 'Making Use of Language Diversity', unpublished paper.

MILLER, J. (1979a), 'Language Diversity: the Implications for Policy and Curriculum', unpublished paper.

MILLER, J. (1979b), 'Language Diversity and Examinations', unpublished paper.

MILLER, J. (1980), 'How do you spell Gujarati, Sir?', in Michaels, L. and Ricks, C. (eds), *The State of the Language*, University of California Press.

MINKER, T.F. (1982), 'An Account of Some of the Languages spoken at Vauxhall Manor School', in the Talk Workshop Group's *Becoming our Own Experts* (available from ILEA English Centre).

MITCHELL, R. (1978), 'Bilingual Education of Minority Language Groups in the English Speaking World', DES University of Stirling Seminar Papers (4).

MITTINS, W.H. (1980), 'Language Study in Secondary Education – Some Comments', *English in Education*, vol. 14, no. 1, spring.

NAIPAUL, V.S. (1962), *The Middle Passage: The Caribbean Revisited*, André Deutsch.

NAIPAUL, V.S. (1979), *A Bend in the River*, André Deutsch.

NATE (National Association for the Teaching of English) (1979), *The Teaching of English in Multicultural Britain*, NATE Multicultural Commission.

PEAL, E. and LAMBERT, W.E. (1962), 'The Relation of Bilingualism to Intelligence', *Psychological Monographs*, no. 76.

PIAGET, J. (1964), *Six Psychological Studies*, Hodder.

POLANYI, M. (1958), *Personal Knowledge*, Routledge & Kegan Paul.

PRIDE, J.B. and HOLMES, J. (eds) (1971), *Sociolinguistics*, Penguin.

QUIRK, R. *et al.* (1972), *Grammar of Contemporary English*, Longmans.

RALEIGH, M. and MILLER, J. (1979), *Languages*, ILEA English Centre. A new edition of this, *The Languages Book*, was published in 1981.

RALEIGH, M. and SYMONS, M. (eds) (1980), *Our Lives*, ILEA English Centre.

REIGEL, K.F. and FREEDLE, R. (1975), 'What does it take to be Bilingual or Bidialectal?' in Harrison, D. and Trabasso, T. (eds), *Seminar on Black English*, Hillsdale, New Jersey, Erlbaum.

RICHARDS, J.C. (ed.) (1974), *Error Analysis: Perspectives on Second Language Acquisition*, Longmans.

RICHARDS, J.C. (ed.) (1978), *Understanding Second and Foreign Language Learning: Issues and Approaches*, Newbury House.

RICHARDSON, D. (1979), *Pilgrimage*, 4 vols, Virago.

RICHMOND, J. (1982), 'Talking and Writing – Connections? – an Instance', in the Talk Workshop Group's *Becoming our Own Experts* (available from ILEA English Centre).

RODRIGUEZ, R. (1980), 'An Education in Language' in Michaels, L. and Ricks, C. (eds), *The State of the Language*, University of California Press.

ROSEN, H. (1979a), 'Dialect Diversity and Education', *Dialekt og rikssprak i skulen*, Universitet i Oslo.

ROSEN, H. (1979b), *Comparative Study 1: Language and Literacy:*

Education for Multicultural Societies. England and Wales, for Organisation for European Cultural Development.

ROSEN, H. and BURGESS, T. (1980), *Languages and Dialects of London Schoolchildren: An Investigation*, Ward Lock.

ROSEN, M. (1978), 'In their own voice', *Issues in Race and Education*, no. 16.

ROTH, H. (1976), *Call it Sleep*, Penguin.

RUBIN, J. (1977), 'Bilingual Education and Language Planning', in Spolsky, B. and Cooper, R. (eds), *Frontiers of Bilingual Education*, Newbury House.

SALMON, P. (ed.) (1980), *Coming to Know*, Routledge & Kegan Paul.

SAVILLE-TROIKE, M. (1973), *Bilingual Children*, Child Development Associate Consortium, typescript.

SAVILLE-TROIKE, M. (1976), *Foundations for Teaching English as a Second Language*, Prentice-Hall.

SCHOOLS COUNCIL PROGRAMME THREE ACTIVITY, Language for Learning project, based in the English Department of the University of London Institute of Education, coordinated by Jean Bleach.

SCHUTZ, A. (1964), 'The Stranger: an Essay in Social Psychology' in *Collected Papers*, vol. 11, The Hague, Nijhoff.

SCOTT, S. (1973), 'The Relation of Divergent Thinking to Bilingualism: Cause or Effect?', unpublished research report, McGill University.

SEGALOWITZ, N. and GATBOUTON, E. (1977), 'Studies on the Non-fluent Bilingual' in Hornby, P.A. (ed.), *Bilingualism, Psychological, Social and Educational Implications*, Academic Press.

SEGALOWITZ, N. (1977), 'Psychological Perspectives on Bilingual Education' in Spolsky, B,. and Cooper, R. (eds), *Frontiers of Bilingual Education*, Newbury House.

SELINKER, L. (1974), 'Interlanguage' (1972) in Richards, J.C.(ed.), *Error Analysis*, Longmans.

SHARP, D. (1973), *Language in Bilingual Communities*, Arnold.

SHARP, D. *et al.* (1973), *Attitudes to Welsh and English in the Schools of Wales*, University of Wales.

SHERRY, N. (1966), *Conrad's Eastern World*, Cambridge University Press.

SHUY, R.W. and FASOLD, R.W. (eds) (1976), *Language Attitudes: Current Trends and Prospects*, Georgetown University.

SIMOËS, A. (ed.) (1976), *The Bilingual Child*, Academic Press.

SLIPP PROJECT (Second Language Learners in Primary Schools), see Hester, H.

SMITH, D.M. and SHUY, R.W. (eds) (1972), *Sociolinguistics in Cross-cultural Analysis*, Georgetown University.

SMITH, F. (ed.) (1973), *Psycholinguistics and Reading*, Holt, Rinehart & Winston.

SMITH, F. (1975), *Understanding Reading*, Holt, Rinehart & Winston.

SMITH, G. (1977), 'Language and Society in Newham', unpublished conference paper for Language and the Inner City.

SPOLSKY, B. (ed.) (1972), *The Language Education of Minority Children*, Newbury House.

SPOLSKY, B. and COOPER, R. (eds) (1977), *Frontiers of Bilingual Education*, Newbury House.

STEINER, G. (1975), *After Babel: Aspects of Language and Translation*, Oxford University Press.

STEINER, G. (1979), 'The Everyday Business of Translation', *London Review of Books*, vol. XXVI, no. 18, 22 November, a review of Kelly, L., *The True Interpreter*.

STEWART, W.A. (1968), 'A Sociolinguistic Typology for Describing Multilingualism' in Fishman, J., *Readings in the Sociology of Language*, Mouton.

STORK, F.C. (1980), 'Language Study in Secondary Education', *English in Education*, vol. 14, no. 1, spring.

SUTCLIFFE, D. (1976), 'Hou dem taak in Bedford, Sa', *Multiracial School*, vol. 5, no. 1.

SUTCLIFFE, D. (1978), 'The Language of First and Second Generation West Indian Children in Bedfordshire', unpublished MEd thesis, University of Leicester.

SWAIN, M. (1978), 'Home-School Language Switching' in Richards, J.C. (ed.), *Understanding Second and Foreign Language Learning: Issues and Approaches*, Newbury House.

THE TALK WORKSHOP GROUP (1982), *Becoming our Own Experts* (available from ILEA English Centre).

TARONE, E.E. (1978), 'The Phonology of Interlanguage' in Richards, J.C. (ed.), *Understanding Second and Foreign Language Learning: Issues and Approaches*, Newbury House.

TORBE, M. (1980), 'On Language Study', *English in Education*, vol. 14, no. 1, spring.

TORRANCE, E.P., WU, J., GOWAN, J.C. and ALIOTTI, N.C. (1970), 'Creative Functioning of Monolingual and Bilingual Children in Singapore', *Journal of Educational Psychology*.

TOSI, A. (1979), 'Semilingualism, Disglossia and Bilingualism: Some Observations on the Sociolinguistic Features of a Community of Southern Italians in Britain', *Lingua e Contesto*, no. 4, Manfredonia: Atlantica.

TRUDGILL, P.J. (1974), *The Social Differentiation of English in Norwich*, Cambridge University Press.

TRUDGILL, P.J. (1975), *Accent, Dialect and the School*, Arnold.

TRUDGILL, P.J. (ed.) (1978), *Sociolinguistic Patterns in British English*, Arnold.

TUCKER, G.R. (1977), 'Some Observations Concerning Bilingualism and Second Language Teaching in Developing Countries in North America' in Hornby, P. (ed.), *Bilingualism: Psychological, Social and Educational Implications*, Academic Press.

TUCKER, G.R. (1978), 'The Implementation of Language Teaching Programs' in Richards, J.C. (ed.), *Understanding Second and Foreign Language Learning*, Newbury House.

UNIVERSITY OF LONDON INSTITUTE OF EDUCATION, ENGLISH DEPARTMENT (1980), *Linguistic Diversity and Standard Written English*, report on day conference, Language and the Inner City, January.

URE, J. (1974), 'The Bridge Course. A Ghana Anthology with Bilingual Exercises in Akan, Ewe, Ga and English', pilot edition, limited circulation.

URE, J. (1977), 'The Range of Language Use Among Primary School Teachers in Ghana', unpublished paper, University of Ghana.

URE, J. (1980), 'English Language and the Community: an approach to the teaching of English through bilingual and bidialectal skills, with projects on practical language work in the community, and a proposal for a mode 3 syllabus at CSE or O level', revised draft presented to LSC/BAAL/LAGB seminars, Bromsgrove, April.

VYGOTSKY, L.S. (1962), *Thought and Language*, Massachusetts Institute of Technology Press.

VYGOTSKY, L.S. (1975), 'Multilingualism in Children', trans. Gulutsan and Arki, Centre for Eastern European and Soviet Studies, University of Alberta, mimeo.

WATT, I. (1980), *Conrad in the Nineteenth Century*, Chatto & Windus.

WEINREICH, U. (1953), *Languages in Contact: Findings and Problems*, Mouton, 2nd edn 1979.

WELLS, J. (1973), *Jamaican Pronunciation in London*, Blackwell.

WHORF, B.L. (1971), *Language, Thought and Reality*, Massachusetts Institute of Technology Press.

WIDDOWSON, H.G. (1978), *Teaching Language as Communication*, Oxford University Press.

WIGHT, J. (1971), 'Dialect in School', *Educational Review*, vol. 24.

WILKINS, D.A. (1976), *Notional Syllabuses*, Oxford University Press.

WILLIAMS, F. (ed.) (1970), *Language and Poverty*, Markham.

WILLIAMS, R. (1975), *The Long Revolution*, Pelican.

WILSON, A. (1978), *Finding a Voice: Asian Women in Britain*, Virago.

WRIGHT, J. (1978), 'Bilingualism and Schooling in Multilingual Britain', *Junction*, CUES.

Index

Achebe, C., 174, 177

Bain, B., 145
Bashevis Singer, I., 173
Beckett, S., 173, 179, 183, 186
Bell, R., 127, 134, 138
Bellugi, U., 140
Ben-Zeev, S., 6, 97, 144–9, 168, 171
Blau, H., 184
Bloch, M., 113
Borges, J. L., 173
Britton, J., 172
Brod, M., 175
Brown, D., 141
Brown, R., 140
Brumfit, C. J., 163
Bullock Report, 156, 196
Burgess, T., 3, 103, 154, 165, 170–1, 194
Burstall, C., 128

Cazden, C.B., 194–6
Chevrillon, A., 181
Chomsky, N., 127, 130, 169, 182, 194, 198
Christian, C. C., 195
Claydon, L., 136, 153
Coe, R., 183–4
Conrad, J., 173, 179–81, 186
Corder, S. P., 43, 109, 139–41, 192
Council of Europe Directive 77/486/EEC, 153, 196–7
Cromer, R. F., 134
Cummins, J., 143–5, 148

De Gaulle, C., 138
Derrick, J., 156
DES, 196
Dixon, J., 169, 172
Donaldson, M., 6, 13, 150–1, 168
Doughty, P., 168
Dummett, M., 198

Edwards, A. D., 156
Edwards, V. K., 117, 124, 156, 166
Eisner, D., 185
Elbaja, M., 21
Eliot, T. S., 174
Emecheta, B., 177–8
Ervin, S., 132
Ervin-Tripp, S. M., 18, 44, 92, 110, 135, 141, 170
Evans, S. J., 149, 197

Fanon, F., 68
Field, A., 185, 198
Fishman, J. A., 12, 149, 154, 156–7
Ford, F. M., 180

Gerhardie, W., 181, 186
Gessner, N., 184
Gogol, N., 176–7
Goodman, K. S., 130
Goodman, Y. M., 130
Gulutsan, M., 144–5, 148
Gunn, T., 41

Halle, M., 194
Halliday, M. A. K., 125, 169–70
Halligan, D., 167–8, 171
Haugen, E., 111, 112
Heaney, S., 173
Heller, E., 175
Higonnet, P., 95
Hymes, D., 127

Ianco-Worrall, A., 145
Ilams, T. M., 197
ILEA, 157, 165, 194, 196

Jackson, B., 11, 38, 116
Jackson, G., 68
Jones, W. R., 149, 194
Joyce, J., 173, 185

Kafka, F., 173, 175–7, 179, 191–2

Khan, V. S., 143, 156, 196, 198
Kingston, M. H., 116, 187, 190
Knight, T., 136, 153
Kolers, P. A., 148–9

Labov, W., 196
Lambert, W. E., 132, 143–5, 194, 197
Leavis, F. R., 174, 180–1
Leopold, W. F., 91, 113, 139, 145
Levine, J., 159
Lewis, E. G., 113
Luria, A. R., 195
Lyons, J., 125, 129

MacDiarmid, Hugh, 173
McLeod, A., 196
Macnamara, J., 132–4, 142, 144, 157
Malinowski, B., 116
Marx, K., 179
Miller, J., 95, 165, 171
Mittins, W. H., 198

Naipaul, V. S., 173, 187–90
Nabokov, V., 173, 179, 181, 185–6, 198
Narayan, R. K., 174, 177–8

Osgood, C. E., 132

Peal, E., 143–5, 194, 197
Piaget, J., 44, 133, 144
Polanyi, M., 182–3
Pushkin, A. S., 176

Rado, M., 136, 153
Raleigh, M., 95, 165, 171, 196
Ray, S., 174
Richards, J. C., 38, 137, 197
Richardson, D., 177
Richmond, J., 195–6
Rodriguez, R., 179
Rosen, H., 3, 103, 154, 156, 165, 194, 196

Roth, H., 175–6

Sapir, E., 134–5
Saville-Troike, M., 149
Schools Council, 159
Schutz, A., 114–15, 117–18, 125, 175
Segalowitz, N., 135
Selinker, L., 46, 109, 130, 136–7, 140
Shakespeare, W., 53, 54
Sharp, D., 156, 194
Sherry, N., 180
SLIPP Project, 159
Smith, F., 130
Steiner, G., 131, 181–3, 197
Stork, F. C., 170
Symons, M., 196

Thatcher, M., 11
Thorpe, J., 85
Tolstoy, L., 87, 94, 116
Torbe, M., 198
Torrance, E. P., 146
Tosi, A., 156, 160, 196
Tucker, G. R., 139
Turgenev, I., 176

Ure, J., 198

Vygotsky, L. S., 133–4, 144, 151–2

Weinreich, U., 60, 111–12, 118–19, 132, 195, 197
Whorf, B. L., 60, 108, 132, 134–5, 182, 197
Williams, R., 94
Wilson, A., 38, 39, 120–1
Wordsworth, W., 54
Wright, J., 156–61, 168, 196

Yeats, W. B., 41
Yudovich, F. Ia., 195